Management Masterclass

This new edition in paperback first published by
Nicholas Brealey Publishing Limited in 1998

36 John Street
London
WC1N 2AT, UK
Tel: +44 (0)171 430 0224
Fax: +44 (0)171 404 8311

17470 Sonoma Highway
Sonoma
California 95476, USA
Tel: (707) 939 7570
Fax: (707) 938 3515

First published in hardback by
Nicholas Brealey Publishing Limited in 1996
Reprinted 1996, 1997

Library of Congress Cataloging-in-Publication Data
Glass, Neil M.
    Management masterclass : a practical guide to the new realities of business
    / Neil M. Glass.
    p.   cm.
    Includes bibliographical references and index.
    ISBN 1-85788-109-5
    1. Industrial management. I. Title.
    HD31.G5377 1996
    658--dc20
                                          96-19788
                                                CIP

ISBN 1-85788-109-5
British Library Cataloguing in Publication Data
A catalogue record for this book is available from the British Library.

Printed in Finland by WSOY

Acknowledgements are due to Corel Mega Gallery for the clipart used in this book.

Management Masterclass

A practical guide to the new realities of business

Neil M. Glass

n*b*

NICHOLAS BREALEY
PUBLISHING

LONDON

A practical guide to the new realities of business

Overview

Contents

Introduction to the New Edition

A great deal has happened in the world of business since the first edition of *Management Masterclass* was published in 1996. For example, business process reengineering (BPR) – the big idea of a couple of years ago – seems to be slipping quietly from view and other concepts are taking its place: emotional intelligence, a new emphasis on the importance of personal effectiveness, open book management, economic value added, supply chain management and a focus on innovation and growth, rather than the dramatic cost cutting that often accompanies BPR.

I originally wrote *Management Masterclass* because I was concerned that there were too many false prophets preaching to managers. In the attempt to market themselves and differentiate their products from those of their competitors, many of these idea-mongers seemed too concerned with promoting their offering as the 'great breakthrough', although most were either useful but limited tools or just smart repackaging of existing ideas or common sense. I hoped to redress the balance by presenting a wide range of these ideas and trying to assess their real value.

Management Masterclass is not trying to sell any big new idea or present any pet theory. Instead the book takes a much broader view and examines a wide range of the main ideas and techniques in ten key areas of management.

In some cases, I am convinced that well-known classical methods have successfully withstood the test of time and I therefore propose how they can be used as effectively today as when they were first put forward. In others, I will try to show the power of many of the new ideas. However, with some supposedly leading-edge ideas, I will attempt to demonstrate how they have turned out to be misleading or even harmful to the organizations in which they have been applied. And when I feel there are no adequate answers available, I suggest a number of approaches of my own which I believe provide original ways forward.

In this updated edition, I have added those new ideas that seem to me to be the most important and have still tried to provide as unbiased a view as possible of their usefulness for managers. Good management practice is continually developing as new, richer concepts are contributed both from within management itself and from a wide variety of other subjects, such as mathematics which gave us chaos theory or psychology which has proposed emotional intelligence. So there will never be a single, definitive management book or approach – in spite of the immodest claims of certain self-promoting gurus – there will only be a number of more or less useful concepts.

From managing chaos to rethinking organizational design, from guiding change to reinventing marketing, from encouraging creativity to revolutionizing the way we measure results, from building teams to restructuring around networks – *Management Masterclass* will help managers see clearly how to choose and apply the best thinking available to achieve major improvements in performance.

The ten parts of this book are organized around three main themes – ideas, people and tools. However, all these interrelate so you can start at any point in the book – you can read right through or dip in and out. It can be used as a reference book and as a practical handbook. However, I recommend you read Chapter 1 first to gain an overview of the historical context of today's management ideas.

All the chapters in the book are in a sense dependent on each other. They are all constituents of a single, broad-minded approach to management.

You cannot inspire innovation, for example, if you retain a ponderous, hierarchical, functional structure, which prevents departments from working well together. Nor can you build customer focus if you have a directive, top-down, inflexible way of developing strategy which takes no notice of the input and experience of those who are closest to the market. And you can't fuel teamworking and networking if your measurement and reward systems encourage your functional managers to build private empires and work for their local departmental interests.

Managing and being managed can be irritating, frustrating and stressful. But it can also be challenging, exhilarating and above all fun. I hope you enjoy *Management Masterclass*.

Neil Glass
London, February 1998

Part One

Keeping Up with Leading-edge Thinking

1
Making the Most of the Masterclass

In order to make sense of today's management world, it is helpful to understand some of what has happened in the past. This introductory chapter explains the main ideas in management thinking over the last 40–50 years to provide a context for the themes and concepts which are explored in more depth in the rest of the book.

Understanding where we come from

With so many, often conflicting, theories being put forward by both recognized and self-proclaimed business gurus, it is easy to be cynical about the current vogue for 'management how to' books. However, not all the theories have been bad. Many, of course, were just common sense dressed up as wisdom. But others were based on sound thinking and can be extremely powerful tools when applied effectively. And each theory naturally tends to reflect the economic realities of its time – what was useful in the low-competition, high-growth years of the 1950s and 1960s may be less applicable in the highly competitive, economically stagnant 1990s.

There has been a tendency for management ideas to be picked up, tried for a while and then dropped in favor of the next fashion. It's not unusual to find a large organization simultaneously delayering, running a total quality program, starting business process reengineering and investing in training of cross-functional teams. With so many initiatives being launched, it's not surprising that each new management project is sometimes seen by employees as just another passing fad. Meanwhile, by trying to find quick and easy solutions, managers are often being distracted from dealing with the deeper problems underlying many organizations' failure to compete.

It is always dangerous to try to pigeonhole the past into neat, clearly defined periods. For a start, there will be conflicting views on what constitutes a period and when any one period started and ended. Moreover, different organizations will tend to move at different speeds depending on the far-sightedness of their management and the degree of competitive or regulatory pressure they are under. Twenty years ago car manufacturers and consumer goods companies were experimenting with 'Japanese' management techniques which are only now being adopted by pharmaceutical companies and government departments. And, of course, different cultures will have particular characteristics which will affect how they apply certain concepts – Germany, the Netherlands and the Scandinavian countries have long since implemented ways of involving workers in decision making, in which they are many years ahead of countries such as Britain, France and the US.

Nevertheless, if we are fully to appreciate the relevance and power of many of today's best ideas, it is necessary to place them in a broad historical perspective. I propose a model which splits the last 40–50 years of management thinking into five main periods (Figure 1.1).

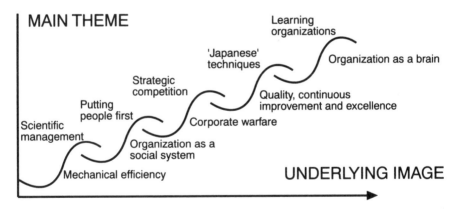

Figure 1.1   One possible way of segmenting trends in management thinking

Scientific management

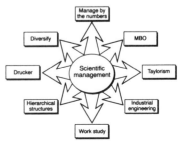

Up until at least the 1950s management was viewed as a science. Financial numbers and hierarchical structure were seen as the way to run an organization. Achieving profitability through mass production and economies of

Pages 212–14

scale drove most organizational policy. Theory X was the dominant management style – authoritarian management by the numbers. The ideas of F.W. Taylor (Taylorism) also had a great influence. He believed that work should be broken down into small, repetitive tasks, carried out by different people and even in different areas, creating the one most efficient way for each job.

Organizations were seen as machines which should run as efficiently as possible. This was the heyday for corporate bureaucrats, and the huge diversified companies that they built have dominated the world economy for more than half the twentieth century. However now, in a much more turbulent environment, some have disappeared and others are still struggling to break free from the constraints of centralized controls.

In the fairly stable political and economic environment of the 1950s, with steady economic growth and rising consumer demand, the major corporations tended to have large centralized planning departments. The belief was that 'the corporate center knows best'. These central planning departments produced the organization's long-range plans, which were then handed down to the operating divisions to be carried out.

Peter Drucker is generally attributed with this period's most influential theory of how to manage – management by objectives (MBO). Executives had their goal set through a process of negotiation with their immediate superior. These goals were usually expressed in quantified targets against which actual performance could be clearly compared. In fact, Drucker was

Pages 22–33

already giving clear warnings in 1955 that measurement systems had to be much broader than the traditional fixation with a few largely financial or productivity figures, but it was not until many years later that companies began to try to put more balance into the way they measured their performance.

Diversification was seen as the way forward for large companies. They believed they had 'scientific' management skills which could be successfully applied to any business. So to protect themselves against cycles in demand for their original products, they embarked on a spree of buying up often totally unrelated businesses, and then imposed their centralized control and supposedly 'transferable' management skills on them. In the 1990s some conglomerates – such as Thorn-EMI, Hanson, AT&T and General Motors – are still trying to unravel themselves and split themselves back up into identifiable businesses.

Putting people first

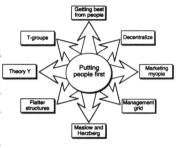

In the 1960s the management pendulum seemed to swing in the opposite direction. Influenced by thinkers such as Maslow and Herzberg, the organization began to be viewed less as a machine and more as a social system. Now it was proposed that success came more from helping employees realize their full potential than from tightly controlling their productivity. Managing 'people' rather than just 'the numbers' became the central issue for managers. The 1950s Theory X – authoritarian management by the numbers – was now replaced by Theory Y – getting the best from your people through helping them develop and satisfy their self-fulfillment needs.

One influential tool was the management grid, developed by Robert Blake and Jane Mouton. This was a matrix used to help classify managers according to their 'concern for people' and 'concern for results'. At the time, the most common outcome was that managers were found to be too results oriented and had to increase their awareness of people's needs, particularly their understanding of group dynamics and effective teambuilding. Managers were sent away to T-group sessions to be trained in how to be sensitive to others – the so-called touchy-feely style of management.

As part of this move toward focusing on people issues, many firms started to decentralize power, giving those lower in the organization greater freedom of action and responsibility. Large, centralized planning staffs came to be seen as a liability, and operating divisions were given some (although often limited) control over their destiny.

Putting people first was not only applied to firms' internal operations but also to their relations with their customers. In a ground-breaking article in 1960 called 'Marketing myopia', Theodore Levitt argued that companies needed to move away from a 'sales focus' (using advertising and promotions to shift their mass-produced products) and instead build a 'marketing focus' (identifying real consumer needs and then making products to satisfy these).

Strategic competition

As competitive conditions hardened, the focus of management seemed to move away from an emphasis on people and the internal working of the organiza-

tion, and toward trying to discover which strategy would enable the organization to compete
most effectively.

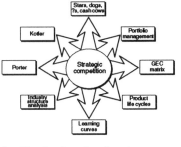

In the 1970s there were two major oil crises
and subsequent recessions, high levels of inflation in the industrialized countries and the
emergence of serious competition from Japan.
These were seen as turbulent times and long-

Pages 269–70

range centralized planning finally died a death. Corporate
headquarters no longer 'knew best'. Instead, the move was
toward breaking larger companies up into strategic business
units (SBUs), in the belief that an SBU could be more aware
of, and thus more responsive to, changes in its environment
than could a massive corporate HQ. Instead of being viewed as a large mono-
lithic entity, the firm was now seen as a portfolio of businesses, each of which
had its own strategic plan depending on its position in its particular market.

To help companies develop strategies for their often numerous and often

Pages 261–3

very different SBUs, strategic planning matrices were
developed by two major companies – McKinsey and the
Boston Consulting Group (BCG). The BCG matrix, with its
classification of SBUs into dogs, stars, cows and question
marks, is the best known of these. Other techniques such

as industry structure analysis, product life cycles and learning curves also
came into vogue. The way many companies used these strategy tools seemed
to be based on a belief that, if they could only find the right strategy, they
would achieve sustainable competitive advantage. Many strategies based on
this approach failed. Often the tools were applied too mechanistically, and too
much management energy went into the search for the right strategy while too
little attention was paid to how it could be successfully operationalized.

'Japanese' techniques

The most important influence on management
theory and practice during the 1980s was the
realization that Japanese companies were
clearly and consistently doing something a
great deal better than their reeling western
counterparts. This new focus led to many leading western organizations implementing tech-

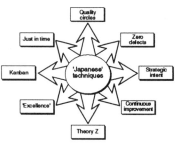

niques such as quality circles, just-in-time manufacturing and kanban (a system of cards to indicate when stock needs to be called forward in a production process). Quality linked to continuous improvement became the goal for many firms. The old attitude of 'inspecting quality in' and x defects per thousand parts was replaced by the total quality concept of 'building quality in' and zero defects. While these methods are often thought to have originated in Japan, they were in fact developed there by a US statistician, W. Edwards Deming.

There was also a focus on building effective teamwork within and across functions. The people side of management returned to the surface. Theory Y was replaced by Theory Z – Japanese-style involvement in decision making and organizational concern for the welfare of employees. Managing corporate culture became a big issue, and so there were corporation mission statements and intrapreneuring (encouraging 'small company' entrepreneurial behavior in a larger organization), and analysis tools such as McKinsey's Seven Ss, which considered the balance of strategy, structure, shared values, symbolic behavior, systems, staff and skills.

Western strategic planning models of the 1970s also came under increasing criticism. At the start of the 1980s, writers such as Kenichi Ohmae began to give warnings that too much of western strategic thinking was mechanical and lacking in creativity. It was blamed for producing predictable, generic strategies, which too many companies followed giving none any sustainable competitive advantage. Developed from studying successful Japanese companies such as Honda, Canon and Komatsu, strategic intent (setting a general direction and ambition for the organization) started to replace strategic planning (setting highly detailed, centrally produced plans).

Another finding from this period was that Japanese and western companies (mainly US and British) were managed according to quite different mental models. Many western managers had a tendency to see problems in a narrowly functional way and to apply simplistic managerial solutions to meet short-term budgetary or profitability targets. The Japanese, on the other hand, were credited with having a more cohesive view of the organization and its employees; a circular, longer-term concept of time; an approach focused more on gaining market share than on immediate returns for shareholders and managers. Oversimplifying, you could say that while western managers sought to ensure long-term survival through generating short-term profits, Japanese companies ensured profitability through building a long-term future based on market domination.

Learning organizations

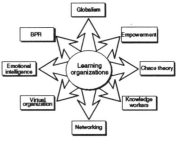

Recent management thinking has been heavily influenced by developments in the natural sciences. Concepts such as non-linearity, uncertainty, repeating patterns and chaos have begun to replace the mechanistic, mathematical and geometric models with which most of

Pages 34–5

us grew up. We have moved from seeing the world as inherently stable and predictable to viewing it as chaotic – subject to unexpected shifts and changes, which can suddenly create huge opportunities for the prepared and sometimes fatal threats for slow movers.

As many markets have reached saturation and competition has become increasingly global, organizations are finding that the pace of change is accelerating. One expert talks of a new era of 'hypercompetition'. This move from national and international to global competition has given organizations a new structural

Pages 232–45

challenge – how to remain responsive to local or national markets while at the same time gaining the benefits of operating globally. Many firms are currently struggling with what structures to put in place and where to allocate decision-making power as they try to balance the needs of local

businesses with the economies of scale which a global operation can offer.

In order to adapt to this new turbulence, the concept of 'finding the right strategy' has been replaced by the idea of 'strategic flexibility' – being able to

Pages 248–57

set a clear general direction yet also being capable of adapting and learning as customer requirements change and new competitive threats or opportunities arise. Employees are being viewed more as critical knowledge workers than as easily replaceable salaried staff, as key

assets rather than costs to be continually reduced. Empowerment, networking and building the capacity to learn are seen as the way to create the necessary flexibility. With the competitive environment becoming more complex and subject to more rapid change, size, which had once been seen as an essential competitive weapon, has become in many cases a clear disadvantage. The controls and bureaucracy which seem such an integral part of large organizations appear to stifle organizations' ability to adapt and develop.

In addition, many organizations have developed a much more holistic view of themselves. Instead of being based around a series of clearly delineated functions, they conceive of themselves as a collection of customer-facing processes. Business process reengineering (BPR) has preached that we should focus, not on how individual departments work, but on how they work together to deliver value to customers – on how information and products flow through the organization. Some organizations are now trying to manage themselves as part of a broader supply chain that extends way beyond their boundaries, rather than as a collection of functional departments.

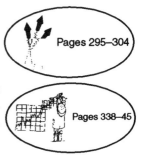

Pages 295–304

Pages 338–45

The boundaries between organizations and their environments have also become much more fluid. Organizations are moving towards being a series of relationships and 'virtual' organizations rather than formal structures as they build networks with outside experts and with other organizations. Value chains are being linked and hardly a week goes by without some new strategic alliance being announced, either between former competitors or between companies in complementary industries. The idea of partnership, rather than competing interests, is now beginning to drive the relationships between organizations, their competitors, their operating environment, their public and their employees.

Page 140

There is also a new emphasis on developing people and improving human relations. Ideas such as accelerated learning, emotional intelligence and neurolinguistic programming have all been proposed as ways of helping us build our own and our people's skills – what has been termed our 'human capital'.

Pages 195–206

The organizations we work for make a considerable investment in measurement – in us. And we spend a great deal of resources following such measures as return on capital employed, return on assets and return on investment. It has been proposed that one measure we overlook is the return on our efforts, what has been called 'return on management'. Are we clearly focused on key strategic targets, continually aware of the critical few performance indicators, efficient in our use of time and highly effective in our interpersonal relationships. Are we developing improved capabilities and methods rapidly enough?

The predictable career paths and well-defined management methods which many of us grew up with will never return. We must all adapt to a more turbulent environment and this will require us to be flexible and continuously to upgrade our skills. The concept of 'lifetime learning' will replace a model where a period of education is followed by a life of work. *Management Masterclass* hopes to provide some contribution to this process of continuous learning by presenting many new ways in which we can master, rather than be caught out by, the challenges of the complex, chaotic and exciting future.

2

A New Understanding of Intelligence

Within the last decade we've rushed into a new era – an era when technology can bring us information much faster than we can absorb it.

We can no longer rely on the knowledge we acquired between the ages of 8 and 25 to be sufficient to support us throughout our working lives. Some of us will find that the jobs we trained for disappear and many of us will have to change careers several times. Society may well be split into an educated élite of knowledge workers who can continue to learn and a disadvantaged group who are unable to find a role – a society split into the 'knows' and the 'know nots'.

Our future strength, and often survival, will depend less on physical or financial assets and increasingly on our capacity to learn and develop new skills. This shift from financial to human capital has put a new emphasis on how we understand and develop our capabilities. Key to this is how we think of, assess and cultivate intelligence.

Intelligence – a moving target

Our concept of what constitutes human intelligence is constantly evolving. It's probably a useful simplification to say that during the last few decades there have been four main phases in the popular understanding of human intelligence (Figure 2.1).

Each of these concepts has built on previous ideas to give us a much broader and more useful understanding of human intelligence. And the more profound our understanding of human intelligence becomes, the more likely

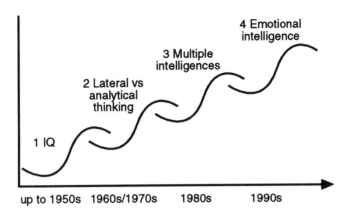

Figure 2.1   Four main phases in the development of our view of intelligence

we are to find the right strategy for successfully developing our human capital.

The basic building block – IQ

The best-known test of intelligence is the IQ test, developed by French psychologist Binet towards the end of the nineteenth century as a way to help children from poorer homes enter higher education. He realized that those children who moved on to higher education came almost exclusively from the wealthier classes because of their privileged backgrounds. IQ tests were evolved so that he could find a more objective way of identifying intelligent children whatever their social class.

IQ tests have become increasingly discredited as an objective measure, most recently by the focus on emotional intelligence discussed below. It is not surprising that they have fallen out of favor. They were developed when much less was known about the human brain. Nowadays they are rightly accused of being too limited and even repressive, as they focus only on specific mathematical and logical skills and fail to take account of or measure the wide range of people's abilities. Regardless of all the criticism of the weakness of IQ tests, however, we must not forget the huge advance they represented when they were first used.

Many people are also aware of an intelligence test called the GMAT, widely used by business schools to sort through and help choose applicants. And those who have taken GMAT will probably know that the more you practice on previous years' papers, the better you tend to do in the exam. So it is unclear whether tests like IQ and GMAT measure real ability or merely how much practice time you've managed to put in before the actual test.

The challenge of lateral thinking

Perhaps the first significant attack on the view of intelligence as purely a restricted set of analytical skills came from the proponents of what has been called lateral (or creative) thinking. They took as a starting point the fact that

the human brain is split into two main hemispheres – left and right. The left is generally associated with analytical, logical and mathematical functions and the right is seen as the source of creativity, humor, emotional expression and non-verbal ideas.

Those who advocate this view claim that traditional education and the organizations in which most of us work fail to take sufficient account of the power of the creative side of our intelligence. A powerful new set of techniques were developed to help people break free from the restrictions of classical,

logical thinking. The best known of these techniques are probably brainstorming, mind-mapping, structured problem solving, idea generation, associative thinking, visualization and use of metaphors. Most managers are familier with these ideas.

Our eight intelligences

A major breakthrough in how we view intelligence came in a book published in the early 1980s. The author, Howard Gardner, proposed that we have eight types of intelligence (Figure 2.2). These eight types of intelligence, and the areas in which they are most typically applied, are:

+ **Linguistic** – reading, writing and communicating with words: journalists, authors, comedians.
+ **Logical/mathematical** – reasoning, calculating, working through problems in a logical, systematic way: scientists, engineers, lawyers, accountants.
+ **Visual/spatial** – thinking in pictures, visualizing a final result: artists, architects, photographers.
+ **Musical** – composing music, keeping rhythm, remembering music: musicians, composers, music therapists.

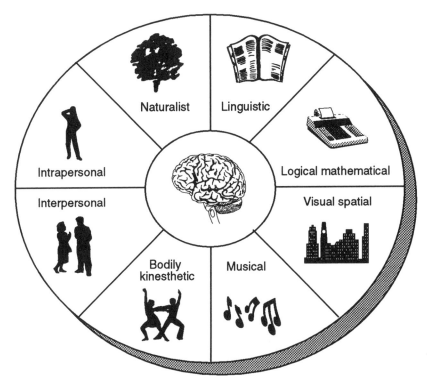

Figure 2.2 Gardner's eight types of intelligence

✦ **Bodily/kinesthetic** – using your body in building things or athletics, dancing and acting: athletes, surgeons, mechanics.

✦ **Interpersonal** – working effectively with others, using empathy and understanding: teachers, managers, salespeople, religious leaders.

✦ **Intrapersonal** – analysing and understanding ourselves, planning and setting our goals: high performers in many fields.

✦ **Naturalist** – using our understanding of the natural world productively: farmers, environmentalists, botanists.

We require a wide range of skills (or types of intelligence) to prosper. Moreover, different occupations will require strengths in different types of intelligence. The traditional approach to measuring intelligence, IQ tests, only really covers two (linguistic and logical/mathematical) of these kinds of ability. Moreover, our education system tends to focus to a large extent on these two skills plus, of course, the ability to memorize and regurgitate pieces of information. Gardner proposed that we must broaden our view of human intelligence, accept that all these types of intelligence are equally important and ensure that we recognize where people's skills lie and value and develop them accordingly.

The latest development – emotional intelligence

In the last few years a further development in our understanding of human intelligence has been proposed. This has been called emotional intelligence (EI) and is our ability to understand, master and work with both our own and other people's emotions.

The proponents of EI explain that to lead fulfilling lives our level of emotional intelligence (our EQ) is as important as, if not more important than, our level of IQ. EI can be pictured as having three levels (Figure 2.3):

1. **Mastery of the inner self** deals with our ability to understand our own emotions, to manage them and to motivate ourselves.
2. **Perception of others** addresses our capacity to understand other people's emotions and to empathize with them.
3. **Interaction with others** considers our social skills – how successfully we interest, motivate and lead others.

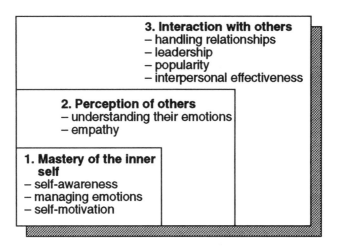

3. Interaction with others
– handling relationships
– leadership
– popularity
– interpersonal effectiveness

2. Perception of others
– understanding their emotions
– empathy

1. Mastery of the inner self
– self-awareness
– managing emotions
– self-motivation

Figure 2.3   The three levels of emotional intelligence

A starting point for understanding EI is an awareness of the potential mismatch between the speed of development of the human brain and the recent acceleration in the speed of development of our society over the last century. The human brain has evolved over millions of years and tens of thousands of generations. During this process it has added new, higher layers. But within the brain are also the basic primitive parts, which we share with other animals and which determine our instinctive 'fight or flee' reactions to external stimuli.

Our brain reacts to external signals on two main levels – instinctive and rational. Instinctive 'fight or flee' reactions are those which ensured our survival when we were faced with a threat. But instant rushes to fear, anger, aggression, timidity, jealousy or whatever are clearly inappropriate in our complex modern society. People with low EQ are those who tend to react instinctively and excessively without sufficient rational analysis of the situation and with insufficient control over their emotions. We can see in the many daily incidents of unprovoked aggression (inability to work with others, loss of control, rage, crime, violence etc.) how many people lack full emotional mastery. It is absolutely normal to feel emotions (hope, delight, anger, fury, disappointment or whatever) but it is how we react to those emotions that is critical. Self-control, self-motivation, empathy with others' emotions and the ability to interact with others are what make up EI.

We can look at how EI works in two types of situation – immediate response and longer-term response.

Immediate response

Faced with an external stimulus, particularly one that elicits strong emotions, we will experience a conflict between an instinctive, emotional reaction and a more rational response (Figure 2.4).

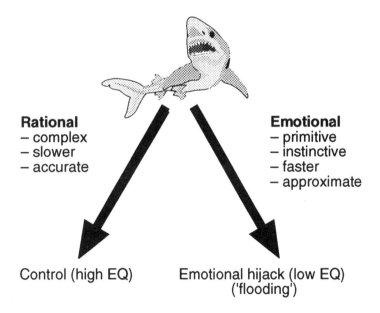

Rational
– complex
– slower
– accurate

Emotional
– primitive
– instinctive
– faster
– approximate

Control (high EQ)   Emotional hijack (low EQ)
                                ('flooding')

Figure 2.4   Our two ways of responding to external stimuli

As part of our evolution, our survival, "fight or flee" instinct (the amygdala) operates more rapidly than our higher-level, more rational mind (the neocortex). Whether our rational mind enables us to take control of our emotions or we allow our emotions to hijack us depends on our level of EI. Too often, when faced with quite trivial incidents – a driver who cuts in front of us, a colleague who disagrees with our proposals, a partner whom we believe has let us down, a child who irritates us – we allow our emotions to take over, the hormones epinephrine and norepinephrine flood through our bodies and we lash out, verbally or even physically, in a way we may later come to regret.

Longer-term response

We can see a similar situation in how we react to general aspects of our environment – success, love, poor results, problems with relationships and so on (Figure 2.5). We can either master the situation and react appropriately, or we can start to lose control of our emotions and overreact, becoming depressed, demotivated, frightened, excessively optimistic or whatever. Again, the higher our level of EI, the more likely we are to find the appropriate response.

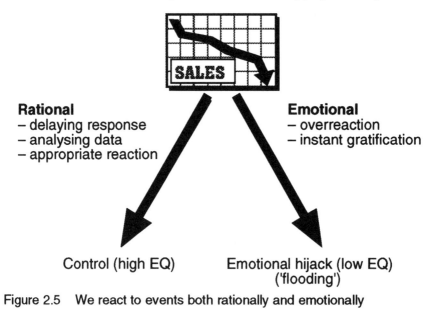

Rational
– delaying response
– analysing data
– appropriate reaction

Emotional
– overreaction
– instant gratification

Control (high EQ)   Emotional hijack (low EQ)
                                 ('flooding')

Figure 2.5   We react to events both rationally and emotionally

In a sense, advertising tries to appeal to our emotional immaturity. It bombards us with images, promising instant beauty, popularity, success, happiness or whatever, provided that we buy a certain product. Our rational mind may tell us that the promises are unrealistic. But the success of so many supposedly new perfumes, diets, cars, drinks, shampoos etc. bears witness to how many of us do succumb to advertising's blandishments.

Applying emotional intelligence

It is clear that understanding and mastery of our own and other people's emotions is just as critical to both personal effectiveness and our relationships as the level of our IQ. By and large, upbringing and education can only have a limited effect on our IQ. However, we can all learn to make significant improvements in our EQ.

Personal effectiveness

In our professional and personal lives, we will face challenging situations. When this happens our brains galvanize our bodies to achieve greater performance (area A on Figure 2.6) and we feel a surge of emotion. However, if we are unable to master this emotion we become overwhelmed, tired, demotivated, unfocused and our performance declines (area B on Figure 2.6). It is not uncommon to see people paralysed into inactivity if they feel they cannot cope with a situation – an exam, a personal loss etc.

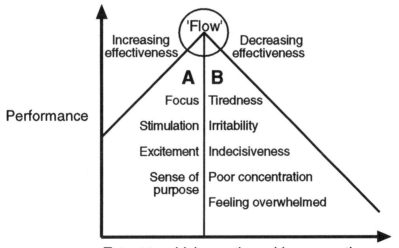

Figure 2.6   Emotion can both increase and decrease performance

The more control we have over our emotions, the more we will be able to use the surge of emotional energy to our advantage and not allow it to become a handicap.

The area at the top of the performance peak has been called 'flow'. This is when we are operating at maximum effectiveness because of our interest, excitement and involvement in some activity – work, sport, making love or whatever.

Relationships

We have probably all seen relationships that have fallen into destructive routines – the partners keep repeating patterns of behavior that in more rational moments they know are counter-productive, and yet they can't seem to break out of it until the relationship collapses. Likewise, we've all seen teams of the brightest fail catastrophically at their tasks and other teams achieve unanticipated success.

There are at least two clear sides to any work or personal relationship – intellectual and emotional (Figure 2.7).

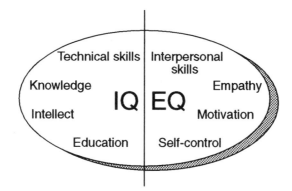

Figure 2.7   The two sides of any relationship

Obviously, the likelihood of success for any relationship or team is the sum of the participants' IQs and EQs. You can gather together the smartest intellects, but if they lack the ability to interact with each other their efforts can only end in failure.

The real contribution of EI is that it has used modern brain-imaging technologies and measurements of bodily activity (heartbeat, pulse, temperature etc.) to trace more accurately how emotions actually work in our brains and bodies. This has given a much greater understanding of how the primitive emotional (amygdala) and the more highly developed rational (neocortex) minds interact with each other and has allowed the development of ways to help people understand and increase their EQ, and thus their likelihood of leading fulfilling lives.

Summary

Life can be seen as a series of projects that we tackle in partnership with family members, friends or work colleagues. These projects will require a wide range of skills. Yet for many of us, our education will have been limited to a series of facts or calculations to be learnt by heart and regurgitated on command on exam day.

Many people, both inside and outside the education system, are becoming aware that our current approach fails to give children either the knowledge or (much more importantly) the desire to keep on acquiring knowledge that will be essential to them in leading fulfilling lives. One reaction is to demand a 'back to basics' approach, a return to traditional teaching methods for reading, writing and arithmetical skills. This will probably do some good in ensuring that all children are at least equipped with some core skills. But it falls far short of preparing them for the rapidly moving, knowledge-intensive world they will have to navigate.

In a more complex society, with continually increasing quantities of information, we need to take a broader view of human intelligence and give ourselves and our children the type of education that enables them to build the intellectual networks that turn information into understanding and the interpersonal skills that ensure successful relationships.

Recommended reading

Edward De Bono (1982) *Lateral Thinking for Management*, Pelican.

Howard Gardner (1983) *Frames of Mind: The Theory of Multiple Intelligences*, Basic Books.

Daniel Goleman (1996) *Emotional Intelligence: Why It Can Matter More than IQ*, Bloomsbury.

3
A Revolution in Performance Measurement

The way successful companies operate today is far different from their counterparts in the 1950s and 1960s, and light years away from the leading organizations of the 1920s and 1930s. Yet almost without exception, they measure their performance using exactly the same criteria and methods as their predecessors of up to half a century earlier.

Company performance measurement is still dominated by the requirements of financial accounting, itself based on double-entry bookkeeping which has been around since the fifteenth century. Some organizations, particularly conglomerates such as Hanson and BTR, have done extraordinarily well by using tight financial control to drive up the performance of their acquisitions. But others have cost-cut themselves out of existence, addicted to maintaining quarterly financial results and blind to the way their market share was being decimated by competitors offering better products and service.

This is not just a matter of changing accounting systems – it's much more important than that! What you measure (and what you reward people on) is what you will get. If you reward people on short-term results, then that's what they'll give you, even if they've sacrificed the company's future in the process, through cutting back on investment in new products, marketplace recognition and training.

There have been warnings about the strong financial bias of western organizational measurement systems. As far back as the 1950s, Peter Drucker (1955) was writing about the need to measure actively such areas as 'market standing' and 'innovation' as well as productivity and profitability. And there have been several more recent attempts to define more useful ways of measuring performance (for example, Eccles, 1991; Eccles & Nohria, 1992; Drucker, 1992; Meyer, 1994; Hope & Hope, 1995). Unfortunately, most organizations are still far away from breaking free from the stranglehold of, usually inappropriate, purely financially based measurement systems.

Too often, the major changes that organizations have gone through in the last 30 years or so have simply not been reflected in the way they measure their success:

INDUSTRY SECTOR	TYPICAL CHANGES (1960s to 1990s)
Consumer goods (from food to TVs)	From 10,000 customers making up 80 percent of sales to 10 customers accounting for 80 percent of sales
Aerospace and defense	From 'cost-plus' (where the more you spent, the more profit you made) to fixed-price contracts, often with time and cost penalties where any overrun will damage your results
Pharmaceuticals	From real price increases on drugs of 8 percent a year and market growth of 12 percent a year to real decreases in drug prices and a halving of market growth
Car manufacturing	From making most of the main parts to buying in 70 percent of each car's value and just assembling the final product

Unless organizations reorient their performance measurement systems to take account of the new ways in which they have to work, they cannot expect their people to adapt to quite different operational requirements.

Lag and lead indicators

One powerful way of looking at performance measures is to split them into 'lag' and 'lead' indicators:

✦ **Lag** – How well are we doing now due to actions taken in the past?
✦ **Lead** – How well are we likely to do in the future, given the actions we are taking today?

Most of the main indicators used by organizations are lag indicators. Like profit and return on investment, they tell us how we performed during the last reporting month, quarter or year. This performance will normally be based on decisions or investments which may have been made years before. However, such indicators give us no idea of how we may perform in the future.

The sudden and unexpected collapse of one of London's oldest and most respected banks, Baring Brothers (the 'Queen's bank'), gives a good example of reliance on lag indicators. The Singapore office had rapidly rising profits – a lag indicator – so everyone assumed all was well. With profits being squeezed in other areas, management appeared only too happy to give the successful Singapore office freedom to continue to churn out the cash. A lead indicator might have been the 'risk exposure of the bank' – such a measure would be aimed at assessing how the bank would perform in the future. This would also have shown that its Singapore office alone was gambling more than the total bank's assets were worth: not a healthy position. Had the bank used such a lead indicator, one assumes that management would have been somewhat more vigilant in monitoring what was happening in Singapore.

Further examples of the two types of measure include:

LAG	LEAD
Profit/loss or working capital	Growth/decline in market share
Return on investment, return on capital employed etc.	Time bringing new products to market
Revenue per employee	Time spent with key customers
Number of customer complaints	Percentage of deliveries meeting customers' requested date

A lag indicator measures results of past actions, a lead indicator tries to identify the drivers of future performance. Lag indicators are easy to get: most financial systems churn them out in whatever frequency and form you may want. But their relative abundance should not be allowed to disguise the fact that, on their own, they are inadequate to help you run an organization successfully.

It is critical to understand that this is not a small matter of accounting procedures. In a time of relative stability, such as the 1950s or 1960s, strong financial performance in the past might be seen to give a reasonable guide to the continued probability of good results in the future. In a time of rapid change, however, managing a company purely on lag indicators is like trying to drive a car looking only in the rear mirror – if the road is straight, you're OK. But if there are some sharp bends and a lot of oncoming traffic, you could have problems.

So the indicators we rely on for measuring our performance must change from focusing only on results to shedding light on the processes we use to obtain those results so that we can influence the future. They must, for example, tell us whether we have a growing or declining market share as well as quantifying the money we are making from our business today. And they must inform us whether our projects are hitting cost and time targets and not just how sales of existing products are performing.

Of course, all businesses must measure profit and must be profitable to survive. But there is a difference in the way most western and Japanese companies view profit. For western companies, profit tends to be the starting point against which all actions are judged – for many Japanese companies, profit is the natural result of the way they work. A British survey conducted in 1990 (*Sunday Times*, 22 April) trumpeted that 28 of Europe's 50 most profitable companies the previous year were British. This was given as evidence of the success of the 'Thatcherite economic miracle'. However, any objective observer of the relative performance of Europe's economies knows that British industry is far from healthy and that the country's industrial base is continuing to shrink. The problem was that the survey measured pre-tax profit as a percentage of sales – basically how much money management had managed to extract from their businesses. And the more money is extracted to give to shareholders, the less there is available to invest in future growth. Moreover, six of the most profitable British companies between 1979 and 1989 had collapsed or been acquired after near collapse by 1990. Following the demise of so many 1980s boom companies, the head of the Accounting Standards Board commented that people were taking too limited a view of companies' performance: 'Anyone who still uses earnings per share needs his head examined.' This was probably little consolation to the many investors who had been encouraged by their stockbrokers to invest in supposedly profitable British companies such as Coloroll, Polly Peck and Maxwell Communications.

To compete, we must move from a myopic concentration on profit to what has been called a 'polyocular' view of how we assess performance – a view which looks at several sides simultaneously. Instead of just taking a once-yearly snapshot of the immediate results which are extracted from employees' work (profit), we must try to measure the processes which lead to those results – the reliability of deliveries, new product development times, customer satisfaction, levels of investment in R&D, reject rates, percentage of policies or contracts issued correctly within a certain target time etc. If we manage these well, profit will result.

From single to multiple stakeholders

One way of expressing the need for a much broader approach to performance measurement is to think of an organization as having to satisfy a number of different stakeholders to be successful. Each stakeholder is likely to have different priorities (Figure 3.1).

Figure 3.1   Most organizations have to satisfy multiple stakeholders

Successful organizations are usually those which manage to balance these different interests most effectively – organizations which, for example, both return a reasonable profit for shareholders and invest to keep their staff and to secure the organization's future. When an organization shows exceptional performance on any one measure, such as sudden huge profits or dramatic growth, this is often because one group of stakeholders is being favored at the expense of the others. Although such results can appear impressive in the very short term, they can indicate an imbalance which can threaten the organization's existence. For example, the British company Polly Peck announced profits of £161 million (70 percent earnings growth!) just days before collapsing. In 1995, by seeking to reduce financial liabilities through dumping the Brent Spar oil platform in the Atlantic rather than the more costly option of dismantling it onshore, Shell caused a consumer backlash which resulted in a severe decline in sales in a number of European countries and undid years of advertising its environmentally friendly image. And by granting huge pay rises and bonuses to their management, the privatized utilities in the UK caused consumer pressure for more regulation of their activities and greater control over their prices. One chairman of a privatized utility even had to give up a bonus scheme worth millions of pounds because of concerns over how the public would react.

In each of these cases, by focusing too much on satisfying one narrow group of stakeholders, the organizations involved damaged their overall positions.

The changing role of measurement – from control to support

In the classical large hierarchical company, measurement had two main purposes – to control the organization and to report its results. Top management decided strategy, set targets and measured the organization against them. Here strategy was a one-shot process – once it was decided, the organization got on with implementing it.

However, if we believe even part of what we say about the need to move to less authoritarian and more customer-responsive structures, then setting strategy should become a more flexible process. Top management still sets the general direction or strategic intent, but this must be adjusted to take account of operational, market and competitive changes. This requires a continuous flow of information both up and down the organization, so that people can learn and adjust their plans.

Pages 248–57

Matching measurements and strategy

The choice of measurement system is becoming a critical issue for managers, especially as IT is now able to provide an almost infinite amount of information about an organization's operations. Too often we hear of people being swamped by data, rather than assisted by information. The new American manager of an oil company's European operation was attracted to a new computer system because it would give him a vast range of data from any country in real time on the screen on his desk. He believed this would improve his decision making. But he had mistaken quantity of data for receiving the right information.

At the risk of stating the obvious, we can say that managers need measurement systems to help them implement their strategies. There should therefore be a clear link between aspects of the strategy and the indicators they monitor. A typical situation where an organization's traditional key performance indicators were dislocated from its strategy is given below. Here, although the firm was building an aggressive strategy based on innovation and customer service, it continued to measure its performance with measures not directly showing the success or otherwise of this strategy.

STRATEGY	TRADITIONAL MEASURES	MORE RELEVANT INDICATORS
Build customer base by 10% p.a.	Profit	Number of customers and average spend
Reach 30% of sales coming from new products (less than two years on the market)	Return on investment Revenue per employee	Percentage of sales from new products
Provide better customer service than two main competitors	Share price/earnings per share	Average lead time per order Percentage of orders delivered by requested date

Executive (or strategic) dashboards

One idea is that executives should try to build a kind of dashboard, containing no more than 15 indicators which sum up all the key aspects of their business. This can either be in the form of a monthly report or even portrayed like a car dashboard. There should be a balance between basic financial (lag) indicators and operational (lead) indicators which give insights into how far the elements of their strategy are being achieved.

✦ An FMCG (fast-moving consumer goods) manufacturer whose customer base has consolidated so that 10 retail customers account for 80 percent of turnover might focus its measurements on three main areas – basic financial measures, how it is serving those critical accounts, and general manufacturing and supply performance.

✦ A defense contractor who has moved from cost-plus to fixed-price contracts with penalties for late deliveries would want to balance standard financial measurements with tight monitoring of project performance, particularly of time and cost 'estimates to complete' the main project milestones.

✦ A pharmaceutical manufacturer facing declining prices, declining sales per product and increasing development costs would see a need to offset base financial data with information on price evolution, measures of the rate of uptake of new products in the market, and time and cost results for achieving development milestones.

In most FMCG companies, defense contractors and pharmaceutical manufacturers you will probably not find this type of data (apart from the traditional financials) being considered at top management level. In one FMCG company, the top managers were so dislocated from the new reality of their concentrated customer base that they never even went to visit any of their 10 key customers, despite their importance to the organization's business. And in many defense contractors, project performance is considered an 'operational' issue and thus not worthy of the attention of top executives. Likewise, in some pharmaceutical companies top managers may show some interest in the technical aspects of ongoing projects, but seldom get involved in the 'operational' aspects such as achievement of key milestones or rate of uptake of new products in the market.

The balanced scorecard

Another way that has been proposed for trying to achieve a balance between classical financial and other strategically important measures is the balanced scorecard (Figure 3.2). In many ways it can be seen as similar to an executive dashboard and its inventors even compare it to 'the dials in an aeroplane cockpit' (Kaplan & Norton, 1992). The main difference is that the balanced scorecard specifies the four areas in which a company should measure itself.

The balanced scorecard is built on measuring two external views of an organization (how customers and shareholders will judge it) and two internal views (key process performance and how well the organization is innovating and learning).

Like the executive dashboard, the balanced scorecard tries to move performance measurement away from top-down, mainly financial control and to link it with achieving the organization's strategy. As many of the indicators are lead indicators, they are not just a judgement on the past but are rather intended to be 'actionable' – a guide to influencing the future. With lag indicators, it is

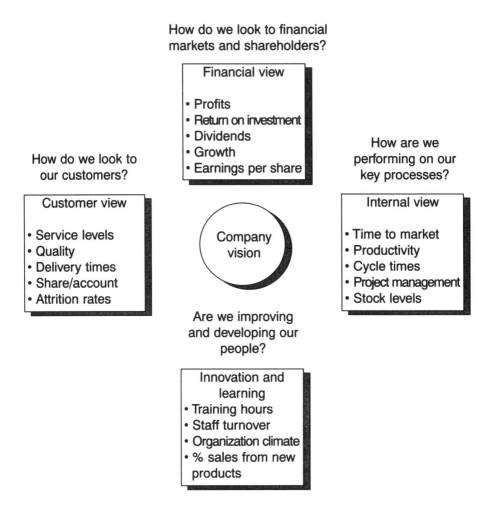

Figure 3.2   An example of a balanced scorecard

often too late to react. Lead indicators, on the other hand, give you more opportunity to understand where you should focus your efforts – if there is good performance in one area, it can be identified and reinforced; if one indicator is dipping, corrective action can be taken.

The strengths of concepts such as the executive dashboard and the balanced scorecard lie both in their use and in the activity of creating them. Few management groups have a single agreed view of their organization's goals. Frequently much executive time is spent defending particular departmental interests or viewpoints. Or else executives sink into a cosy complacency of sharing an easy common viewpoint, which allows for a quiet life. Building an executive dashboard or balanced scorecard with an executive group forces them to face up to, and to come to agreement on, the key issues facing a business – as such it is an excellent way of aligning executives and motivating them to perform the task for which they are paid.

Too often, executives (like politicians) are quick to take the credit for good financial results and even quicker to blame external factors for poor financial performance. We have to make executives more responsible for the future by giving them measurement systems and indicators that help them influence that future. As financial results measure what has happened in the past, executives can easily fend off any criticism and give the impression of intense activity by presenting their plans for improving financial performance in the next reporting period. However, when the next reporting period does come, these plans are sometimes conveniently forgotten or else external circumstances 'out of our control' are blamed for missing targets. By moving executives' focus from the (always backward-looking) lag financial indicators to more actionable (forward-looking) lead indicators, we can give top management the opportunity to become more directly involved in influencing the course of the business and take away many excuses for poor performance.

Measure the process, not the people

Many organizations are rapidly moving towards cross-functional teams to carry out key business functions such as managing improvement programs or serving certain critical customer sectors. Problems can arise when an organization makes these types of fundamental changes to the way it works and does not adapt its measurement systems to match. If this happens, measurement systems can undermine the effectiveness of the changes.

Pages 142–53

When you install cross-functional teams, for example, you are normally reducing the power of the functions – if you retain a system of performance indicators based on functional achievement, you will only exacerbate tensions between the new teams and the existing functions. When you are empowering teams to manage a critical business process, you must move to measuring that process as a totality – just measuring small, functionally based parts of the process will cause people in those functions to act in ways that make their functional results look good, but are dysfunctional to the process as a whole.

To use the three earlier examples:

✦ FMCG – if you have set up a team to manage some of your largest accounts and ensure excellent service, they should not be continually tripped up by, for example, a factory manager who is being rewarded for holding stock levels down or machine utilization up. A couple of failed deliveries to a major supermarket chain will probably lose you more than the low stock holding would ever have gained.

+ Pharmaceuticals – if you have launched a team to take a potentially best-selling extension of an existing drug rapidly to market, you should not permit individual functions to hold back key resources and deploy them on 'higher interest' new drug projects or local area research work.

+ Defense – if you are running the risk of time-overrun penalties on a major contract and you have found a subcontractor who can do some critical path work faster than your in-house specialists, you should clearly use the subcontractor, even if your in-house specialists claim that this will leave them with insufficient work for the following six months. Your traditional measurement system will show a low work loading for that area for a while. But now that you're on fixed-price contracts, with penalties for time overruns and not the old cost-plus system of charging, it is clear that you have to go against what the traditional measurement system values, and act in the interests of the business as a whole.

The above examples may seem obvious, even trivial. Yet time and again, when they try to have controversial decisions taken which are in the best interests of the organization as a whole, cross-functional teams find themselves being entangled in endless political battles against narrow functional interests, fuelled by an out-of-date, functionally based measurement and reward system.

In a simple supply chain (Figure 3.3), there are many performance measures you could put in place (for example, there are more than 60 performance measures available just for order taking and invoicing). Almost inevitably, as each area in the process optimizes its local performance, after a certain point this will tend to harm the effectiveness of the process as a whole – too little stock will affect deliveries, too much pressure to reduce sales costs may harm customer service, extreme focus on low-cost suppliers may have implications for product quality. What many companies are struggling with is how to find the right balance between local optimization and good performance of the whole process.

Summary

The revolution in performance measurement has not yet arrived – not by a long way. In far too many organizations, the linkages between what they are trying to achieve and what they measure are poor. However, the need for

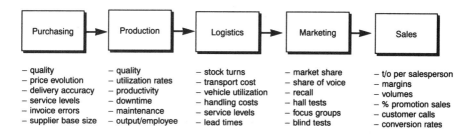

Figure 3.3   Too much focus on measuring all the individual parts of a process can lead to local optimization but poor performance of the process as a whole

change is there, and a few leading companies are seizing the initiative by replacing their old-fashioned, financially based, lag measurement systems with more broad-based, forward-looking and actionable lead indicators.

Whatever position you occupy in an organization, you should review the key indicators against which you are measured and against which you measure others, to see how many are just lag (measuring the results of past actions) and how many are truly lead (helping you actively influence the future). If they are mostly lag indicators, perhaps you should be looking to supplement them with some more useful measures.

Recommended reading

P. Doyle (1994) 'Setting business objectives and measuring performance', *European Management Journal*, Vol. 12, No. 2.

Peter Drucker (1955) *The Practice of Management*, HarperBusiness (US)/Heinemann (UK).

Peter Drucker (1992) *Managing for the Future*, HarperBusiness (US)/Heinemann (UK).

Robert G. Eccles (1991) 'The performance measurement manifesto', *Harvard Business Review*, Jan–Feb.

Robert G. Eccles & Nitin Nohria (1992) *Beyond the Hype*, Harvard Business School Press.

Tony Hope & Jeremy Hope (1995) *Transforming the Bottom Line*, Nicholas Brealey.

IR-RR (1987) 'UK management training and development – too little, too late, for too few', May.

Robert S. Kaplan & David P. Norton (1992) 'The balanced scorecard – measures that drive performance', *Harvard Business Review*, Jan–Feb.

Christopher Meyer (1994) 'How the right measures help teams excel', *Harvard Business Review*, May–June.

4

Chaos and Management

Chaos theory may turn out to be one of the most significant influences on management over the next several years. Like all powerful models, it has the potential to help us:

+ structure and understand what we have observed or sensed
+ clearly express what we have intuitively felt, but not yet put into words
+ develop new insights into the way we view and manage our organizations.

Some definitions

The popular understanding of chaos is that it is a state of complete disorder. The scientific definition is quite different. Scientists distinguish between three states:

+ **Stable equilibrium** – where the elements are always in, or quickly return to, a state of balance. The temperature in a room controlled by a thermostat could be said to be in stable equilibrium: whatever changes there are affecting the room, the thermostat will always return the temperature to a pre-set level. For many years car and soap powder markets were near to stable equilibrium. Of course, one company could improve its product and another could launch a huge advertising campaign. But, in general, when the dust settled market shares between the main competitors tended not to change that much.
+ **Bounded instability (or chaos)** – a mixture of order and disorder. There are many unpredictable events and changes, but the basic patterns of a system's behavior can be detected. Over the last 20 years many car markets have been in chaos. Sudden shocks such as oil price changes, shifts in con-

sumer tastes, pressure from environmentalists, aggressive new competitors and government policies have thrown many forecasts way off course, but general trends can be detected and exploited by faster-moving firms.

✦ **Explosive instability** – there is no order or pattern. Many of the events during the Second World War or in the former Yugoslavia could be seen to be examples of this.

The contention of chaoticians (remember, there was one in *Jurassic Park*) is that many organizations used to operate in something approaching stable equilibrium and are now finding themselves in bounded instability or chaos. Denationalized airlines and banks or many manufacturing industries are good examples – the former are suddenly having to compete to retain customers; the latter are finding the competitive situation increasingly harsh; and all of them are subject to rapid technological change which, if applied effectively, can unexpectedly propel a competitor from being an also-ran into a seemingly unbeatable lead.

If it is the case that organizations have moved from stable equilibrium to chaos, then this has profound implications for how they are managed. But, before going on to that, one more definition, of a non-linear system.

A **linear system** is like the thermostat mentioned above. An action will cause a directly predictable reaction: light a fire in the room and the thermostat will turn the heating down; open a window to let cold air in and the thermostat will turn the heating up.

An example of a **non-linear system** could be a major TV advertising campaign. Launching your campaign, you hope for linear system results – you spend £10 million and you plan to gain three market share points. You've tried this before and it worked. Moreover, your financial models show exactly what market share result and return on investment you can expect from the extra £10 million advertising expenditure. Sometimes things turn out as you had expected.

In reality, of course there are a whole series of other possible outcomes which you may not have planned for – a competitor may fight back and outspend you, or they may beat you for much less money with a more creative campaign, or they may offer a special '2 for the price of 1' promotion and satisfy market demand, leaving you with reduced sales and a big hole in your bank balance. Or a competitor may be aggressive and just go for a low-cost response such as spreading bad publicity about the quality or safety of your product (as with a recent £100 million new soap powder launch), or there may be a spell of good weather so not so many people are watching television.

Why do we need chaos theories?

Most people will accept that organizations' environments, whether global, competitive or regulatory, have become more complex and more prone to sudden, unexpected changes. This looks like being an accelerating rather than a passing phenomenon – in short, it's going to get worse.

In a reasonably stable environment, we can run our organizations in the traditional hierarchical, mechanistic way. Top executives (aided by their consultants and corporate planners) set strategy, middle managers carry it out, and very detailed control and reporting systems pass thousands of numbers back up the hierarchy to inform those responsible about progress.

Unfortunately this model doesn't work very well any more because it is based on three assumptions which are no longer wholly valid:

✦ Assumption 1 – the organization is a simple 'closed system': what it decides to do will generally take place without too much disruption from outside events.

✦ Assumption 2 – the operating environment is stable enough for managers to understand it sufficiently well to develop a relevant detailed strategy and for that strategy still to be relevant by the time it comes to be implemented.

✦ Assumption 3 – in an organization there are a series of clear levers which can be applied to cause a known response (e.g. if you cut staff numbers, profitability should go up, or if you increase interest rates, the value of your currency will rise).

These three assumptions have been replaced by three new realities:

✦ Reality 1 – organizations are complex 'open systems', deeply influenced by and influencing their environments. Often intended actions will be diverted off course by external events or even by the internal political or cultural processes of the organization itself.

✦ Reality 2 – the environment is changing so rapidly (continuously throwing up new opportunities and threats) that top managers cannot expect to have sufficient sense of what is happening to formulate very detailed strategies. Moreover, by the time a strategy moves from concept to being operationalized, key aspects of the environment have often changed.

✦ Reality 3 – the simple linear models of cause and effect have broken down and many actions can lead to quite unexpected (positive or negative) consequences.

Implications for management

If we accept the concept of chaos, there are at least six important implications for the way we manage our organizations and employees.

1. Moving from 'damping' to 'amplifying' actions

In linear systems, 'negative' or 'damping' feedback is primarily used to bring the system back into equilibrium. The belief is that there is a state of equilibrium (unemployment being around 7 percent, or your firm controlling 30 percent of the market, or return on investment being 14 percent) and that it is desirable always to try to return to this state. Your state of mind is 'what actions can we take to return to the desired equilibrium?'. 'Management by exception' is an example of using damping actions – you plan to achieve a state of equilibrium and act only on deviations from that state, rather than continuously looking for opportunities to improve.

In non-linear systems, there is 'positive amplifying' feedback. As the world is seen as inherently unstable, very small actions can be amplified so that they have major consequences. Sudden shifts in technology, taste or regulations – and there have been many in recent years – can hugely amplify small actions. Apple's and Microsoft's incredible growth were the result of breakthroughs in technology matching an untapped market need and being brilliantly exploited. And nobody could have guessed that, by simply changing its focus from large to small bikes, Honda, a virtually unknown Japanese manufacturer, would swamp the US market (see page 42).

Managers' ways of thinking and acting are quite different if they see the world as being in something near stable equilibrium than if they believe they are operating in chaos (Figure 4.1).

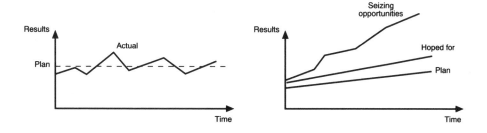

Figure 4.1 Comparing mindsets – stable equilibrium and chaos

In stable equilibrium, managers are constantly trying to bring a situation back to a pre-planned state. In chaos, managers have goals, but are also looking for the kind of positive amplification which can give extraordinary, rather than just ordinary, results.

2. Creating your own self-reinforcing positive spirals

Linked closely to the idea of positive amplification is the concept of self-reinforcing spirals. Often it seems that some organizations can do nothing wrong. Japanese carmakers, for example – if you allow them access to a market, they will compete on better quality and features for a lower price. Yet if you restrict access, they can use the fact that demand outstrips supply to raise prices and extract higher profits. However, there are other organizations that seem to try every trick under the sun, yet nothing can slow down their relentless decline. The continuing deindustrialization of the British economy, in spite of scores of government initiatives to boost industry, investment and training, is an example of this.

In stable equilibrium, actions tend to have very clear outcomes. You increase advertising spend and sales will increase, you add an extra shift and production volume will go up. However, in chaos, actions tend to have expected and also unexpected (both positive and negative) outcomes, because changes or complex interactions of factors amplify consequences. Very quickly, small actions can launch you into vicious or virtual spirals with unforeseen consequences.

> You launch an advertising campaign to gain some market share. A competitor takes fright and reexamines their relations with their advertising agency. They realize that, having been with the agency 10 years, they're no longer a 'glamor' account for the creative department and so are getting poor service from junior staff and an unsatisfactory campaign quality. They move their account to a new agency. Anxious to make its mark, the new agency puts its best people on the account. They come up with a great campaign and you get slaughtered in the market. All you were trying to do was grab a few points of market share to satisfy your newly appointed boss, who wanted to make a mark. But you end up pushing your main competitor into a more aggressive mode, which results in them taking from you the extra market share which you'd hoped to steal from them.

Figure 4.2 shows how this vicious spiral quickly develops.

Intended outcome

Actual outcome

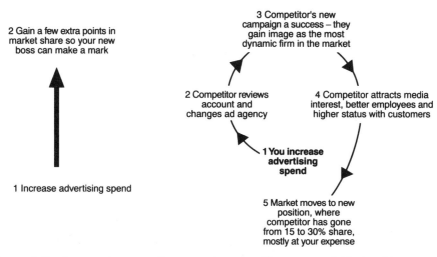

2 Gain a few extra points in
market share so your new
boss can make a mark

1 Increase advertising spend

3 Competitor's new
campaign a success – they
gain image as the most
dynamic firm in the market

2 Competitor reviews
account and
changes ad agency

4 Competitor attracts media
interest, better employees and
higher status with customers

1 You increase
advertising
spend

5 Market moves to new
position, where
competitor has gone
from 15 to 30% share,
mostly at your expense

Figure 4.2   In complex, non-linear systems, actions can quickly lead to
self-reinforcing virtuous or vicious spirals

And, of course, once your competitor gains that extra market share, they
can attract better people, achieve higher profitability by putting more volume through their factories and can use their improved position to
increase their bargaining power with customers and suppliers. This gives
them more to spend on advertising, strengthening their market position,
improving their profitability further and so on. Your competitor is now on
a self-reinforcing positive spiral. It's going to be very difficult for you to
catch them up, unless you can find a positive self-reinforcing cycle of your
own – for example, by launching a new product range. There's no point
trying to follow your competitor on their virtuous spiral as they're already
far ahead of you.

Similarly, a small investment in training order takers and giving them better information about stock availability could lead to their giving better service to a major customer than your competitor does. This in turn could
lead to a gradual shift of orders from the competitor to you, increasing
your sales volumes, leading to higher profits and allowing you to invest in
better equipment. This in its turn helps you become more effective and
gives you a major advantage over the competitor.

Once you start to understand that chaos can so easily lead to self-reinforcing positive or negative spirals:

✦ you're no longer prepared to cede small temporary advantages to competitors, because you understand how quickly these can be turned into self-reinforcing positive spirals for your competitor and negative self-reinforcing spirals for you
✦ you're always on the lookout for small advantages, however insignificant they may appear at the time, because you realize that these can often be quickly amplified into a self-reinforcing positive spiral for you.

3. Using attractor points

While a stable equilibrium mindset has a tendency to see developments in terms of regular trends, chaos thinking views developments as lurching from one temporary state of semi-stability to the next. For example, equilibrium thinking might believe a market will grow by 3–5 percent a year (Figure 4.3a). The chaos view might be that, although it grows by 3–5 percent a year averaged out over the long term, the actual growth will come in fits and starts (Figure 4.3b) with periods of rapid growth and then plateaux. These

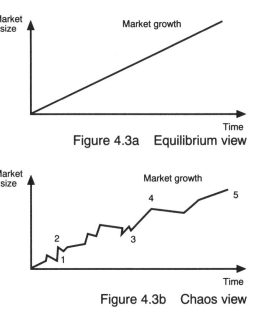

Figure 4.3a   Equilibrium view

Figure 4.3b   Chaos view

temporary plateaux are called 'attractor points', because for a period a system's behavior seems attracted to their level.

Many attractor points are obvious – if a firm brings a new factory on stream, available volume rises to a new level and pressure to lower prices increases; or if consumer taste shifts towards large family transporters or small city cars, then demand for cars may increase for a while to a new level as people move over to the new fashion.

However, too often managers act as if these attractor points or plateaux did not exist:

✦ A carmaker, seeing the growth in large family transporters, entered the market over seven years after a competitor on the assumption that the rapid rate of growth would continue. What actually happened was that initial demand was satisfied by the first manufacturer and sales of these cars levelled off at a new attractor point. So the late entrant significantly overestimated market demand and built expensive excess production capacity.

✦ The customer base of most FMCG companies has shrunk from several thousand retail customers taking most of their volume to about 10 major retailing groups now accounting for up to 70–80 percent of volume. Treat one of those customers badly and get yourself downgraded as a supplier or even delisted, and you don't just temporarily lose a couple of percentage points on sales. You move to a new and much lower attractor point, you give away a heaven-sent opportunity to a competitor and it's incredibly difficult to rise back again to the previous attractor point.

✦ As markets grow, they don't add consumers regularly as in Figure 4.3a. Instead, they add new consumer segments with different needs and tastes (Figure 4.3b). And as each new segment joins, the sales level rises to the next attractor point. So if you are slow in keeping up with a market's development, you don't just miss a few thousand consumers, you may miss a whole new segment and fall irreparably behind.

In chaos, organizations can quickly slip down to or rise up to new attractor points. There is often more at stake with each management move or oversight than most organizations realize. If managers really understood and internalized the potential negative results of inaction – allowing service levels to slip, allowing burned-out executives to while away their time to retirement in key positions, running a boring advertising campaign too long because of the cost and political implications of withdrawing it, or adopting a 'wait and see' attitude with a new technology application in their market – they would not be so laid back about their own or their organization's slowness to act.

4. Building strategy – from detailed planning to strategic intent

If we believe that the environment is not inherently stable, then we know that our industry will be regularly shaken by a series of, to some extent unpredictable, shocks. So it is pointless for executives to lay out an extremely detailed, top-down, five-year strategy. The likelihood is that we'll be thrown way off course long before we've implemented our great plan. Moreover, the people who are going to have to identify and cope with the unpredictable shocks are not only executives, but more often those closest to customers, technology developments and the market. If these people are hemmed in by a very detailed strategic plan, they're going to be unable to respond effectively.

So the development of strategy needs to move from a model where you produce very detailed planning to a more flexible approach based on setting a  fairly clear direction, then continuously adapting the detail to cope with specific events, threats and opportunities. We must move from a strategic planning mentality to the concept of strategic direction or strategic intent (see Part Eight – Developing the Right Strategy). For example:

◆ Komatsu set a strategic intent to 'Surround Caterpillar'. Over the years it used many different methods – low prices, total quality, just-in-time, exploiting unexpected market opportunities and responding rapidly to any moves by Caterpillar. There was no very detailed strategic plan, but everybody in the company knew and shared the one overarching goal.

◆ Honda wanted to make inroads into the export market for large motorbikes. It tried southeast Asia and failed. It tried the US and was having little success until some customers expressed interest in the small 'Supercub' motorcycles which the Honda staff used for their errands. Honda had not tried to market these in the US as 'they seemed wholly unsuitable for the US market where everything was bigger and more luxurious' (Quinn, Mintzberg & James, 1988). Honda quickly responded to this interest, changed focus from large to small bikes and within five years dominated the US market. While other companies would probably have given up or fought an uphill struggle with their original strategy to sell large bikes, Honda had built an organization that could quickly identify and adapt to new opportunities within a general shared goal.

Strategic success in this context derives not from detailed strategy, but from a statement of clear and ambitious goals and from creating a cohesive, entrepreneurial and learning culture, enabling people to seize the opportunities to achieve those goals.

5. Encouraging organizational learning – single- to double-loop

The Honda example earlier illustrates another key implication of operating in chaos – the need for management to create an organization that is capable of learning, so it can adapt to new situations. It is generally thought that there are

two types of learning – 'single-loop' and 'double-loop' (see
Part Three – Encouraging Creativity).

Pages 78–80

✦ **Single-loop learning** is when you meet a situation with
a straightforward reaction – whenever you have peak sales, you increase
overtime for your employees; whenever market share falls below a certain
level, you increase promotional spend; when a supplier delivers poor quality,
you increase the level of control on their deliveries or simply return the faulty
goods and demand a credit.
✦ **Double-loop learning** means reacting, but at the same time questioning
the assumptions behind your reaction.

For example, when you are applying double-loop learning, instead of meeting
sales peaks with expensive overtime, you try to understand the reasons for
those peaks and look for ways of smoothing them out (working with customers or building stock of base-range items). Some firms even find that it is
their own policies of regular yearly price rises or end-of-year rush to meet budget by pushing stock into customers which cause these disruptive and costly
demand peaks. By analysing the reasons behind events you can deal with the
events themselves and not just react to their consequences.

Or, instead of increasing inspections on your problem supplier, you could
set up meetings with engineers from both your organizations to see whether
you could jointly solve the problem and come up with a better way of making
or using the problem parts.

6. Building balanced measurement systems

Stable equilibrium is the perfect environment for old-fashioned, voluminous
management reporting systems. When you know exactly which actions will
lead to which results, then it's worth analysing in detail the detailed weekly or
daily sales trend in every single type of customer segment and geographic area
you cover. Find a variance from plan and you can take action to correct it. And
now, thanks to the wonders of information technology, all the data you could
ever want can be provided instantly in any combination of market, product,
price group, pack size etc. to incredible levels of detail. One great selling point
of a new computer system to executives in multinational companies was that
it would give them access to extraordinary amounts of information, at the
touch of a button, from any or all of the countries where they operated.

Of course, much of this so-called information is useless. Do the top executives of a European company really need to know how well a certain pack size

is selling in a small region of a minor country? Or should their minds be focused on slightly larger issues? Receiving vast quantities of data is a great emotional security blanket. But is it actually helping you, or just drowning you in unnecessary detail? Maybe we need better, rather than more, measures.

If we believe that organizations are moving towards operating in environments which more resemble chaos than stability, then there are two main types of activity the organization must be good at and therefore two main features which our reporting systems should measure:

- ✦ **Current operations** – are we efficiently making, delivering, serving or whatever our core activity is?
- ✦ **Strategic direction** – are we developing our people, customers and suppliers so that when half-expected or unexpected threats or opportunities arise, we are aware of them and able to react to them?

This dual nature of the information we require has led to concepts such as lag and lead indicators, the executive dashboard and the balanced scorecard (see Chapter 3 – A Revolution in Performance Measurement). These are ways of trying to move away from the obsession of most measurement systems with purely quantifying past financial performance toward a focus on ensuring that we are building the capability to succeed in the future.

Pages 22–33

As the faltering performance of many once great companies has shown, while in stable equilibrium past financial results may well have been a good guide to future performance, in chaos (or bounded instability) they can often be a very poor indication as to how we will prosper in even the very near future.

Summary – the way forward

Most managers are having to work in conditions which have some if not all of the attributes of chaos – virtuous and vicious spirals instead of stability, sudden shifts to new attractor points instead of gradual evolution, amplified effects of apparently small incidents, unexpected outcomes from seemingly straightforward actions.

Chaos, with its frequent sudden shifts and lurches, is constantly creating new opportunities and threats. These can allow seemingly small, powerless competitors to dominate a market quickly and can cause apparently invincible incumbents to start stumbling helplessly from one disaster to another.

Too many organizations have not understood the dynamics at work and are repeatedly caught out by events. However, once managers have grasped the basic logic behind events, it is less difficult to anticipate and benefit from the new chaotic environment. By moving towards double-loop learning, working to reach new attractor points and trying to create our own self-reinforcing virtuous spirals, we can achieve the kind of results which would be considered impossible in a more stable environment.

Recommended reading

Kevin Kelly (1994) *Out of Control: The New Biology of Machines, Social Systems, and the Economic World*, Addison-Wesley (US)/Fourth Estate (UK).

P. Ormerod (1994) *The Death of Economics*, Faber and Faber.

D. Parker & R. Stacey (1994) *Chaos, Management and Economics*, Institute for Economic Affairs.

J.B. Quinn, H. Mintzberg & R.M. James (1988) *The Strategy Process*, Prentice-Hall.

R. Stacey (1992) *Managing Chaos*, Prentice-Hall (US)/Kogan Page (UK).

Part Two

Focusing on the Customer

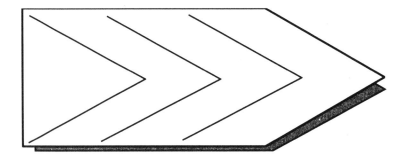

5
The Need for Customer Focus

Some organizations may think they focus on the customer, or claim to do so – others really do it. Which of the following organizations would you prefer to deal with:

✦ A theme park which uses ingenious ways of hiding the real length of queues for attractions – or one which keeps guests informed of waiting times?

✦ A food manufacturer which bombards supermarket chains with one unsought-after 'special price' promotion after another – or one which has set up a partnership with the main supermarket groups to offer continuously low prices?

✦ A motor insurance company, which spends months shunting claims from one department to another – or one which promises to process all claims within two weeks?

✦ A hospital which brings patients in 3–4 times for pre-operation tests and admits them 1–2 days before the operation – or one which tries to organize the tests at times to suit the patients and aims to do as many operations as possible on a day-surgery basis?

✦ A management consultancy which has all kinds of escape clauses written into its contracts to absolve it if hoped-for results are not achieved – or one which guarantees to stay with the client until promised benefits are firmly delivered?

✦ An airline which fights tooth and nail to maintain a monopoly allowing it to charge high ticket prices – or one which positions itself as a champion of open competition and lower prices?

Some organizations are heavy, bureaucratic, old-fashioned and seem to treat their customers as irritants, while others are fast-moving, flexible, exciting and dedicated to providing a different and better service. Although, in the short term, the first kind of organization may achieve some success, it's not difficult to imagine which will eventually win long-term customer loyalty.

Developing true customer focus is no longer a choice for organizations if they want to survive. There are too many derelict factories, empty office blocks and unemployed people left behind by organizations which took their right to exist for granted and prioritized their own interests above those of their customers.

With breathtaking speed, organizations which had previously believed themselves immune to the need to consider their customers' needs are being thrust into an environment in which their customers can now go elsewhere if they are continually let down. Banks, denationalized airlines, medical services, even parts of national and local government are being given the choice – either satisfy their customers or face decline and possible disappearance.

More conventional commercial organizations are also being forced to adapt to more exacting customer demands or be wiped out by more agile competitors. The problems, and in some cases demise, of organizations such as IBM, PanAm, General Motors, British Leyland, Hoover, Rank Xerox, Crédit Lyonnais and many other former household names, which had seemed almost invulnerable institutions, show how rapidly failure to adapt can be repaid.

Relations between organizations and their customers have changed dramatically over the last 40–50 years. Truly successful organizations, in the pub-

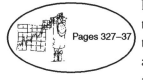

lic or private sector, no longer just 'sell' or 'market' to their customers – they form a kind of partnership with them. To do this, they must be flexible and innovative, and supply 'solutions' to fully understood customer needs and not just 'products' or 'services' for customers to use.

Pages 327–37

The 1990s consumer is discerning and has high expectations. There are many opportunities for organizations which are prepared to respond:

✦ a car insurance company which offered cheaper and more convenient insurance by phone, rather than through expensive commission agents, made its founder a multimillionaire in under three years

✦ manufacturers who have linked their planning systems directly to their customers' forecasting, production management or sales systems have forced out less imaginative competitors

✦ a hospital which actively marketed the short waiting lists and high success rates of its cardiac department to referring doctors gained increased funds, new facilities and higher research expenditure; nearby hospitals had to close their cardiac units due to lack of patients

✦ a bank which was able to offer a personalized customer service by basing its computer systems around the customer, rather than around its different accounts and products, became its country's second largest and most profitable bank in only eight years.

How customer focused is your organization?

It is difficult to produce a blueprint for what customer focus means, as it will inevitably vary from one sector to another. Nevertheless, Figure 5.1 suggests some questions against which to measure your organization or department.

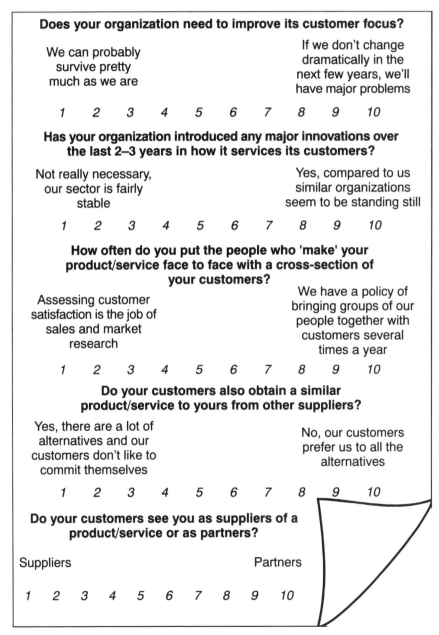

Figure 5.1   A short checklist for assessing customer focus

If your answers fall to the left of the scale, your organization is probably dull, bureaucratic, internally focused and resistant to change. You may well have a strong position in the market or even be in a protected area. Because of this, you may never have felt any great need to improve your customer focus. One major chemical company, for example, conducted a customer satisfaction survey. When executives saw that the results were poor, they made them confidential and didn't reveal them to the rest of the organization. Unaware of the level of customer dissatisfaction, most staff just carried on working as they had always done.

If your answers are towards the right, your organization is probably innovative, dynamic and maybe an exciting place to work. And if you had conducted a customer survey, you probably would have openly communicated the results to your staff and used them as a basis for improving service even further.

Charting changing customer needs

Key to building customer focus is the ability to think through how the needs of customers, potential customers and non-customers will evolve in the future. Of course, you may find that the largest part of the population are probably in your non-customer and potential customer sections. If this is the case, consider whether your organization is being creative enough in the difficult task of attracting new customers or whether you are just content to deal with your existing customer base.

This kind of thinking should serve as the basis for setting or tightening up your short-, medium- and long-term planning as you identify gaps in your organization's existing strategy. The action plan in Figure 5.2 may help.

Taking a holistic process view

Being customer focused requires a dramatic change in the way many organizations structure themselves. Many organizations still have a fairly classical structure, clearly split into the traditional functions and the board made up of the directors of each of the main functions, such as finance, research and development, and manufacturing.

In addition, most organizations still base their decision making on a traditional, functional view of the world:

ACTION PLAN	Now and for next 2 years	Next 2–4 years	Next 4–6 years
Customers	Link supply chains (S/C) with top 5 customers	Increase by 15% Link next 20 customers' S/C	Joint product development with 5 clients
Potential customers	Encourage trial by 30% Retain 10%	Expand range to meet this sector's needs	Further range increase Give 30% of sales
Non-customers	Research ways of reaching this group	Build alliance to target this sector	Alliance giving 20% of sales

Figure 5.2   Laying out a plan to meet changing customer needs

+ if sales are stagnant, it is seen as a problem for sales management to fix
+ if quality is poor or output too low, manufacturing is put on the hot seat
+ if profitability is unsatisfactory, finance will normally push for tighter controls on expenditure and across-the-board cuts
+ if market share is being lost, marketing will probably put pressure on the advertising agency.

This type of knee-jerk thinking is not only common, it is also completely inadequate to deal with all but a few simple situations. It sees problems as being entirely within the control of one or another of the functional areas and looks for a simple, unimaginative, cause-and-effect relationship between problems and solutions.

There is probably nothing wrong with organizing on a classical structure. Few organizations have yet found workable alternatives. And Hampden-Turner and Trompenaars (1994) found evidence that, while many western companies are struggling to flatten their organizations, a large number of successful Japanese companies have retained quite hierarchical structures (see Part Nine, Redesigning the Organization). What is wrong  is allowing the different functions to work almost independently – to have a 'stovepipe' mentality, where true cooperation and understanding between functions are rare and where solutions to problems are sought within rather

True customer focus can only come when the organization's operations are seen as a process or value chain going from identification of a customer need to satisfaction of that need. No single department owns any one part of that process – they all should be contributing to each part (Figure 5.3).

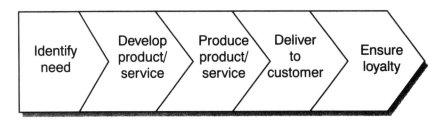

Figure 5.3   A basic customer-focused business process

Some organizations do try to take this process view of their operations and set up cross-functional teams, hold customer awareness training programs and conduct frequent surveys of 'customer satisfaction'. And many are successful. But in too many others, when times start to get difficult, people retreat into their narrow functional viewpoints and the search for the simple, local answer to problems starts again.

From satisfying to delighting

It has become fashionable to talk of organizations trying to ensure customer loyalty by attempting to exceed their customers' expectations. While this may seem fine in theory, if you're in a highly competitive market where price is important, you may feel that your options for 'delighting' customers are fairly limited. One reason firms don't try to delight their customers is that they feel they are blocked by the law of diminishing returns. If, for example, you've invested millions in ensuring high product consistency or quality and you have a customer service level well above 90 percent, you may wonder what else you can do to meet customer needs. Usually, in this situation, achieving further improvements in quality or service levels would be prohibitively expensive and would give little extra customer benefit.

However, one way to break out of this apparent impasse is to split the elements of your relations with customers into two groups – 'satisfiers' and 'motivators'. A satisfier is something you have to achieve to ensure a basic level of customer satisfaction. A motivator would be some special benefit you can bring the customer which your competitors don't offer.

Good quality and high levels of service are usually satisfiers. Although this will sound like heresy to total quality disciples, once you've reached a certain level of quality and service further improvements will be costly (due to the law of diminishing returns) and will bring few if any advantages. To strengthen customer relationships you have to look for a motivator – for example, special packaging so that your products can go straight onto the shelf or into production, or linking together your production-planning systems so customers don't have to worry about reordering as you guarantee constant stock replenishment.

> One shirt manufacturer, for example, offered a supermarket chain a range of shirts with a photo of a model wearing the shirt in each pack. This helped distinguish this range from those of competitors and gave benefits to both the supermarket chain and the supplier.

Too many companies get caught in the trap of endlessly trying to improve their performance on satisfiers and hitting human or technological barriers which require enormous efforts to overcome. Creative companies ensure that the satisfiers are in place, but then try and find a motivator to strengthen their standing with their customers.

Smaller companies are often in a much better position to delight customers than larger competitors. If you have two or three massive production facilities supplying all your markets, you will have difficulty customizing your product offering to meet the needs of different customer groups. Your profitability will depend on fast output, high machine utilization and as little variety as possible. Smaller businesses, on the other hand, will usually be capable of adding an extra aspect of service or flexibility, making them more attractive to customers than their enormous rivals.

Summary

The main messages in this chapter may seem obvious:

✦ organizations and individuals must be customer focused to have a future
✦ true customer focus is a process of imaginatively involving all parts and all aspects of the way an organization works
✦ we must mobilize and involve all of the organization if we are to start overtaking, rather than reluctantly following, the current leaders in our field
✦ we must go beyond focusing only on satisfiers if we are to develop mutually beneficial relationships with our customers.

Yet when you are under pressure to develop a new product, provide a service, arrange a delivery, dream up a new idea, improve financial performance or whatever, it is too easy to be caught up in the immediate, local task and lose sight of the longer-term objective. Most people genuinely try to work well. For example:

> An X-ray department will, of course, try to provide the best service. But its narrow functional view of what 'best service' means might lead it to overlook the importance of coordinating its activities with other departments to provide what could be called patient-focused rather than speciality-focused care.

> Sales departments will try to satisfy customers – that's what they're there for. But if they have insufficient training on handling complex service situations for major customers and a lack of information on how their special offers, promotions and new pack sizes will affect production, they may feed back misleading information, take too many 'difficult' orders and give a hard-pressed manufacturing operation an impossible task.

We must be able to step back from our narrow departmental interests and take a process view, looking at all the main inputs into customer service, if we are to be able to take decisions which meet genuine customer needs. And we must push our thinking beyond matching what competitors can achieve and look for some differentiating feature of our service to protect our relationships with customers.

Recommended reading

Tom Peters (1992) *Liberation Management: Necessary Disorganization for the Nanosecond Nineties*, Knopf (US)/Macmillan (UK).

Gary Hamel and C.K. Prahalad (1994) *Competing for the Future*, Harvard Business School Press.

Charles Hampden-Turner & Fons Trompenaars (1994) *The Seven Cultures of Capitalism*, Doubleday (US)/Piatkus (UK).

6
Reinventing Marketing

Marketing departments are under attack in many organizations. Their contribution is now being questioned, their big budgets and elevated salaries are under scrutiny and their often too close relations with advertising agencies are attracting attention. Sometimes marketing is being taken off the organizational chart altogether, as it is seen as having outlived its usefulness.

By its very nature, marketing should be close to the customer. Everybody knows that. Marketing departments should understand the customer and enable the organization to satisfy customer needs. But too frequently, they are perceived as being disconnected from operational reality and being more interested in an intellectual game rather than the practical day-to-day promotion of an organization's products or services.

As outlined in Chapter 1, over the last 10–20 years most areas of organizations have been through dramatic and painful changes – manufacturing has implemented total quality, distribution is working to just in time, IT has replaced scores of clerical jobs and middle management numbers have been decimated. But marketing departments have emerged from the turbulence, possibly with slightly reduced budgets, but often otherwise unaffected.

Pages 4–11

Now it's marketing's turn to change

Marketing departments grew up during a period of 'mass marketing', when their role was mainly to convince consumers to accept the products firms had to offer. Mass marketing was a consequence of the logic of mass production – the higher the volume of a product a company could make, the lower its unit costs and therefore the more profitable and competitive it could be. Mass marketing was intended to shift the huge volumes of goods which mass production provided.

Now, successful companies are abandoning manipulative mass-marketing techniques and trying to move closer to working with, rather than on, customers. Customers are becoming partners rather than pawns. In forward-looking organizations, customers, like employees, are beginning to be treated as 'resources with something to contribute', rather than faceless 'entities to be controlled'.

Mass marketing is one sided, aimed at satisfying the needs of the marketer. The newer forms of marketing – 'micro', 'value' or 'relationship' marketing – try to be more balanced and to provide genuine benefits for both marketer and consumer.

Some problems with mass marketing

While mass marketing may have suited a certain period, it is now inappropriate in a changed competitive environment. Some of the main criticisms of mass marketing are:

✦ **Concern with form, not substance** – being mainly interested in creating an image for products or services without trying to ensure that the product/service lives up to the image. It's much easier, for example, to spend tens of millions on claiming you're the 'world's favorite' in your field than it is to provide a consistently high level of service, which might genuinely attract customers.

✦ **Me-too advertising** – too much advertising is seen as unoriginal and indistinguishable from that of competitors and often even from products in quite different categories. For example, after spending three years and over £10 million on an electric shaver commercial, the manufacturer's surveys found that viewers thought the ad was for a well-known cigar brand, which the shaver commercial all but copied. Moreover, when advertising agencies insist that clients should spend as much on advertising as their competition, it's clear that the agencies have no confidence in the creative superiority of their work.

✦ **Too simplistic** – according to classical mass-marketing logic, you should find one unique selling proposition (USP) for your product – a reason for your product being different from and better than the competition – and constantly push this USP in your marketing. The reasoning is that consumers will only respond if the advertising message is simple and constantly repeated. As markets become more competitive and consumers more discerning, the single USP approach can be seen as too limited and unimaginative.

✦ **Inappropriate performance measures** – a large part of market research is aimed at measuring advertising effectiveness (share of voice and recall) rather than actual satisfaction with the product or belief in the product benefits which are claimed in the advertising. This is great for telling you if people like your advertising, but gives little clue of customers' reactions to your product.

✦ **Adversarial and patronizing** – most mass marketing, although it may profess the opposite, looks down on and tries to manipulate customers. This is reflected in the patronizing tone of many advertisements and the superior attitudes of marketing departments and advertising agencies.

✦ **Functional focus** – while organizations are breaking down functional barriers and reorganizing around customer-facing processes, many marketing departments are trying to remain aloof from these changes and are defending their functional territory.

✦ **Lack of innovation** – 10–15,000 new products or new variations are launched each year. More than 90 percent don't survive more than 12 months, because few of them really offer any benefits that customers want or value. Most so-called new products are unimaginative and unwanted small variations on existing products, not radically different at all.

The forces for change

There are at least five main reasons for marketing's need dramatically to change the way it works.

1. Decline in advertising effectiveness

It has been calculated (Peppers & Rogers, 1993) that most people in the industrialized west see between 2000 and 3000 commercial messages a day. On radio, television, billboards, newspapers and magazines, we are swamped with competing offers. And most of the post we receive is unsolicited junk mail, which annoys rather than interests many people and usually ends up straight in the garbage. Faced with this daily onslaught consumers are becoming more and more immune to advertising messages. Although we are exposed to so many ads per day, we usually don't notice most of them as they provide a kind of dull background noise, rather than attracting our attention.

Some 200 years ago, Samuel Johnson wrote:

> Advertisements are now so numerous that they are very negligently perused and it has therefore become necessary to gain attention by magnificence of promises, and by eloquence sometimes sublime and sometimes pathetic.

And the situation has not improved since. Some commentators talk of 'increasing advertising literacy' – consumers are catching on to all the advertisers' tricks and it's simply not as easy as it used to be to flog a product through sharp advertising.

Many marketers are aware of the diminishing returns they are receiving from their investments. Surveys have shown that not only does most advertising fall below many people's threshold of awareness (they just don't register it), but when people do take notice of an advertisement, many actively resist the advertising message because they know it's not true and instead turn to competitive products. To try to overcome this resistance, some advertisers have moved away from campaigns spread out over several months and adopted a technique called 'fastmarketing', which is based on saturation advertising backed up by *Blitzkrieg* sales promotion encouraging consumers to try their brands immediately. This has been shown to be effective in some cases – but only at huge cost to the marketer.

Other companies have reacted to the declining power of advertising by putting their faith in sales promotion. It has been estimated that 'above the line' advertising has shrunk from 60 to 40 percent of corporate marketing spend in 10 years, with a corresponding increase in sales promotion ('below the line') activities.

2. Media fragmentation

There are more publications, TV channels and radio stations today than ever before. And their number is still increasing. Moreover, videos and pay-per-view TV allow people to choose what they want to see and, more importantly, what they don't want to see. Of course, advertisers can always get their messages on to the various media available. But given greater media choice, it is going to be much more difficult for them to be sure that we will see those messages. The old certainty that positioning a commercial during a specific program would ensure so many million viewers of a certain demographic type no longer holds true. One of the world's largest food companies, Heinz, has recently said that it would withdraw from TV advertising altogether and put its budget into below the line promotions, as it felt TV advertising was no longer an effective way of reaching its customers.

3. Saturated markets

Most markets today are saturated. Most people have enough refrigerators, televisions, cars, stereos, washing machines etc. Most purchases are replacements, not first-time buys. And unless there is a major technological breakthrough, the rate of replacement is insufficient, in many product areas, to match the volume being produced. So being in a market and having reasonable advertising are no longer guarantees of profitability. There are normally too many other competitors and too much spare production capacity available.

4. Stagnation in consumer spending

During economic booms consumer spending is encouraged by general optimism and the availability of cheap credit. In times of high inflation, spending is rewarded and saving penalized. As the value of savings declines in real terms, people see greater benefits in using their income for consumption rather than investment.

We are now in a period of limited growth with low inflation. Moreover, the economic shocks of the last few years and permanently high levels of unemployment have made consumers more cautious and more inclined to save a larger proportion of their income. In spite of the claims of business leaders and politicians, consumer spending will not quickly return to its previous high levels.

During times of growth, marketing is mostly intended to gain new customers and increase product usage. Mass marketing usually did this through appeals to people's snobbishness, uniqueness or insecurities. But as spending stagnates, the marketing task will move from acquiring new customers toward ensuring the loyalty of the existing customer base. This is a much harder task altogether as it requires continual satisfaction with the product or service on offer – and that can't be achieved by a clever commercial with a famous-name presenter and a catchy tune.

5. Reduction in the value of the brand

In the 1980s there was a great debate among consumer goods companies about what value they should give their 'brands' in their balance sheets. Quite rightly, many of these companies believed that their major brands were valuable assets and that this value was not sufficiently reflected in their accounts.

In the 1990s, however, the brand has come under attack. The power of retailers has grown as they have increasingly dominated many markets. In some countries, five or six companies account for 70–80 percent of consumer expenditure. Now the big retailers can decide which brands are offered to consumers. Moreover, as retailers compete for customers, some retailers are becoming brands in their own right and selling their 'own-label' competitive products, usually at up to 20 percent cheaper than branded equivalents. One cheaper 'own-label' cola, for example, took over 20 percent of a supermarket chain's cola sales within a few months of being launched. And between 20 and 30 percent of all groceries sold in many European countries are now 'own label' (Glemet & Mira, 1993). The main logic for buying a branded product is probably the belief that it will be of a consistent high quality. As retailers position themselves as offering as high a quality as national brands, a key attribute of major brands begins to lose its value. The sudden loss of 10–20 percent of sales can be disastrous for mass-production branded goods firms, which can only be profitable if they sell huge volumes to cover their high fixed costs. However, the retailers' need for firms to supply their own-label products offers a huge new opportunity to smaller local manufacturers. It allows them to compete once again with the major national and international brands which had at one time seemed about to dominate most markets.

Many branded goods companies are finding it difficult to justify why consumers should pay up to 20 percent more for their products – especially when much of this price difference is funneled straight back into advertising. Yet pressure from cheaper 'own-label' products has forced many of them into a frenzy of big-budget campaigns and a stream of special promotions as they try to defend their market share. But this is often self-defeating, as it both increases their marketing costs (thus reducing profitability) and eats away at consumer brand loyalty by encouraging the consumer to value the special offer more than the brand itself.

It may be that in developed economies the power of the brand will stabilize at a lower level than today. However, in developing economies with a rising standard of living, the ability to buy branded products will represent achievement and prosperity (as was the case in the west during the 1950s and 1960s) and so the major brands will retain their power there until everyone can afford them. Then brands will slip too to a lower level of sales as part of their market is taken over by better value, unbranded products.

Marketing's 'golden years'

In a highly influential article written in 1960 – 'Marketing myopia' – Theodore Levitt laid down much of the approach that would underpin marketing for the following 20 years.

The article differentiated between 'selling', which is concerned with satisfying the needs of sellers to turn their products or services into cash, and 'marketing', which focuses on the customer by trying to supply the products the customer wants. The article was a reaction against what Levitt saw as the 'product' rather than 'customer' focus of many mass-production organizations. One of its key messages was that if firms move away from simply trying to supply mass-produced products and towards trying to satisfy genuine customer needs, then this will have major implications for the way they approach their markets.

A **product-focused** mind believes that each product has a lifecycle and that the organization's aim is to maximize the profits from each product's life (Figure 6.1).

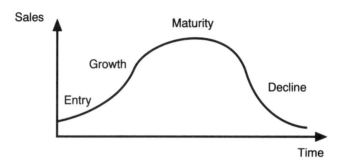

Figure 6.1   Product-focused firms often believe in a product lifecycle

Such companies will bitterly fight to defend their products against newcomers. For example, the railways in the US fought (vainly) to retain customers against the threat posed by airlines, and Hollywood initially saw television as a rival and refused to make programs for it.

A **customer-focused** mind, on the other hand, believes that consumers have certain needs (transport or entertainment, for example) which will be satisfied by a sequence of different products or services as tastes and technology change (Figure 6.2).

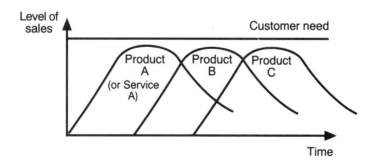

Figure 6.2   Basic needs will be met by different products at different times

Such companies will always be looking for the next way to satisfy an identified customer need, rather than energetically, but hopelessly, defending a particular product or service whose time is past.

If the railways, for example, had been customer focused, they would have viewed themselves as satisfying the need for transportation and not just providing one product – rail transport. Then it would have been natural for them to expand into offering air travel, rather than fighting against it. After all, they had a network of offices and staff who were experienced in running a transport organization, so they had a ready-built, but unexploited, advantage over the newcomers who were setting up airlines. Likewise, if Hollywood had seen itself as providing entertainment and not just films, it would have been much quicker to offer films and series to TV, instead of almost being destroyed by it.

The famous 'four Ps'

The mantra of marketers from the 1960s on has been the 'marketing mix', commonly known as the 'four Ps' – product, price, promotion and place:

✦ **P**roduct – what product are we trying to market?
✦ **P**rice – what is an appropriate price level?
✦ **P**romotion – what are the most effective promotion media and messages?
✦ **P**lace – what distribution channels should be used?

In itself, there is nothing wrong with the marketing mix. It is a sound, logical way to approach building a marketing strategy. However, often it has been used far too mechanically, as a substitute for imagination rather than as an aid to it. The lackluster advertising, uninteresting competitions and endless 'few pennies off' promotions on which many companies spend millions are frequently the result.

One possible problem with the four Ps is that they take the product as their starting point. It's as if the product had some divine right to exist. However, as the failure of more than 90 percent of new products shows, many products are simply not wanted. If marketers were to force themselves into the discipline of always having an N (consumer need) before the four Ps, some new products might be more successful and some marketing campaigns might be more convincing.

Micro-marketing and mass customization

While most experts are agreed that the 1960s to 1980s constituted the era of mass marketing, opinions are divided about what has followed. The next wave has been called 'micro-marketing', 'mass customization', 'value marketing' and 'relationship marketing'. But whatever the name, it seems that marketing now has to exhibit a number of new characteristics, such as better understanding of customer needs and better provision of real value, if it is to respond to the challenges it faces and have a useful role to play in the future (Figure 6.3).

Figure 6.3   Marketing will have to change if it is to maintain its key position

1. Closer and deeper understanding of customers

Consumer markets

Many marketing departments and advertising agencies are still working with oversimplistic definitions of their customers. Some continue to use the old basic demographic categories (A, B, C1, C2, D, E) for classifying their markets. Others have developed lifestyle or psychodemographic profiling – consumers are now Full nest 1, Full nest 2, Full nest 3, Empty nest 1 etc., or Mainstreamers, Aspirers, Succeeders, Reformers, or maybe just Volvo-driving suburbanites or whatever. And yet others use very detailed geodemographic analyses based on the areas in which people live.

These groupings may give a reasonably accurate portrayal of customer lifestyles and consumption patterns (although this is doubtful in many cases).

However, too often they are used in the mass-marketing spirit of 'What can we sell to which group? How much and how often?' rather than to help identify what customers actually want.

> GM and Ford probably had demographic and psychodemographic analyses coming out of their ears in the 1970s and 1980s. But that didn't help them anticipate the demand for smaller cars, nor counter the successful European and Japanese incursion into the US market.

> Similarly, US home electronics and appliance companies had probably analysed their market profiles every which way. But again, because this information was used primarily to target selling, rather than to target understanding, it proved useless when competitive conditions hardened and consumer tastes changed.

Too often, the availability of ever-more detailed and imaginative psycho- or geodemographic analyses fools marketers into believing they understand a market. After all, if you've got 25 kilos of computer-generated statistical analysis, what more can there be to learn about your market? But all this ingenious analysis only has value if you use it as a basis for listening to, as well as selling to, your customers. New products fail because, while marketers know exactly who bought what, they don't spend enough time finding out if the key groups actually wanted to buy their brilliant ideas.

Commercial markets

Twenty years ago, most commercial companies would have aimed at having at least two to three suppliers for each product or component. This allowed them to have a fallback if one supplier had problems and also to play one supplier off against the other in negotiations to get the best price and payment conditions. In this environment, it was not difficult to convince a customer to switch suppliers, providing there was a clear commercial benefit in doing so.

Now the trend is towards having fewer suppliers and building partnerships with customers and suppliers. Instead of just selling to and buying from each other, firms are linking together for their mutual benefit.

These can be information links:

> Supermarket chains link up their electronic point of sale (EPOS) systems to suppliers' forecasting systems, and manufacturers link their production planning systems to component suppliers' planning systems.

Or physical links:

> Component suppliers and chemical companies may keep stores at a customer's site. The supplier has the responsibility to keep these replenished and the customer only pays for the quantity used.

> Engineering companies may set up joint product design teams with suppliers.

> Branded goods firms may have a customer service person working full time at a supermarket chain's head office.

Once a potential customer has established these kinds of links with suppliers, the costs of switching suppliers increase and the customer is more likely to remain with an existing supplier. Obviously, establishing these kinds of links with your customers requires you to develop an understanding of their business and how you can best fit in with their goals.

> A minor branded goods company analysed the market positioning and competitive strategies of its five main customers and then tailored a slightly different product offering for each of them.

> A car components manufacturer could see that one customer tended to give it more complex and thus more expensive designs than its competitors. By making suggestions about how designs could be simplified and better adapted to its particular manufacturing set-up, it provided cost benefits to its customer and gradually obtained an increasing share of the business.

2. Expand the 'product/service envelope'

Linked to the idea of genuinely trying to understand your customers' needs is the concept of expanding your product/service envelope – that is, adding more features to the product you offer or adding more service characteristics to a product. For example, the supermarket chain that also offers cheap gas from a gas station in its parking lot, an engineering company that provides design services, a food product company that prints recipe ideas on packages, retailers who offer home delivery – all these are trying to gain some competitive edge by offering more than their rivals do.

Increasingly, the ways in which firms can expand the product/service envelope go far beyond the traditional areas of marketing. For example:

> A flooring manufacturer was under increasing price pressure from whole-
> salers. The manufacturer's margins were already so low that it couldn't
> afford any further price concessions. So, instead of relying on skillful
> negotiating, it tried to understand why wholesalers were suddenly squeez-
> ing it so hard on price. An analysis of the economics of its wholesalers'
> operations showed that the larger wholesale groups, which were taking
> over the industry, were bearing heavy financial costs from having to stock
> all items at each of their stores.
>
> As the production process required quite large minimum order sizes,
> the wholesalers were having to carry large stocks of many slow-moving
> items. By offering to hold stocks of slow-moving items centrally and guar-
> anteeing deliveries within 24 hours, the manufacturer could significantly
> reduce the wholesalers' stock-financing costs, without a major increase in
> its own stockholding. This partnership with wholesalers would help
> reduce their demands for lower margins and would benefit both parties.

This expansion of the service aspect of the product is a much more sophisticated approach than the search for a traditional USP. It requires an organization to take a multifunctional, rather than just selling-based, view of how to
interact with customers. In many cases, it threatens the territory which marketing had traditionally seen as its exclusive domain. In some cases, it may
even question the need for a separate marketing function.

3. Move from defensive to expeditionary marketing

An organization's marketing strategies can be classed as either defensive or
expeditionary (Hamel & Prahalad, 1991).

Traditional marketing aims at establishing a brand and then defending it
against competitors and 'own-label' products. In defensive marketing, you constantly analyse your advertising effectiveness and you monitor your positioning
against other brands, using tools such brand-image maps and multiple discrim-
inant analysis. You continually refine your advertising and media buying to
improve advertising effectiveness and hit rates. You probably believe that you are
close to your customers, as you are continuously analysing how they view your
products and your advertising compared to those of your competitors.

Expeditionary marketing goes further. Here you don't rely so slavishly on
your market research. You are aware that consumers can only comment on
what they know and that most could never have imagined products like the

Sony Walkman, Apple Macintosh or Ice Cream Mars before they were launched. Expeditionary marketing uses the corporate imagination to invent new product concepts instead of focusing mainly on defending existing ones. It tries to back away from the product or brand itself to deal with the customer need which the product or service is aimed at satisfying. So it focuses not only on improving the existing product (and its marketing) but also on new ways of satisfying the customer need. With expeditionary marketing, you measure things like 'share of shelf', 'share of pocket' or 'share of stomach', rather than just 'share of market'.

> Suppose a supermarket wants to launch a new range of its own-label pet food. The defensive marketer would see this as a threat to its branded product. An expeditionary marketer, being less focused on the branded product, would see this as an opportunity to increase its share of consumers' pet food expenditure. The defensive marketer would fight tooth and nail with all kinds of promotions and advertising to defend its market share – the expeditionary marketer would probably offer to manufacture the 'own label' in addition to its branded products, thus capturing a greater share of shelf.

In a sense, traditional marketing can be seen as fairly reactive, done purely by the marketing function and built on following customers. Expeditionary marketing tries to find new ways in which all parts of the organization can be channelled into providing customer benefits and to lead customers proactively.

4. Reorganize along customer-facing processes

Organizations, particularly those which are running business process reengineering projects (see Part Nine – Redesigning the Organization), are increasingly moving away from departmental structures and basing their operations around cross-functional, customer-focused teams.

Pages 295–304

Most branded goods companies now have 5–10 main retail customers who make up more than 70 percent of their business, instead of the several thousand they might have had 15–20 years ago. If such a company sets up key account managers backed up by cross-functional teams, this can mean a changed role for marketing. Some of the options are:

✦ maintain marketing as a separate function, to ensure a consistent presentation of the brand across key account groups

- ◆ integrate marketing as part of key account management teams
- ◆ put senior marketing management into some of the key account manager positions
- ◆ remove marketing altogether and replace it by a brand management team made up of key account managers.

One option which is frequently chosen is to move from a concept of 'brand' managers to 'category' managers. A brand manager is normally only responsible for one brand – a soap powder, for instance. A category manager would be responsible for a number of brands in one product group – for example, all a company's different soap powders and other cleaning materials. The main advantage of moving towards category management is to ensure consistent and logical positioning of all the different brands a company may offer in a product group. It also fits in better with most customers' view of the world, as supermarket chains tend to be organized around product categories. The old brand manager model would probably have several sales representatives from one supplier all calling on one supermarket chain buyer and no coordinated strategy for dealing with that buyer. By organizing around categories, a supplier can ensure a single point of contact with the buyer. This can then be used as the basis for building a much more cohesive relationship strategy.

5. Build 'customers for life'

Economic conditions and a static birth rate in the west have deprived companies of the possibility of rapidly increasing their customer base in most markets. Some marketers are protecting their existing customer base through the idea of building customers for life. Common-sense calculations have shown that an average car user can potentially be worth over $100,000 during their life, that a supermarket customer can buy thousands of dollars of groceries a year and that it can cost at least five times as much to gain a new customer as it does to retain an existing one.

However, it is much easier to entice someone to try your product a couple of times than it is to provide such a consistent level of satisfaction that a customer stays with you forever. The first can be achieved by some clever advertising, the second requires that the product or service lives up to the claims of the advertising – this is clearly a challenge for the whole organization and not just for marketing.

Studies of airline and car rental customers have shown that the 80/20 rule generally applies – 20 percent of your customers account for about 80 percent of your business. Companies in these areas have understood this and are falling over each other to offer free air travel, gifts and extra services to secure the loyalty of the critical 20 percent of high-spending customers.

The 80/20 rule may be less applicable in areas such as groceries, financial services or consumer durables. However, the principle that customers are too important to be carelessly discarded is still relevant. Most marketing budgets are aimed at a possibly mythical figure – the new customer, who is not yet aware of a particular product's benefits. Of course, these people exist. But the main part of a company's market will be customers who have already tried and know the product. For example, many customers know that a certain southern European state-owned airline is a shambles and no amount of expensive advertising will convince them otherwise. And while the various parts of the British railway system may enjoy spending millions to tell us how wonderful they are, the commuters crammed into dirty, overcrowded, unhygienic carriages and forced to suffer their incompetence will not be made any happier seeing commercials of supposedly happy, relaxed travellers comfortably seated in clean, spacious compartments.

Keeping customers for life demands more from marketing than hard selling or eloquently seductive campaigns. It requires marketers to broaden their view of their role from the narrow concept of promoting products to the wider and much more difficult task of ensuring consistent consumer satisfaction with the product or service being offered.

Pages 327–37

Direct marketing – a dangerous panacea?

Five or ten years ago any direct mailing which had a conversion rate over 1–2 percent was considered a success. However, the increasing processing power and declining cost of computers is turning direct mail into a much more targeted and formidable marketing weapon. By buying a geodemographic database and cross-referencing it with public records and a few address lists bought from the many available, direct mailing companies can build up frighteningly accurate 'taste profiles' of individual households and thus target groups for many products. One US company, for example, went through court records to compile a list of people convicted of drunk driving and mailed them an offer of a $200 drink-control device. Four thousand were sold.

The increasingly accurate targeting potential of direct marketing is obviously attractive. TV and the press are very blunt instruments. With them the vast majority of people seeing your offer will not be interested in the product – not many people reading a newspaper, for example, will be about to buy a new carpet or video recorder (probably less than 1 percent), yet newspapers constantly carry ads for these products. With well-targeted direct marketing, you can almost guarantee that most of the people you reach will be users or potential users.

Many companies will have great success switching to direct marketing channels. However, some consumers are becoming concerned about the invasion of privacy and the ecological waste caused by the thousands of direct mailings and leaflets they receive each year. For the moment, marketers are touting junk mail as a powerful new competitive weapon. But it may well be that people will increasingly resent direct selling which is too accurately targeted. This supposed solution to marketing's problems could turn out to be less effective than hoped and in some cases even a liability – consumers may start going to the courts to protect their privacy or politicians may even start to act against the excessive power of junk mail.

In a few years, so many marketers will be using and abusing direct marketing that it will, like other forms of promotion, lose its power. Then marketers may be reluctantly forced to find some other way of reaching their potential customers. Of course, companies will always need a certain level of advertising and promotion. But perhaps the best form of marketing is ensuring consistent delivery of high-quality products and services that consumers want. If this is the case, then the task of marketing goes far beyond the role that most traditional marketing departments set themselves. Marketing will need to concern itself with the whole process of building and delivering value to the customer, rather than with creating an image for the product to make selling easier.

Summary – can marketers really move with the times?

In some businesses, the question of whether marketing can adapt is not a problem. A reduction in the number of customers, the building of closer relationships with customers, the reorganization around key customer groups and the blurring of the distinction between the firm and its customers have made the marketing function largely irrelevant. In many of these firms, marketing as a function may disappear and be replaced by a team of key account managers.

In other organizations marketing will still be necessary, but it will have to change radically the way it thinks and works. The staff of many marketing departments and advertising agencies are generalists. In the age of mass marketing, the ability to conduct some market analysis, develop a USP, research some product and advertising concepts and run a few big-budget TV campaigns with some printed press back-up was sufficient to survive. With all its psychodemographic profiling, hit rates and attribute mapping, marketing often seemed to speak a different language from the rest of the organization. Frequently it kept itself apart, particularly from the sales department, whom marketers saw as their intellectual inferiors.

With media fragmentation and consumer saturation, simple big-budget campaigns are no longer as effective as they used to be. The generalists in marketing departments and advertising agencies must learn more about their products and customers to establish more balanced, mutually advantageous relationships. And getting closer to customers often requires functions other than marketing to become involved. Many marketing departments and marketing managers will have great difficulty adjusting to these new conditions. Some companies will suffer, as their marketing department battles to defend their status and power. Others, however, will adapt their marketing approach and build success on new products and services which correspond to identified customer needs. In these companies, marketing will be something in which all areas are involved, not just the aggressively guarded preserve of the marketing department.

Recommended reading

F. Glemet & R. Mira (1993) 'The brand leader's dilemma', *The McKinsey Quarterly*, No. 2.

Gary Hamel & C.K. Prahalad (1991) 'Corporation imagination and expeditionary marketing', *Harvard Business Review*, July–August.

Philip Kotler (1977) 'From sales obsession to marketing effectiveness', *Harvard Business Review*, November–December.

Theodore Levitt (1960) 'Marketing myopia', *Harvard Business Review*, July–August.

D. Peppers & M. Rogers (1993) *The One to One Future: Building Relationships One Customer at a Time*, Doubleday.

Part Three

Encouraging Creativity

7

Moving from 'Machine' to 'Brain'

Rich networks rather than hierarchical structures, intelligent insight rather than simple cause-and-effect thinking, multilevel interpretation rather than binary logic, the ability to learn rather than mechanical or calculating power, managing complex systems rather than using a few simple levers – these are some of the ways in which brains differ from machines or computers. These are also some of the characteristics which differentiate fast-moving, innovative organizations from ponderous, oppressive bureaucracies, and successful economies from countries in industrial and competitive decline.

Faced with challenges such as changing customer bases, falling prices and competition in new areas, the old-fashioned, 'steady as she goes', arthritic hierarchies are struggling and declining. New, faster-moving and innovative organizations and countries are taking their place. Successful organizations and economies are now looking less and less like efficiently functioning 'machines' or 'computers' and more like thinking and learning organisms – 'brains' (Figure 7.1).

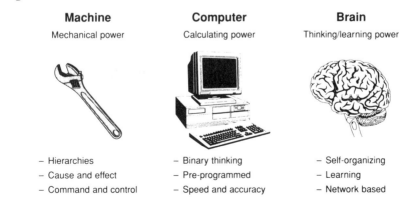

Machine	Computer	Brain
Mechanical power	Calculating power	Thinking/learning power
– Hierarchies	– Binary thinking	– Self-organizing
– Cause and effect	– Pre-programmed	– Learning
– Command and control	– Speed and accuracy	– Network based

Figure 7.1   Moving from machine and computer to brain

The brain-based organization

In the early part of the twentieth century, F. W. Taylor's 'scientific management' tried to apply the key features of machines to organization structure and management – fragmentation of tasks, deskilling, humans as completely replaceable parts, monotony, regularity, one most efficient way for carrying out each task, clear measurable targets for every job. Economics also tried to develop a similar scientific basis. In an attempt to emulate physics and chemistry, it tried to reduce people's and firms' behavior to a series of mathematical relations. And this 'scientific' approach is still apparent in many organizations and most economic theories today. With environments becoming more turbulent and requiring more flexible reactions, it may now be time to take another model – the brain, a thinking, organic rather than mechanistic entity – and to start trying to build our organizations, management approaches and economic models according to the principles by which it works (Figure 7.2).

The following sections consider how the attributes of the brain can be applied to 'intelligent' organizations and economies.

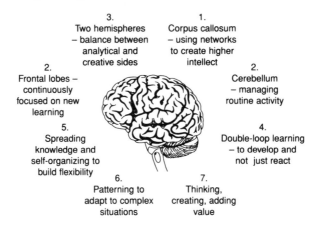

3.
Two hemispheres
– balance between
analytical and
creative sides

1.
Corpus callosum
– using networks
to create higher
intellect

2.
Frontal lobes –
continuously
focused on new
learning

2.
Cerebellum
– managing
routine activity

5.
Spreading
knowledge and
self-organizing to
build flexibility

4.
Double-loop learning
– to develop and
not just react

6.
Patterning to
adapt to complex
situations

7.
Thinking,
creating, adding
value

Figure 7.2   Some key attributes of the brain applicable to thinking organizations and economies

1. The corpus callosum – networks not physical size

Within the brain, connecting the left and right hemispheres, is a group of about two hundred million nerve fibers called the corpus callosum. These nerve fibers play a vital part in enabling brain cells (neurones) to make their hundred thousand possible connections with other neurones. It is now believed that what mainly distinguishes humans from animals is not brain size

Species	Index
Man	3.12
Chimpanzee	1.79
Elephant	1.11
Dolphin	0.93
Horse	0.70
Lion	0.67
Fox	0.62

Figure 7.3
Calloso-bulbar index

– elephants have significantly larger brains than humans, yet humans are (we think) more intelligent. The real difference is in the relative number of collosal fibers to the size of the brain. A measurement known as the calloso-bulbar index (Blinkov & Glezer, 1968) has been used to compare the human brain to those of other species (Figure 7.3).

So the ability of the brain to make connections is more important to thinking power than is the actual number of neurones in the brain. The same can be said for organizations and countries. Fifteen to twenty years ago, General Motors and IBM were vast organizations with extraordinary financial power and high-quality people and the US and European economies dominated the world. Since then, thinking, networked organizations such as Microsoft have come apparently from nowhere to be as large as the previous generation's commercial giants and a whole series of 'Asian tigers' are racing ahead of some floundering western erstwhile competitors.

Increasingly, the strength of both organizations and countries is coming not from the size represented in the balance sheet or GDP figures but from the knowledge capital held in its people.

Pages 87–8

Huge hierarchical, bureaucratic structures are designed to provide compartmentalization and control. But, in the process, they fragment and divide up knowledge. This often leads to subgroups (manufacturing, marketing, sales, a country subsidiary and so on) losing sight of the whole organization's strategic direction and to them pursuing local subgoals which are not aligned to the organization's overall welfare. Similarly, in economics, social divisions can lead to destructive battles between interest groups which have little understanding of each other's views.

In contrast, by involving trade unions in company decision making, countries such as Germany and Sweden probably avoided the several decades of union/management conflict which did so much damage to the British economy. Building a large number of networks between people and organizations helps information to flow freely, gives people a more holistic understanding of other areas' points of view and builds common goals. There is less internal conflict and the organization or country can direct its energies towards a common purpose.

2. The frontal lobes and cerebellum – learning to deal with and encode new situations

Experiments using PET (positron emission tomography) to measure activity levels in the brain have shown that, as subjects learn new skills or get used to carrying out unfamiliar exercises, the level of effort required by the brain falls rapidly. The brain quickly learns to set up new networks to cope with new experiences, so that activities which at first might have required a lot of concentration become almost subconscious or automatic.

Some experts have proposed that unfamiliar or difficult activities tend to be handled by the brain's frontal lobes. But as these activities become learnt and thus more routine and subconscious, they are gradually handled further and further back in the brain – functions basic to life (breathing, for example) are managed right at the back near the base of the brain, in the cerebellum. As we learn to drive, our frontal lobes are very active. When driving has become an almost automatic, 'background' occupation, the frontal lobes are hardly used and so are free to handle other tasks (the most common nowadays probably being talking on a mobile telephone).

An organization can also be split into routine activities and new challenges. A number of functional tasks (budgeting, market planning, standard manufacturing, order handling) could be seen as activities which the organization should be able to do almost subconsciously, whereas activities such as managing cross-functional, customer-facing processes, reacting to a sudden shift in the market or absorbing the benefits of a new technology may pose new challenges, which require the organization's mental energy. In too many cases, key managers and potential thought leaders (the 'frontal lobes') continue to put most of their energy into activities which should be second nature and so don't have the time or motivation to look for new opportunities to learn:

✦ Marketers spend most of their time poring over excruciatingly detailed sales figures and neglect the search for new market openings or improving advertising creativity.

✦ Hospital administrators are able to tell you down to the last penny how much each patient meal or bed-night cost, while the hospital is shrinking under their very noses because it is not providing adequate service or because waiting times are too long.

✦ Top executives may have spent months developing their new strategy in mind-boggling detail thanks to expensive consultancy help and a number of 'workshops' at luxury country house golfing hotels. In the meantime, competitive conditions have changed and the great new strategy is mostly worthless.

An organization has two main areas of activity on which it must focus:

✦ Is it managing and controlling routine activities efficiently?
✦ Is it building the human and technical capability to succeed in the future?

If it mostly uses its frontal lobes for routine, detailed tasks – only managing and controlling existing activities, for example – it will block all chance of learning and developing. It may function efficiently and profitably now, but it may also have neglected to build its future.

In economies like Britain and the US, where there are 20 to 30 times as many accountants and lawyers as there are in more successful, engineering- and production-focused economies, there has been and still is a tendency to place a lopsided emphasis on quantifying, controlling and legislating for current routine activities and too little effort put into preparing for the future.

3. The two hemispheres – balance between analytical and creative sides

It is generally recognized that each of the two hemispheres of the brain has a bias towards certain types of activity:

✦ left hemisphere – analytical, doing calculations, solving puzzles, source of language and grammar
✦ right hemisphere – creativity, comprehension of metaphors and humor, non-verbal ideas, emotional intonation for language.

People who suffer brain damage in one hemisphere will tend to display unbalanced behavior – either having a too literal interpretation of language and expressing themselves in a flat, uninteresting way (right-side damage) or having difficulty with basic calculations or structuring logical sentences (left-side damage).

Organizations should keep a balance between their left brain (financial control, asset management, cost reduction) and their right brain (growth, market expansion, new product ideas). There are two main ways in which performance can be improved (Figure 7.4).

Many western companies and countries have been accused of displaying unbalanced behavior by being too left-brain focused – always concentrating on the cost side of their results, the 'denominator' (Hamel & Prahalad, 1994). Denominator managers get results by downsizing, reducing expenditure, divesting and controlling. When ambitious managers plan to spend only two

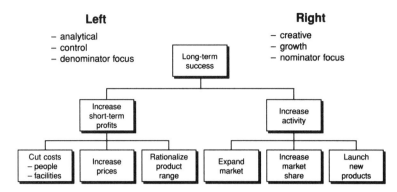

Figure 7.4   Comparison between left- and right-brain management

to three years in any position in their urgent scramble on their way to the top, it is natural for them to gravitate towards left-brain, denominator management – that's the quick way to show results to secure that next promotion. Likewise, politicians, eager to show quick results such as tax cuts, will tend to try to fund these from short-term cuts in public expenditure, rather than from creating real economic growth.

Right-brain, nominator strategies are more difficult and longer term. They're all about generating growth. It's easier to cut new product development costs than it is to develop successful new products; it's simpler to close a factory than to build markets so the workers have something to make; it takes less time and effort to reduce staff than it does to build them into value-adding teams. Basically, it's simpler to retrench and claim that you're a victim of circumstances beyond your control than it is to build the capability to adapt successfully to a changing competitive environment.

Ultimately, as many organizations and countries have found, you cannot cost-cut yourself back to economic health. Of course, productivity and efficiency are important. However, an excessive focus on cost control, without a sufficient plan to balance it with growth, may appear to give positive short-term career-enhancing or politically attractive results, but is ultimately a recipe for failure.

4. From single- to double-loop learning

Pages 42–3

One of the key strengths of the brain compared to machines or computers is its ability to perform what has been called double-loop learning (see Part One – Keeping Up with Leading-edge Thinking).

A thermostat, for example, is capable of single-loop learning. If the temperature goes too high or too low, the thermostat will respond to bring it back to a chosen level. However, a thermostat is unable to decide what the ideal temperature target should be or to think whether this should be changed in different circumstances (summer vs winter, for example).

Many traditional organizations and countries have been described as using a single-loop learning approach (Figure 7.5a). The top management group or educated elite, in their supposedly infinite wisdom, set policies, budgets, sales targets and cost objectives and cascade these down, level by level. Then each organizational level monitors how the level below performs against these targets, identifies variances and deals with any deviation. In these organizations the various levels seldom get the chance or have the knowledge to question the validity of those targets or their fit to a changing environment. Management by objectives (MBO) systems often exhibit the features of single-loop learning.

Unlike a thermostat, the brain is not only capable of identifying variances from a plan or expected situation, it is also able to question the plan itself and make any readjustments to take account of changing circumstances (Figure 7.5b). Double-loop learning is thus a much higher level of thinking.

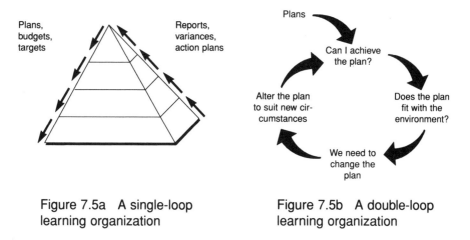

Figure 7.5a A single-loop learning organization

Figure 7.5b A double-loop learning organization

There are still plans and targets and budgets in a double-loop learning organization. However, the difference is that these are no longer 'set in stone'. Now they are part of the organization's general strategy (its strategic direction or intent). But it's up to those closest to the coal face (the factory, the market, new technological developments and so on) to interpret those plans and alter them if necessary to take account of local knowledge and significant changes in circumstances.

By specifying to a supplier the exact measurements, materials and manufacturing method of a car part, engineers would demonstrate single-loop learning. They would have given precise targets and only be open to discussing the price. On the other hand, engineers could define the space a component will occupy, its key interfaces and its required performance characteristics, but leave it up to the supplier, with their particular expertise, to decide what materials to use and how to make it. This would be double-loop learning, as the engineers are allowing general guidelines to be interpreted and applied by the person who has the most up-to-date knowledge and will then learn new methods from the supplier's solution.

Organizations need to be capable of double-loop learning to respond to changes in their operating environment. But most hierarchical, bureaucratic organizations are not able to apply double-loop learning for two main reasons:

✦ Their detailed plans and budgets do not allow those at the coal face the discretion to apply them flexibly.
✦ As knowledge is fragmented into specialities, those at the coal face usually don't have a sufficient view of the organization's overall goals to use any freedom they might be given in the organization's best interests.

By taking action such as moving its focus away from functional hierarchies to cross-functional, market-focused teams, an organization can start to move from simplistic single- to more productive and responsive double-loop learning. Similarly, by encouraging training and education instead of restricting it to a chosen few, a country can create a workforce capable of actively applying double-loop learning in adapting to changing competitive conditions.

5. Building flexibility through spreading knowledge and through self-organization

In an experiment with rats, an American psychologist Karl Lashley discovered that he could remove up to 90 percent of their cortex without any major deterioration in their ability to find their path through a maze (Morgan, 1986). Clearly, you could not do this with most machines or computers and still expect them to function. Many don't function particularly well, even with all their parts intact.

Although most human activities are generally located in specific areas of the brain, people can suffer significant brain damage and either not lose or start to recover the functions linked to the damaged areas. This is because the brain has a level of overcapacity built into it and can reorganize itself to deal with any new situation – it can lose physical areas without necessarily losing abilities. Overcapacity and the ability to reconfigure itself are useful to any organism or organization. They allow it to cope with varying levels of activity – sudden peaks in demand or periods of high stress – without any fall-off in performance.

There are two main ways of building overcapacity into a system or organization:

✦ You can put in excess resources, additional management levels and extra physical facilities – power plants often have back-up systems in case of failure or surges in demand, factories can work overtime or bring in part-time workers to meet high-volume periods.
✦ You can spread knowledge so that there is greater flexibility to respond to different activity levels – in a self-managed, multiskilled production team, the absence of one member or the need to adapt to a temporary peak in workload can usually be covered by the rest of the team.

The brain develops its overcapacity by spreading knowledge and by self-organization, creating new rich networks. So the loss of one part can quickly be compensated for by the interconnections formed by remaining areas.

When problems arise in heavy, overspecialized functional organizations, the general attitude tends to be 'that's production's (marketing's, finance's) problem'. If the particular area under stress has no built-in extra resource, it is likely that the problems will affect performance. In networked, team-based organizations, with a better spread of knowledge and richer levels of interconnectivity between specializations, problems in any one area are usually much more easily dealt with. People reorganize themselves around the problem and have the knowledge and skills to deal with it.

 Pages 131–41

6. From binary cause and effect to complex patterns

Automated machines can produce more consistent quality than can manual workers. Computers can clearly do mathematical calculations faster and more accurately than can most people. In fact, my pocket calculator, which cost less than the price of two beers, has more calculating power than my brain will ever be capable of. Machines can respond to instructions in a regular and repetitive way, with little deviation. Computers can perform incredibly complex calculations, providing there is at the base a series of binary operations.

The brain, however, works quite differently. Instead of trying to find simple cause-and-effect relations between events or pieces of information, the brain can use its vast number of networks to form rich relationships between data and discover new or original patterns and meanings.

Functionally specialized, bureaucratic structures are like machines or computers. They may be efficient at carrying out a number of well-known motions or routines. But they also compartmentalize people and knowledge. Individuals and departments within them will tend to only have a narrow view of the world and will interpret events through their narrow and often over-simplified functional filters:

✦ When production problems arise the solutions will tend to be sought in production alone, whereas in reality they may be due to unrealistic promises made to customers by sales or inadequate time spent by development on testing the manufacturability of new products or on poor design or whatever.

✦ Dips in sales may be due to changing consumer taste, quality and delivery issues or even customers' annual cycle of spending and financial reporting. If the sales director only focuses on pressuring the salesforce to do better, the real issues will not be dealt with.

✦ A fall in the value of a currency may be due to the long-term competitive decline of a country's industry. Simple measures such as putting up interest rates to protect the currency, although common in some countries, are clearly inadequate to deal with the situation. In fact, they usually make it worse by increasing industry's borrowing costs and thus further harming its competitiveness.

By trying to emulate the brain in looking for meaningful patterns in events, rather than seeking narrow functional or simplistic, one-dimensional explanations, managers and politicians can come closer to developing appropriate responses.

7. Thinking, creating, adding value

Once US industry was the envy of the world. US companies dominated most areas of business. Now that has changed. In underarm deodorants, fast foods, colas, chewing gums, washing powders and other simple consumer products, the US probably still leads. But when it comes to microchips, faxes, VCRs and so on – products which are more complex and contain higher added value – the US has lost the lead. The US may make the impressive computers, but many of the components come from Japan. The US makes the film, but Japan makes the cameras. The US makes TV programs and microwave food, but the TVs and microwave ovens are produced by companies based in Asia.

What has happened is that the mechanistic, scientifically managed US companies have managed to compete on more basic, standardized products where massive economies of scale can still give a competitive edge. But, apart from the entertainments industry, these organizations have been unable to set up the human infrastructure required to compete on more knowledge-intensive products – information-sharing networks, flexibility to adapt to technical and market changes, the ability constantly to learn and adapt from experience. As companies such as Microsoft have shown, western companies resembling brains can be built and achieve incredible success. But, until most western companies break free of their mechanistic command-and-control heritage and move towards a culture based on thinking and learning, they will continue as suppliers of low value-added, 'no-brain' products and services.

Pages 305–14

Moving from a mechanistic to an organic world

Economists' theories are mostly based on fairly mechanical models. Many of these models may be incredibly sophisticated and contain thousands of variables, but ultimately their relationships are mechanistic. Raise this and that will happen. Control money supply and x will be the result. Increase public spending on infrastructure and y will automatically follow. They see the economy as a machine which can be simply speeded up and slowed down by applying pressure on the appropriate levers. With this mechanistic view of the world, economists usually have a set of targets for inflation, unemployment and so on and are using what are called damping effects to bring the economy back to a state of equilibrium which they believe is desirable.

Pages 37–9

In reality, of course, things are nothing like this. In reality you have to take account of people's behavior. If you slow an economy down, people lose jobs, homes and a sense of security. So, when you try to accelerate growth again, people are cautious and the hoped-for growth doesn't materialize. This then reinforces people in their view that things are not getting better and they remain pessimistic, further hindering economic recovery.

Reality does not behave mechanistically, but rather as a series of self-reinforcing positive or negative spirals. Each positive or negative influence fuels the next. Basically, success breeds success and failure feeds failure.

The more optimistic someone feels, the more they will tend to spend. The more educated they are, the more productive they will tend to be, the more educated their children will tend to be and so on. The more workers and managers have common goals, the more competitive the organization will be, the more new products they will develop, the better customer service will be, the more jobs will be created etc.

Take two firms. Both are under economic pressure. The first has a mechanistic mindset. It believes that all it has to do is to cut staff costs and profitability will return to a desired level. It lays off 10 percent of its staff to achieve planned profits. People feel insecure, become inwardly focused and service levels decline. Moreover, the downsizing encourages some of the best employees to leave and join more successful companies. Because reality tends to work in self-reinforcing spirals and not mechanistically, this negative action does not improve results but actually sends the firm further down a spiral of decline. The second firm believes in positive and negative self-reinforcing spirals. It sees its people not as a source of unnecessary cost but as a key competitive weapon. It tries to enter a positive self-reinforcing spiral by investing in, rather than disposing of, its people.

Mechanistic management tools

This mechanistic view of the world has led to the development of a whole series of 'tools' for managing the economy and organizations. Only simplistic mechanistic thinking could make us believe, for example, that monetarist policies, such as manipulating interest rates and money supply, could really help improve a country's long-term competitive position.

A similar process has happened in management. Only this kind of thinking could bring our leading experts to accept that a firm can only compete on either cost or differentiation – Japanese carmakers compete on both of these simultaneously, and on quality, better customer relations, closeness to the market, innovation and so on. Likewise, it is this mindset which has led to the development of strategy models like the BCG or GE matrices, where all you have to do is to class your operations into one of four segments and automatically your strategy (hold, harvest, invest, divest) becomes clear. How many times have we seen companies abandon supposedly 'mature businesses' which they had classed as 'dogs', only to see a foreign competitor relaunch the sector through applying new design or new technology? And finally, it is this kind of thinking, where we are convinced that there is a simple answer to every problem, which is pushing organizations into a lemming-like rush towards the new management 'Holy Grail', business process

Pages 258–75

reengineering. Unless we can radically change our mindset, this latest idea will turn out have just as little effect on improving our competitiveness as most of its predecessors.

Summary – time to change our model

For about fifty years, we've lived, consciously or subconsciously, with the concept of the organization and the economy as a machine. This has had a major influence on how we manage our companies and countries – although we all want flexibility, innovation, learning and increased competitiveness, too often our mechanistic mindset seems to push us toward constantly trying to impose order, quantification, consistency, efficiency and control. All these are aspects of a simple closed system or a machine.

If we decide to change the metaphor which underlies our concept of the organization and the economy from machine to brain, this should help change how we work and manage. Of course, we still need efficiency and control, otherwise there would be anarchy. However, by taking up the metaphor of the brain, we can start to think about new ways of working which have been proved to be more successful in many environments than is tight bureaucratic control.

You can't move overnight from a mechanistic to a thinking organization and economic regeneration can take years. But you can start trying to replace some of the more mechanistic processes and economic models by approaches which are more similar to how a brain might work. Some small moves in that direction can have a liberating effect and can start to put you, your department or your organization on to the kind of self-reinforcing positive spiral of growth currently enjoyed by your most successful competitors.

Recommended reading

A. Baddely (1983) *Your Memory: A User's Guide*, Penguin.

A.M. Blinkov & I.I. Glezer (1968) *The Human Brain in Figures and Tables*, Plenum Press.

Gary Hamel & C.K. Prahalad (1994) *Competing for the Future*, Harvard Business School Press.

Gareth Morgan (1986) *Images of Organization*, Sage.

C. Temple (1993) *The Brain*, Penguin.

8

Inspiring Innovation

At the end of 1994, a so-called shareholder revolt, led by a group of American investors, forced the removal of Maurice Saatchi from the advertising agency Saatchi and Saatchi, which he had co-founded with his brother Charles in the 1960s and rapidly built up into one of the world's largest agencies. The reason for his displacement could appear logically sound. Maurice Saatchi had presided over a tenfold collapse in the agency's share price and had now tried to link his bonus to a doubling in that share price. Some investors felt this was unsatisfactory. The only problem was that three top directors followed Maurice Saatchi to the new agency he decided to start. Then a whole series of major clients, including Mars and British Airways, started to quit, either to follow Maurice Saatchi or to head for other rival agencies.

Threats of court action against Maurice Saatchi and the other three directors, for poaching staff and clients, flew thick and fast. And the Saatchi and Saatchi share price fell even further. Within six months, the share price had halved. The fund manager who had originally made the proposal to oust Maurice Saatchi tried to put a brave face on the situation by claiming that the share price was 'the result of a misconception that the company is weaker now than it was before Mr Saatchi left'. However, it seemed as if the stock market took a different view. All in all, it appeared to be a somewhat Pyrrhic victory for the investors who had organized Maurice Saatchi's removal.

So what has this to do with inspiring innovation?

Advertising agencies tend to have few capital assets – their strength lies in their reputation and their client base. And these are both dependent on their people. If they start to lose those whom the market perceives as their best people, their reputation and client accounts will often disappear as well – sometimes with surprising and disconcerting speed. The investors, in expelling

Maurice Saatchi, had probably underestimated the value of his knowledge, experience, contacts and ideas and overvalued traditional performance measures such as turnover and cash flow.

There have been a number of takeovers in the last two decades (consultancies, banks, stockbrokers, advertising agencies, leading-edge biotech and computer companies, among others) which have been unmitigated disasters. The acquirers have found too often that dissatisfied key people have resigned and they have been left with empty and sometimes worthless shells. Again, they mistook figures such as turnover, growth rates or market share for concrete assets, not realizing that the acquired companies' assets lay in their people's heads and relationships.

Increasingly, an organization's strength is coming not from its balance sheet but from knowledge capital held in its people (Figure 8.1).

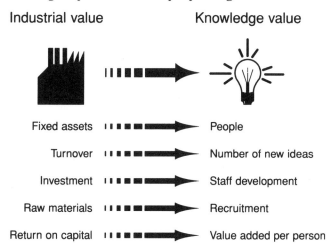

Figure 8.1   Value is moving from the balance sheet to knowledge capital

If you lose the people the apparent value of the business seems to disappear into thin air. Traditional accounting systems, with their emphasis on measures such as return on capital, often make these knowledge-based companies look extraordinarily profitable – after all, with few classical capital assets, they can easily generate returns on capital of 30–40 percent and look very attractive to a predator. Unfortunately, accounting systems fail to take account of how mobile and fragile the knowledge assets are. So with depressing but entertaining regularity, large and supposedly smart companies gobble up small innovative firms, pay substantial amounts to the founders and then proceed to irritate them by imposing heavy control systems on them. Frustrated with their new owners, the founders take their money and their latest ideas and go off to start yet another small, innovative company, leaving their surprised acquirer with an expensive and humiliating vacuum.

In highly structured, 'industrial model' organizations, jobs are designed with such clear task definition that the quality of the person employed is often not that important – for example, certain well-known fast-food chains have cash tills with pictures, rather than words or numbers, so that they can employ people who can't read.

With knowledge-intensive organizations, competitiveness depends on attracting the right quality of people. So developing your assets is now less a matter of investing in new plant or machinery and more one of ensuring that your people's knowledge and creativity are fully developed and used. You must learn to invest in knowledge, rather than physical assets. Building your people's capability to think more creatively is a key part of that investment. In some people-based businesses (law, consultancy, advertising), competitiveness is more about successful recruitment of human assets than building capital assets. As one manager said, 'competitiveness ends at the first interview'.

Three main types of thinking

The most useful studies of creativity tend to split the way we think into two main types, which have each been given various names:

analytical	vs	creative
convergent	vs	divergent
vertical	vs	lateral

While analytical/convergent/vertical thinking is about moving logically from one idea to the next, working on the basis that there is one right solution to each problem, creative/divergent/lateral thinking tries to break out from a problem to generate as many solutions as possible, even if many, at first, don't seem logical (Figure 8.2).

A simple but effective way to show the difference between analytical and creative thinking is to ask a group of people how many uses they can imagine for a paperclip – usually there will be 20 to 30 ideas. Then ask them how many things they couldn't use a paperclip for – often there aren't that many. This forces the group to understand how a logical, analytical approach can blind them to the rich variety of solutions which an alternative way of looking at an issue can provide.

This analytical vs creative split reflects the work done in neurosciences on

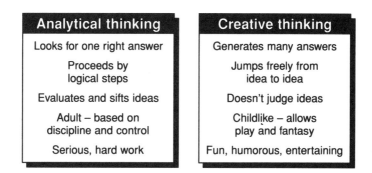

Figure 8.2   Key differences between analytical and creative thinking

analysing the brain's functioning discussed in Chapter 7. Given that there were the two clearly defined hemispheres of the brain with their different abilities, it was a fairly logical step to assume that there were also two main types of thinking.

Pages 74–8

Newer approaches, based more on the types of problems faced in organizations than on neurosciences, have proposed a third type of thinking particularly required in more complex and cross-functional situations. This is integrative thinking, the ability to take a large number of inputs from quite different functional areas or parts of the external environment and to merge all these into a balanced point of view (Figure 8.3).

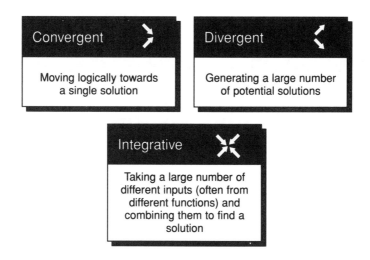

Figure 8.3   The three main types of thinking

The key is, of course, to be aware of the three types of thinking and to apply them selectively according to the situation.

De-risking innovation

There is a sad paradox with innovation. The greatest risk an individual can take in their career is probably to propose an innovative idea, as most innovative ideas will seem to threaten the organizational *status quo* in some way or other. Yet the greatest risk an organization can take is not to innovate at all. Too often organizational innovation comes from individuals taking the risk, because of their deeply held belief that they genuinely have something new to offer, rather than because the organization had actively encouraged innovative behavior. If they are to succeed in innovating, organizations must find ways to take the risk out of creativity so that it is encouraged rather than hindered.

Clearly, many smaller businesses have an advantage. Provided that they are not run by dominating autocrats, unable to consider other people's opinions, they won't suffer from the multiple levels of hierarchy and vested interest in the *status quo* which suffocate innovation in larger organizations. The last 20 years have been full of examples of small firms which have experienced explosive growth through developing innovative products or services which much larger and more powerful competitors were unable to produce.

Helping individuals think more creatively

Much has been written (see, for example, de Bono, 1992, and von Oech, 1983) about how our education system inhibits rather than encourages creative thinking. At school, we are generally taught nothing about the human mind or about improving memory and learning. Moreover, in many of the subjects we are taught (history, mathematics, economics etc.) the stress is usually on learning a series of answers off by heart and not on how to use our minds more productively. When we sit exams, it is usually those who can cram a vast number of facts into their short-term memory who excel, even though most of those facts are often forgotten a few months later. Two hundred years ago, such an education system might have been relevant. But today, when knowledge expands much faster than any individual's ability to absorb any more than a fraction of it, it is ludicrous to propose that an ability to memorize lists of facts is a useful preparation for life.

Numerous interesting and original techniques have been proposed to liberate our innate creativity. But not every manager wants to sit in meetings wearing different colored hats to represent different thinking states, using made-up words to indicate they are moving into a creative thought mode or dreaming up metaphors to stimulate an executive group's creative juices. In fact, in most organizations you'd be classed as certifiably insane for trying any of these methods. So here we'll propose a few methods for expanding people's mental productivity which can be used in the sober reality in which most of us still work.

Problem solving

Although managers don't always have the chance to adopt a fully structured approach to solving a particular issue, an awareness of the main stages of effective problem solving and the type of thinking required for each can help avoid some of the most common pitfalls (Figure 8.4).

Phase	Type of thinking		Most common pitfalls
1. Defining the problem	Integrative		Taking a narrow, functional view Being too broad to generate some effective responses
2. Generating solutions	Divergent		Starting out looking for the one correct answer Shooting down solutions that don't immediately appear logical
3. Choosing a solution	Convergent		Allowing politics and emotions, not logic, to decide the outcome Continuing to be creative, not applying sufficient analysis and judgment

Figure 8.4   The three main phases in problem solving and some common pitfalls

Phase 1: Defining the problem using integrative thinking

Delivery performance is slipping, a new product is not moving forward fast enough, patients/customers are waiting too long, an advertising campaign is not giving the hoped-for results or production levels are below plan – typical problems most managers will have to deal with. The two most frequent errors are:

✦ **Being too detailed:** Assuming there is a single department or area responsible – for example, just looking to manufacturing if deliveries are behind schedule, instead of studying where the whole supply chain might be under pressure; or only reorganizing a hospital accident and emergency department if casualties are waiting too long, instead of understanding all the many functional blockages preventing patients getting the care they require.

✦ **Being too general:** Selecting such a general reason – for example, the changing nature of the market/the economic situation – that finding any implementable solution becomes pointless.

Obviously, if you define a problem wrongly you can only develop the wrong answer. With many of the kinds of issues facing managers today, the solution is no longer in a series of narrow functional responses (put pressure on sales, shake up manufacturing, reorganize development etc.). Instead, situations often require a much broader, cross-disciplinary approach covering all the ten areas on which this book is based. The essence of defining the problem is to be able to integrate a large amount of possibly conflicting data from different areas in order to assess what the real issue is, so you deal with the problem and not just its symptoms.

Phase 2: Generating solutions

The skill in this phase lies in using divergent thinking to try to develop a large number of solutions, rather than working logically towards one right answer. It's here that the well-known techniques of creative thinking come into play:

✦ **brainstorming** – to generate a large number of ideas
✦ **blue sky thinking** – building what the ideal answer would be and then seeing how near you can get to it in reality
✦ **using metaphors, turning the situation on its head, Delphic processes, putting yourself in someone else's shoes, playing, taking risks etc.** – all methods for trying to break out of our normal, limited incremental way of thinking.

If you succeed in being creative, your solution can be quite original. One company, for example, found that it could dramatically improve customer service by reducing, not increasing, the level of stock and the number of warehouses.

The greatest mistake you can make at this stage is to gun down any idea that doesn't immediately seem practical. You may not know the whole story and may be destroying an excellent solution. For example:

A proposal to increase the sales of a product was shot down by the manufacturing manager because he believed there was no capacity to make any more. What he didn't know was that the 'capacity' problem was actually a 'yield' problem (the yield was an unacceptably low 60–65 percent). So, instead of solving the problem of why yield was so low, it was decided to maintain sales at their existing levels, and millions of pounds were lost.

A bright spark at a British car-parts manufacturer suggested that the company go into a strategic alliance with its main German rival to fight off a coming threat from a Japanese company, which had licenced European technology to build up capability in preparation for attacking the European market. 'Over my dead body!' the chief executive exclaimed. What he could not know was that the German manufacturer was coming to the same conclusion – the two companies would have to cooperate to survive. Five years (and many job losses) later, under a new chief executive, the alliance was announced.

Phase 3: Choosing a solution

Once you have generated a large number of potential solutions, you have to apply convergent thinking to ensure that the solution you end up with is useful and practical. By this point, those involved tend to have a high level of ownership of their particular solution. The skill is to get them to overcome their political or emotional attachment to their preferred answer and analytically arrive at a shared view of the best way forward.

The following is a typical example of how a semistructured problem-solving approach was used to break out of a simplistic reaction to a situation:

A European car manufacturer had to react to compete with growing Japanese imports. They had already improved productivity and quality and had cut labor costs drastically. Now they decided to put pressure on their suppliers to reduce prices by 5 percent a year.

◆ Mistake 1 – in defining the problem, they assumed that the high cost of components was the fault of their suppliers.
◆ Mistake 2 – they generated one solution only: put pressure on suppliers to reduce costs.

When this 'solution' didn't yield the hoped-for results the problem was revisited. A new way forward came through applying the three phases of problem solving and the three types of thinking:

+ **Defining the problem** – through discussions with suppliers, they learned that suppliers considered the car manufacturer's designs overcomplex and often difficult to produce, and that they saw the manufacturer's design engineers as inflexible. The parts thus ended up being expensive compared to those made for competitors. The suppliers felt that if they could have more freedom to interpret the manufacturer's requirements, they could find better and cheaper ways of making the parts. So by applying integrative thinking and looking across the various groups involved in the final design of parts, it was discovered that one key reason for the high cost of parts was the poor relationships between the engineering department and suppliers.

+ **Generating solutions** – the first attempt to solve the problem was by getting groups of engineers from the manufacturer's buying department and suppliers to meet to discuss particular components (exhaust systems, brake units, car bodies etc.). These meetings quickly became bogged down, involved in detailed technical discussions about a particular specification, material or manufacturing method. The breakthrough came when the meetings were split into three parts:
  - Part 1: participants generated ideas about all the possible ways of designing and making the individual parts of a component such as an exhaust system or dashboard. They also estimated the complexity, performance and price level of each method.
  - Part 2: they compared the method and materials used for the car manufacturer's components to the whole range of possibilities. Naturally, they found that often the most economical or best method had not been used.
  - Part 3: using the whole range of solutions they had generated, they jointly redesigned each component, producing cost savings 2–3 times greater than the manufacturer had originally hoped for

+ **Choosing a solution** – this proved extremely difficult, as the buying department engineers had to go to the enormously prestigious and powerful engineering department to try to get them to work differently with suppliers, for whom the corporate engineers often had little respect. This ended up as a tough political and emotional battle as the proposals were seen by the engineering department as an attack on their competence. Only by rigorous use of logic and evidence of the improvement potential could the resistance be partially overcome.

Mind mapping – applying associative thinking

First proposed by psychologist, broadcaster and writer Tony Buzan (1974), mind mapping is an extremely powerful way of capturing a wide number of features of an issue rapidly (Figure 8.5). It can be used to generate ideas, memorize a complex subject, as a basis for giving presentations and for many other applications. Here the focus will be on how it can help move from a narrow, functional view of a problem to a broader, richer, cross-disciplinary one.

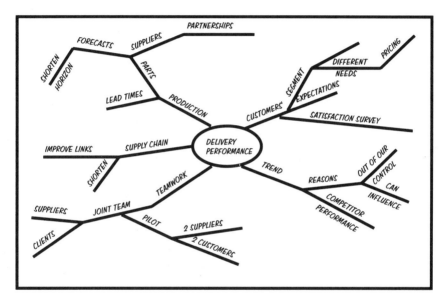

Figure 8.5   An example of a mind map

Linear and associative logic

When asked to prepare a report or analyse a problem, we often take a linear approach – we tend to write a few headlines and then try to fill in a bit of detail beneath them. The form of the written word on the page almost forces us to think in this way. Yet our minds work in an 'associative' way – any sound, smell, word or thought can spark off a whole series of (possibly logically unconnected) thoughts and images. By freeing us from the straitjacket of linear form, mind mapping helps release some of the richness of which our minds are capable.

At its most basic, a mind map entails writing the subject or issue in the middle of a page and then building a whole series of branches around themes as ideas occur.

Mind maps are particularly useful when working on improving cross-functional business processes with groups of people who represent the individual functions involved. To be successful in your process redesign, you need to move people from viewing the world through the filter of their functional interests to seeing how the whole process must serve business needs. Alternatively, you can build a mind map yourself to test whether you are taking a broad or narrow view of a problem.

Process mapping – brown-papering

Process flows of how work is done or how information or products pass through an organization are powerful ways of bringing out the real workings of a system and showing where improvements can be made. Two potential dangers with process flows are that they are frequently drawn up by specialists, rather than the people who do the work, and that they often end up showing how work should be done, rather than how it happens in reality – they reflect the corporate procedures manual rather than the messy reality of day-to-day working.

One way of overcoming these problems is to use a technique called brown-papering. In today's high-technology, computerized world, each time we propose to construct a brown paper of a business process, we are met with incredulity. People cannot believe that such a basic and simple method can add anything to what are usually very complex business situations. However, once the first draft is completed, you usually find you have converts for life. Brown-papering has been called 'low tech, high touch' – a low-technology tool that allows a very high level of people involvement.

 Some typical business processes which you might want to brown-paper are the order-to-delivery cycle, the new product development process or the administration and activities involved in dealing with a customer, guest, patient or client.

The construction of the brown paper (Figure 8.6) might proceed as follows:

1. Interview a few people connected with the main parts of the process you are brown-papering to understand the main activities, information flows, connections, volumes and measures. Normally you would just draw this out on some sheets of A4 paper.
2. Stick up a large sheet (usually about 4–6 meters long and 1–2 meters high) of brown paper along a wall. Then (using Post-it notes, sheets of paper and documents from the process) draw out the process on the brown paper.
3. Invite the people first interviewed to review the process flow on the brown

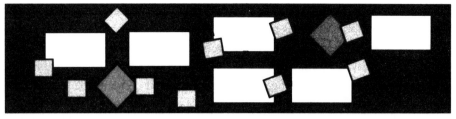

Figure 8.6 Building a brown paper

paper to check you have correctly represented their descriptions and to start getting some ideas on where the process could be improved. You can highlight these ideas by writing them on a different color of Post-it notes.

4. Now you're ready to invite the people who work in or are affected by the process to 'walk through' the brown paper (either individually or in groups of 6–8) giving their ideas on the areas for improvement. These can again be written up on Post-its. By the time a few people have been past the brown paper, you'll usually have at least 50 ideas of how the process could function better.

5. Finally, when you have collected all the improvement ideas, you can use the brown paper as a basis for building the new process.

Although extremely simple, brown-papering is a highly productive way of involving people from all parts and levels of a process in analysing and redesigning the way they work. By making the flow of often complex processes very physical and visible, you enable people to see the processes in a new way and to realize where they can contribute to improving them.

For many people, the brown paper will be the first time they have visualized the whole of the process within which they work. Due to functional or geographic boundaries, they may only know the part of the process which directly concerns them. So by bringing together people from all parts of a process in front of a brown paper, you help them gain an understanding of each other's operating problems and how they can help simplify life for other people involved in different parts of the process.

Helping organizations think more creatively

People who work in large organizations are no less creative than those in smaller ones. In fact, with their huge resources and their ability to offer varied international careers, larger organizations can often attract the 'best' people. Yet somehow, with their carefully partitioned functional departments, their religiously guarded hierarchical levels and their tendency (despite claims to the contrary) to end up promoting those who fit in rather than those who stand out, many large organizations seem to suppress new ways of thinking.

While Asian economies are seen as 'tigers' because of their ability to change, adapt and grow, people think of most large western organizations as 'dinosaurs' and 'elephants' – heavy, slow-moving and condemned to eventual extinction. Normally, it is only in conditions of crisis that they deign to change their ways. Very few seem capable of gradual positive development – when they do move forward, it's usually in great, painful lurches and only under extreme stress.

To change a large organization usually means finding some way to change the lens through which it views itself and its environment. And this requires ways of breaking out of the mental models held by top management. There are a number of techniques available for helping managers move from a defensive, 'steady as she goes' approach to a more ambitious way of designing their future.

Building on leverage not economic power

Agile small competitors have repeatedly shown large organizations that big does not mean powerful any more. In fact, with rapid change continuously catching them on the wrong foot, large organizations now appear vulnerable rather than awesome. People even feel sorry for them and wonder if some of them will be around for that long.

While large companies take comfort in the abundance of their resources, agile, once small competitors have often achieved astounding results by building on leverage rather than economic power:

> If Honda had 'stuck to the knitting' or restricted itself to its 'core competences', it would have remained a motorcycle manufacturer. But it did not allow itself to be limited by what it knew how to do and instead is a leading maker of cars, motors for boats and many other products.

> Likewise Yamaha, another motorcycle maker, did not limit itself to known markets and is now a world leader in electronic keyboards and pianos.

Apparent power creates complacency, ambition builds inventiveness. Managers need to move from trying to build static strategies, based on what  they know the organization can achieve with little effort, to developing 'ambition' strategies aimed at what the organization could achieve if it was to set 'stretch' goals (Figure 8.7).

Pages 248–57

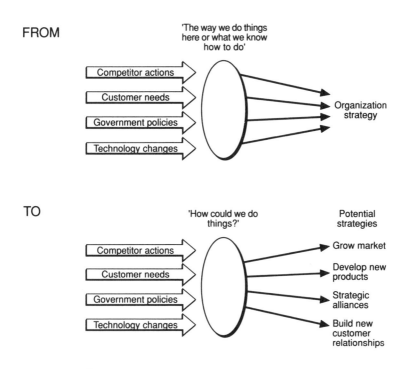

Figure 8.7   From 'fit' to 'leverage' strategies

S-curve models

Too often, managers become trapped in viewing their industry in a particular way and are unable to imagine how it might develop. They fight new competitive battles with yesterday's mindset and weapons. By building an S-curve model of where their industry has come from and what the next probable stage of development might be, they can start to open their minds to the new challenges and opportunities they have to face.

> For example, in fast-moving consumer goods (FMCG), sales of branded products are declining and many companies are caught in ever more expensive advertising, price and promotional wars. All this is much to the delight of their main customers, the supermarket chains, who both benefit from better prices and in the meantime put pressure on the FMCG companies by substituting cheaper and more profitable own-label goods for the branded products.
>
> By building an S-curve model of the FMCG market, you could come to the conclusion that what is happening is not just another of the peri-

odic brand wars which companies often engage in to gain temporarily a few precious market share points from their rivals (Figure 8.8).

In reality, a major shift in the market may be occurring away from more expensive branded products towards 'better value' own-label competition. With sometimes 30 percent or more of their potential market about to disappear, FMCG companies may be wasting time and money slugging it out over a declining and decreasingly profitable market. The time may have come for them to change their mental picture of their own role from, for example, being a branded cleaning products manufacturer to being a cleaning products producer. The brand may have to be replaced by the product itself as their core competence, even to the extent of becoming a manufacturer of own-label products.

The benefits of becoming product rather than purely brand focused can be significant — more volume through factories, less need to spend so much on advertising, moving from competitor to partner with the supermarkets, ensuring that an FMCG company will now fight in the larger total market for its products, and not just in the declining branded section of it.

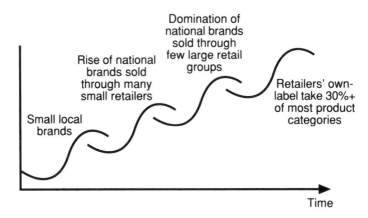

Figure 8.8   Typical development phases for an FMCG market

You can build on an S-curve model and gain additional insights by analysing what the critical success factors, strategy, management approach, organization structure, measurement systems and so on should be for each of the curves.

Moving from functional to process innovation

In too many organizations, innovation is seen as a slightly unpredictable, functionally based activity. R&D can come up with an exciting new product concept, marketing can develop a powerful new campaign idea or manufacturing can design a more effective production process. This is probably the common perception of innovation – something which is largely unplanned and which happens in individual departments or comes from so-called creative individuals. Moreover, as many of these innovations may require other areas to change the way they work, they are often met with hostility and suspicion and many are killed prematurely by political opposition.

But other innovations can come from taking a cross-functional view of the process of serving the customer and reinforcing horizontal communication. For example, customer service staff will tend to view the difficulties which customers are having with ordering products and paying invoices as the normal trials and tribulations of their work, rather than as opportunities to be communicated so that their employer can redesign the way customers are served.

> A chemical company found that customers were increasingly being visited by more than one salesperson and receiving several invoices from different product areas. While competitors just accepted these complications as a fact of life, this company selected those customers who were ordering a number of products from different divisions and established single account managers and a single ordering and billing point for them. This allowed the company to coordinate deliveries, improve communication and strengthen their relationship with these customers.

Likewise, confronted by modifications which a customer has made to a piece of equipment, repair engineers working with standard repair manuals, a limited kit of tools and spares and to a tightly controlled schedule will tend to see these modifications as an unwanted complication to their work rather than as an opportunity to learn some new techniques and to pass these back to their organization.

It is no longer sufficient for organizations to rely on an individual or single department stumbling on the 'great creative breakthrough'. This happens too infrequently and the outcomes are often fragile. There are a wealth of potential innovations which can be much more systematically found by communicating information and ideas horizontally across the organization and by building the capability to solve problems in cross-functional groups.

 Pages 131–41

Using simple images

Sometimes a business becomes so complex that many parts of it seem to lose contact with its underlying purpose. By building a simple image of the business, it is possible to help all its areas recapture some of the sense of common purpose they may have lost.

At a company in the tourist industry support staff numbers were extremely high, as were their costs. However, like all centralized corporate functions, the administrators were expert in justifying the absolute necessity of all the many activities which occupied their time and the weighty reports they often produced. By drawing a seasonality chart (Figure 8.9) showing customer flow against administrative staff numbers (administrative staff mostly took their holidays in the peak holiday months), even they could see that there were some anomalies and they became slightly more amenable to discussing better control of their costs.

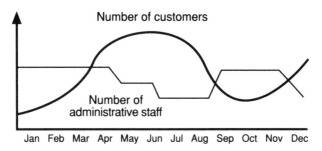

Figure 8.9   A seasonality chart

Summary

A great weakness of British and American companies is their obsession with detailed numbers and facts. Strategic plans are often monstrous documents which pretend to be scientific through an overload of quantitative data. The fact that so many managers have MBAs reflects this belief in management as a scientific pursuit which can be learned in a classroom rather than through experience. Yet 'business administration' is not clearly adding any value to end customers, it is not productive and it is internally focused. Administration is an activity which feeds on itself, grows continuously and often sucks up considerable time and resources which could be better employed on more productive, value-added activities. We have to move some of these managers away from the pseudo-scientific theories and models they have learned at business school and reduce their need for numbers as an emotional security blanket before they can take any decision. And we have to let them experience adding value through building on their own ideas and the ideas of their people, rather than on conducting detailed and ultimately useless analyses to the nth decimal place.

If we accept that we need to build flexibility and adaptability into our organizations, then there is a clear need to improve the way we arrive at solutions to problems. Individuals and organizations can be taught to be more creative – brown-papering, building S-curves, using structured problem solving and constructing a simple picture of a business are just a few powerful techniques which can be quickly and easily applied. And usually people trying these methods are surprised at how quickly they produce results of a much higher quality than many traditional and often more labor-intensive analytical approaches.

Recommended reading

Tony Buzan (1974) *Use Your Head*, BBC Books.
Edward de Bono (1992) *Serious Creativity*, HarperCollins.
V. Nolan (1987) *The Innovator's Handbook*, Sphere.
R. von Oech (1983) *A Whack on the Side of the Head*, Warner Books.

Part Four

Managing Change

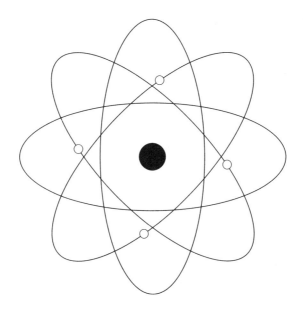

9

Implementing Change Successfully

Over the last five to ten years, managers have been bombarded by a cacophony of advice – we must 'reorganize every two years', 'each organization must continually reinvent itself' and 'revolution must replace evolution'.

Apparently now we must all change to survive. Anyone not involved in changing something, and changing it radically, is assumed to be a managerial dinosaur headed for rapid extinction.

The changemongers would have us believe that everything is changing so fast that all our existing structures and methods rapidly become outdated. But we should be careful of these new prophets of change – most of them have a vested interest in the message they preach. Of course, major technological and environmental changes do take place. But put in a historical context – compared to the generations who lived through either of the world wars or the Great Depression – we've had a pretty easy ride so far.

Too many organizations have now become 'initiative weary'. Managers have difficulty keeping up with the flavor of the moment – is it reducing new product introduction time or getting close to the customer? Is it reengineering or creating a learning organization? Or maybe different departments are each pursuing their own particular favorite. Moreover, what priority should be given to the day-to-day running of the business, when an ever-increasing proportion of staff time is spent on doing (or avoiding) the latest 'improvement' initiatives?

So, instead of rushing around changing everything to keep up, we need to take a balanced view of what changes will affect us and how we need to react to them. In telling us what all the 'excellent' organizations are doing differently, the changemongers often omit to tell us what they have kept constant. Few organizations can cope with continuous change – too much change makes them internally focused and distracts them from their customers.

In any case, the real problem with many organizations may not be that managers have failed to understand the need to change. It is more likely to be that many management groups have been unable to transform their knowledge of what needs to be done into effective action. The 'what' of change is often not that difficult to ascertain – it is over the 'how', the implementation, that most organizations stumble.

Change programs

Most change programs produce disappointing results. Whether it's downsizing, just in time, total quality or business process reengineering, surveys generally show that less than one in three programs are considered successful (for example, Fuchsberg, 1992; CSC Index, 1994). Different organizations obviously fail for quite different reasons. Nevertheless, one common theme which seems to run through most less than satisfactory change programs is that organizations put too much time and effort into intellectualizing about what they want to change and far too little on the most difficult part – how they are going to carry out that change.

With all our brilliant tools for market segmentation, strategic planning, competitor mapping, channel analysis Pages 258–75 and so on (see Part Eight – Developing the Right Strategy), we've become pretty good at working out where we want our organizations to go – the 'content' part of change. However, we tend to be much weaker at change implementation – the 'process' of change.

There are scores of books and hundreds of articles available on the process of managing change. And however many steps there are in the model they propose, most agree on some key points. For a change program to be successful, you need such things as:

✦ top management commitment
✦ constant, consistent communication
✦ employee involvement at all levels
✦ a shared vision of the future
✦ understanding of the need to change
✦ management of political networks.

There are already sufficient summaries of the theory of change management in existence. Rather than repeating what is so readily available, this chapter will describe the main phases of how one might manage a change program, giving details of some tools, meeting agendas, team structures, communication plans and so on, in the hope that this will give a better idea of what good change management should look and feel like.

'Change program' is not intended to mean a small local initiative such as increasing the productivity of an area of a factory by 10–20 percent, reorganizing a single department or improving the performance of a customer service unit. Here we are talking about major organizational change, such as:

✦ reducing the purchasing costs for a car manufacturer, through working more closely and in partnership with several hundred suppliers
✦ reducing the development and launch time for a major new product by about two years
✦ restructuring an organization with several thousand employees from being based on functional departments to being organized around serving market sectors.

Focus on improvement, not cost

In spite of the noble-sounding names many management groups think up for their change programs ('Project 2000', 'Fast-track', 'Top 5 by '95' etc.), the basic driver is too often the need to reduce costs – usually personnel costs. This focus on cost reduction will tend to cripple most change programs from the start, for two fairly obvious reasons. First, staff may pay lip-service to the program but are hardly likely to be motivated to contribute enthusiastically to a project which will deprive them or their colleagues of their jobs. Second, excessive costs are normally the result of poorly operating processes. If you reduce staff without fixing the processes, you will tend to find that the remaining staff will be unable to support the workload and that service levels will fall and costs gradually drift up again.

On the other hand, you could launch a change program which is genuinely targeted at process improvement. You may find that you start a self-reinforcing positive spiral, where the improvements made create opportunities for the staff who are no longer needed to operate the new more efficient processes. You may, of course, genuinely need to reduce costs. There is nothing wrong with that. The mistake is to target this too directly. Real performance improvements can often take away the original need for personnel reductions (Figure 9.1).

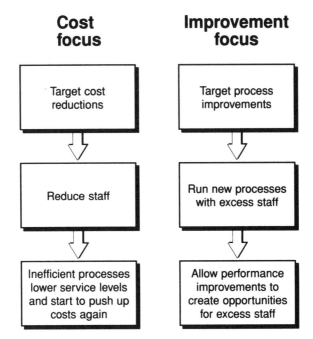

Figure 9.1   Few change programs succeed if they are aimed too
directly at cost reductions

Change management team structure

Many organizations set up part-time cross-functional groups which meet
weekly or monthly to drive their change effort. The main advantages of this
approach is that the team remains close to the reality of the business through
also performing their regular jobs, and thus cannot be portrayed by the opponents of change as a group of theorists with smart but impractical ideas. The
problem with this method is that a part-time group, however talented, can
rarely develop the speed and critical mass which most major change programs
require.

A better method is to set up a full-time cross-functional change team led by
a change manager. This team should work between three main groups of people – the executive team, functional/process managers and staff, and expert
resources (Figure 9.2).

The size of the change team can be anything from five to twenty people,
depending on the complexity of the task and the size of the organization. In
the fast-moving and trying environment of a change program, teams larger

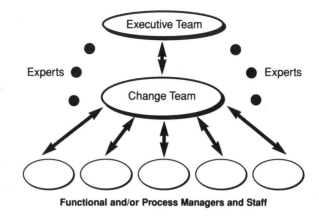

Figure 9.2   Change management team structure

than fifteen to twenty people start becoming unmanageable. If you find, at times, that the team needs specialist skills it doesn't have, you may find it easier to appoint a part-time (or even full-time) expert for a couple of weeks or months, rather than looking to expand the team's size permanently – more bodies don't necessarily mean more effectiveness.

The basic change process

You can split a change program into any number of steps, depending on the level of detail you wish to go down to. The model to be used here has five main phases (Figure 9.3):

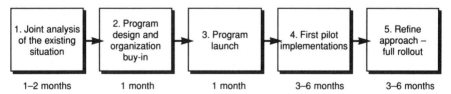

Figure 9.3   The basic change process

The model also gives approximate timings for each phase. Obviously these will depend on the complexity of the situation. Programs which are multisite or multinational, which are technologically difficult, which rely on changing organizations outside the targeted organization (customers, suppliers, regulatory authorities etc.), which are conducted when the organization has a strongly resistant culture or when an organization feels no real need to change – all of these will tend to take longer.

Phase 1 – Joint analysis of the existing situation

Purpose

This phase is deliberately called joint analysis, because the purpose is not just to find out what must improve, but to do this jointly with people who work in the key business processes, so that your conclusions represent their operating reality and also so that the people you involve in the analysis process begin to share the understanding of why things should be changed. From this phase, we want to:

+ identify where improvements/changes should be made
+ check whether the organization's strategy/vision (if it has one) is appropriate given market realities and existing competences and ability to learn
+ help people begin to build a shared view of what can be improved
+ open up the organization to the need for change (start what Kurt Lewin calls unfreezing)
+ start to identify the components and priorities for the change program.

Approach (Figure 9.4)

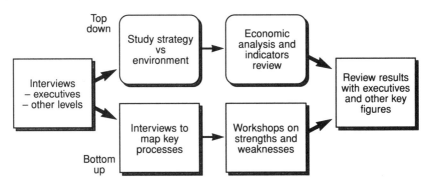

Figure 9.4   Joint analysis of the existing situation

Start with a series of interviews with executives and interviews and/or group discussions with middle management and staff. These give an idea of:

+ where each group sees the main strategic and operational problems
+ what the potential benefits opportunity is if those problems are fixed
+ to what extent the different organizational levels are in agreement over the issues and solutions.

The next step is to start two series of studies:

- ✦ top down
  - – look at the organization's strategy vs the environment vs people's opinions of the fit of strategy and environment
  - – conduct a rapid financial analysis of the business looking at what both 'lag' and lead indicators tell (see Part One – Keeping Up with Leading-edge Thinking)
  - – examine which performance indicators executives are judged on: if these indicators are from the past and are less relevant to today's business, it's likely that they're leading to the wrong behaviors
- ✦ bottom up
  - – identify the key customer-facing processes, interview experts on these processes, map out how these work in reality and then through interviews with users and brainstorming workshops try to establish the main strengths and weaknesses of these processes. A possible agenda for one of these workshops is given in Figure 9.5.

Workshop agenda – analysis of a key process	
Objectives and personal introductions	10 mins
Capture participants' expectations	5 mins
Background and purpose of the study	15 mins
General opinions on strengths and weaknesses of the organization	15 mins
Presentation of the process flow	20 mins
Idea generation – strengths and weaknesses of the process	40 mins
Summing up and invitation to attend next workshop – 'Design of a future key process'	15 mins
Total	2 hours

Figure 9.5   Workshop agenda – key process analysis

To end this first phase, the conclusions of the interviews, analyses and workshops should be discussed in one-on-one meetings with executives and with key thinkers or influencers to ensure that the right conclusions are being drawn and to start bringing them to a common view of the issues.

One-on-one meetings are proposed because the purpose is not to have big set-piece presentations for the change team to show how smart they are, but rather to start building a consensus around the way forward. During these meetings, in spite of their no doubt worthy desire to communicate all they have discovered, the members of the change team must listen to the questions, doubts and views of their interlocutors. Change teams are normally dealing with some quite sensitive issues. If they fall too quickly into a 'broadcast' rather than 'receive' mode, they will only alienate the organization, however devastatingly brilliant their insights.

Phase 2 – Program design and organization buy-in

Purpose

The purpose of this phase is to:

+ involve as many people as possible in building a first rough view of what the new working methods and structures should look like
+ design a change program to move to these new methods and structures
+ ensure that the change program design suits the organization's particular position in the market, skills and political make-up
+ ensure that key figures have the chance to contribute to, but not derail, the design and that they are generally in agreement with it
+ have executives approve the program plan, supply of adequate resources and funding.

Approach (Figure 9.6)

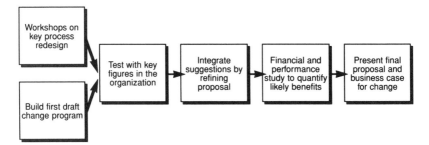

Figure 9.6   Program design and organizational buy-in

This phase consists of:

+ running cross-functional workshops around the key processes to start to build a future model of how they should work
+ laying down some ideas of what the areas of work should be in the change program
+ testing these ideas with executives, key thinkers and department managers.

Future process design workshops

At this point, the aim is not to produce a finalized design of the future processes, structure and supporting systems. We are just trying to involve the local process experts, customers and users in broadly outlining the way they would like to see the processes work, so we can:

+ see what degree of change will be necessary and build this into the change program
+ have a base against which to start estimating the financial and operational benefits of the new ways of working.

There are three main parts to the workshop (a sample agenda is given in Figure 9.7):

+ agreeing on the analysis of the strengths and weaknesses of the existing process
+ developing an idea of how the 'perfect process' could work
+ outlining how near to the 'perfect process' the participants think the organization could realistically come.

It is critical that people do not try just to fix the existing process. If they do, they will only end up proposing small, incremental improvements, whereas if they first start to imagine a perfect process, then move back to a realistic design, they are likely to be much more ambitious and imaginative in their thinking.

Build first draft change program

The main elements of the change program will probably include those shown in Figure 9.8.

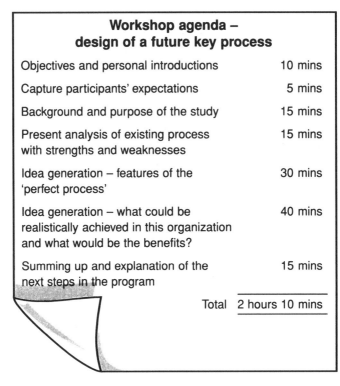

Figure 9.7   Workshop agenda – design of a future key process

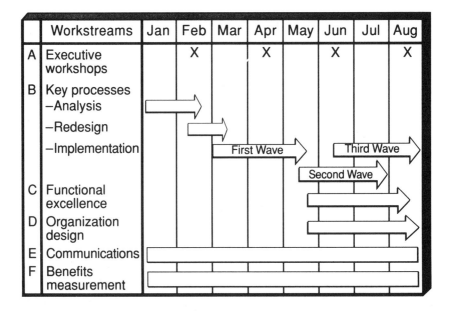

Figure 9.8   A typical change program

✦ 3–4 executive workshops to ensure executives are continuously in agreement with the way the program is starting and progressing (A)

✦ 4–6 key processes being analysed in more detail, redesigned and the new methods implemented (B) starting 2 processes first. You need to spread your risk, so if one process gets bogged down you'll have another one still being worked with. Usually not more than 2, as you'll first want to test your approach before applying it to all the key processes (B)

✦ a stream of work focused on the future role of the functional departments (C). If like most organizations you're moving away from being structured around functions to being based around key processes, the role and power of the functions will change, from being the main owners of budgets and resources to being centers of functional expertise which exist only to support the key processes (C)

✦ a stream of work aimed at producing the new organization design and supporting reward and promotion systems (D)

✦ a communications group to ensure that the purpose, progress and successes of the program are properly broadcast (E)

✦ a benefits measurement group to put in place performance indicators and baselines to measure progress against and to monitor continuously whether the program is achieving its targets (F).

When should the organization structure be changed?

This is a key question which always arises in designing change programs. Traditional practice proposes that you should put in place your new organization structure and at the same time, or immediately after, work with people to change the way they operate so that it fits your new structure. This approach fits quite closely to the classic strategy model where 'structure follows strategy' (Chandler, 1962) – when you have decided your strategy, this will guide you as to what structure you should adopt (see Part Nine – Redesigning the Organization).

Pages 278–80

However, you cannot know what structure you want to put in place until you have worked out in some detail how you want your key processes to operate. So you start working on key process redesign and implementation and from this you draw out the implications for structure.

In the change program outlined in Figure 9.8, the functional excellence and organization redesign streams of work don't start until the second wave of redesigned process implementation has begun, since the experience of implementing the redesigned processes will guide the organization redesign.

While this brief piece on structure may look like a matter of semantics or slightly differing models, it is vitally important. Basically, instead of top management deciding the 'appropriate' structure and the change program being all about implementing it, the change program will be aimed at implementing improved work processes and the teams designing these processes will themselves propose to management the structure they think is most suitable.

Phase 3 – Program launch

Purpose

The purpose of this phase is to:

+ communicate to the organization the program structure and aims
+ ensure that people understand how the program is likely to affect them and what their required contribution might be
+ enable people to start to discuss their concerns about the proposed changes and also to alert the change team to other opportunities which may not have been fully recognized during the initial joint analysis phase
+ continue the process of opening up the organization to the need for change.

Approach

How you decide to communicate the program will depend on how you normally handle this kind of information – large meetings chaired by executives, a video shown to all, cascading communications down each function and level or a letter sent to all staff are all possible methods. Given the importance of a major change program, you might want to think about using a communication method which is not usual for your organization. This may help to differentiate this program from the many other improvement initiatives which most organizations have already undertaken with differing degrees of success.

Phase 4 – First pilot implementations

Purpose

The purpose of this phase is to:

+ test the approach to redesigning and implementing the new ways of working
+ prove that the new ways are better than what existed before
+ start dealing with some of the emotional and political problems which will

have to be overcome for the program to be successful
+ achieve benefits from implementing one or two key business processes
+ train the first groups of people to adopt the new kinds of behaviors which will
be required to work with the new processes (e.g. customer instead of internally focused, or business process instead of functional loyalties)
+ serve as a learning laboratory to improve the way the next series of processes
should be redesigned.

Approach

Normally most pilot implementations will follow a fairly similar pattern
(Figure 9.9):

Figure 9.9   First pilot implementations

+ **Finalize analysis of the existing situation** (2–3 weeks) – take the initial
process analysis conducted at the program start and review it with a wider
audience to ensure that the real sources of problems, rather than just the
symptoms, have been identified. Also, conduct deeper studies and statistical,
financial or operational analyses to capture exactly how current performance
can be measured and what the results of redesign should be.
+ **Confirm the perfect process** (2 weeks) – take the initial views of how the
process could work and, again using a wider audience and examples from
other companies and industries, build the 'perfect process' design.
+ **Gap analysis** (2 weeks) – identify what would have to change to move from
the existing situation to the perfect process.
+ **Build proposal** (2 weeks) – based on the existing situation analysis, the perfect process picture and the gap analysis, put together a recommendation as
to how the process being worked on should operate in the organization's
particular environment.
+ **Gain approval** (2 weeks) – through one-on-one meetings and set-piece presentations, build support with executives and key managers to the proposed
new process.
+ **Implement new methods in a pilot area** (1–3 months).

Phase 5 – Refine approach and full rollout

Purpose

The purpose of this phase is to:

+ take what has been learned on the pilot implementations and reconfigure your change management approach to take account of these lessons
+ fully implement all key business processes
+ implement any required organizational and system changes
+ measure quantifiable business benefits.

Approach

The time required for this phase will depend very much on whether the roll-out is concerned with moving on to different business processes or just taking processes which have already been reconfigured and repeating the same implementation in different geographical locations. Also, the extent of necessary organization structure and information systems change will have a major effect on the workload. The main steps are (Figure 9.10):

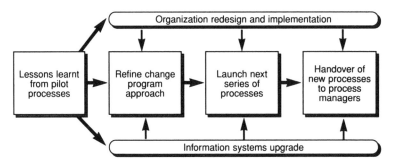

Figure 9.10   Refine approach and full rollout

+ Review pilot implementations with both the change team and the people involved. Establish what went well and what went badly. Also draw out implications of the implementations for organization structure and information systems.
+ Launch next series of process redesign and implementation.
+ Launch organization restructure and information system upgrade work.
+ Work with functions to adapt them to their new role as supporters of the redesigned cross-business processes.

Of course, all this should work – provided that you successfully manage the thousand and one ingenious ways in which people resist, block, undermine, avoid, circumvent, obfuscate and otherwise obstruct even the most well-meaning change program. Change programs tend to start off like a hundred meter race, gradually develop into a marathon and often end up like wading through particularly sticky molasses. To try to avoid this you should never, ever underestimate how extraordinarily inventive people are in thwarting any change, however minor management may believe it to be (see Chapter 10 – Overcoming Resistance to Change).

 Pages 120–9

Recommended reading

R. Beckhard & R.T. Harris (1987) *Organizational Transitions: Managing Complex Change*, Addison-Wesley.

M. Beer, R.A. Eisenstat & B. Spector (1990) 'Why change programs don't produce change', *Harvard Business Review*, Nov–Dec.

A.D. Chandler (1962) *Strategy and Structure*, MIT Press.

CSC Index (1994) *State of Re-engineering Report*.

Gilbert Fuchsberg (1992) 'Quality programs show shoddy results', *Wall Street Journal*, 14 May.

10

Overcoming Resistance to Change

One thing is certain with any change program. However well it is planned and communicated, most people will aggressively oppose it. And almost any manager who has been involved in a change program, whether it was successful, mediocre or disastrous, will admit that they underestimated people's ability to resist (Miller, 1990). Sometimes despairing managers will dream of how successful their programs would be, if only a small part of the energy and ingenuity people used resisting change could be transferred to supporting it. The question of why resistance occurs has proved fascinating for psychologists and sociologists, but is more than frustrating for most managers.

Resistance can be seen as both an individual and an organizational phenomenon. Sometimes the organization as a whole is able to change, but key individuals, for a variety of reasons, put up a ferocious rearguard action and sink or at least bog down the initiative. This often happens when organizations which have had strong functional department 'barons' find themselves trying to move from a function-based to a process-based structure. Top management and front-line staff understand the need for change. But the already powerful barons, facing a loss of power and influence, tend to mount impressive opposition.

At other times, individuals may be frustrated and anxious for change, but the organization seems stuck in a certain, sometimes almost manic, behavior pattern which cannot be altered. Many organizations with a centralized power structure and close contacts to customers can find themselves in this position. Those close to the customers are aware daily of how the organization is failing to meet competitors' levels of service – but every request for improvement coming from 'the field' is seen by the central power structure as a criticism. Faced with what it sees as 'unwarranted' attacks from people whom it believes have only a partial picture and don't understand the whole business view, the center tends to become more closed in on itself and more impervious to the warnings from the field.

Individual resistance to change

Emotional, political and rational responses

There are many ways of looking at how and why individuals are so well motivated, perhaps perversely so, when they see the threat of change coming in their direction. One model for analysing the different reasons for resistance is to group people by how well they understand the reasons for change and how emotionally or politically involved they are in the change itself (Figure 10.1).

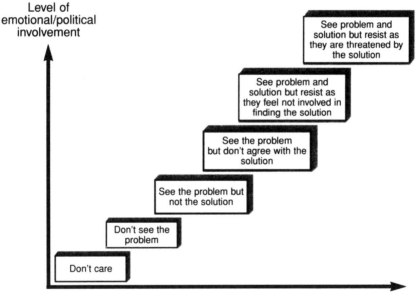

Figure 10.1   Some of the key reasons for resisting change

Whatever people's reasons for resisting change, they are seldom 'logical' – a result of analysing the change proposed and having a good basis for believing the changes are not appropriate. People respond to change on three levels:

✦ **Emotional** – What will this change mean for me personally? How will my life change? Will my position in other people's eyes be different? Will I be able to cope with the changes to my role? and so on.

✦ **Political** – Will I lose control over resources/people/decisions? Will I still be part of some key groups? Will I still be able to influence the decisions that affect me and my area?

✦ **Rational** – Is this change right for the organization?

With depressing regularity, managers try to gain acceptance for change by appealing to their people's logic, while staff consistently interpret any change through the filter of their emotional and political anxieties (Figure 10.2).

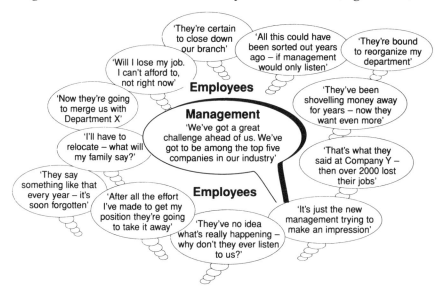

Figure 10.2   A typical breakdown in communication as managers announce a change program

Not surprisingly, the quality of the communication in these situations is quite poor. As the change program progresses, each side becomes increasingly frustrated and irritated with the other. Managers start to wonder if their people are too bloody-minded or simply too stupid to understand the need for change, while staff will tend to get increasingly angry with management for not addressing what they believe are valid concerns.

Executive defense mechanisms

Resistance to change is seldom direct. There are very few people who will openly say to management why they are opposing some proposal. What happens instead is a sometimes very elaborate kind of game, in which people hide their real opposition behind an apparent willingness to cooperate 'if only circumstances were right'. The trick here for managers is to avoid being side-tracked and to deal with the real reasons for people being against your proposals.

A possibly entertaining and useful approach to looking at how resistance to change manifests itself is to begin to class some of the main types of response you get, as you start the often seemingly thankless task of trying to convince colleagues to move from an old behavior pattern to a new one. For example, animal caricatures can be used to distinguish some of the more creative ways in which people resist, yet try to disguise their opposition as helpful cooperation:

The Wise Owl

✦ Always knows better than you and tries to discourage you.
– Complicates the issue: 'Absolutely right, but what about conformance to safety standard 2183723 and acceptability to our industrial derivatives customers?'
– Adopts the moral high ground: 'I can understand that marketing might want to work that way, but in accounts we must take a more professional approach.'

The Eager Beaver

✦ Tries to put pressure on you by wanting the solutions right away or tries to throw you off the scent by claiming the problem has been sorted out.
– Demands the answer: 'We could have all told you that, the question is what exactly are you proposing we do about it?'
– Has sorted out the problem: 'Don't worry, as soon as I heard, I put a team right on to it. We won't have that problem any more.'

 ### The Busy Bee

✦ Has a thousand and one important things to see to first and uses these to fob you off.
– Puts customers first: 'I'd like to help you, but I've all the customer orders to see to first. After all, we're here to serve our customers.'
– Hasn't got time: 'Just now is not the moment, but I like your ideas. When I get time, we should get together and see what we can work out.'

The Sly Fox

✦ Always attempts to divert attention from their area, hopefully embroiling you in such political and personal battles that you lose your desire to change anything.

- It's someone else's fault: 'Yes, but if only production could change the way they do things, I don't think we'd be having all these problems, do you?'
- Management must act: 'If management would just tell us what the strategy is, we'd have no problems sorting things out.'

The Snake in the Grass

✦ Hides behind personal attacks on others.

- Blames colleagues: 'I personally agree with everything you say. But, between you and me, with Johnson in charge of marketing, things are hardly likely to get better. He's a nice person, just a bit out of his depth.'
- Criticizes their former boss, often conveniently forgetting that they used to be second in change of the area: 'I'm all for it, but I've only been in this job for two years and I spend most of my time sorting out the mess I inherited.'

The Procedural Elephant

✦ Professes support, but uses systems, procedures and controls as a way of slowing you down.

- Change is OK, providing it is controlled: 'I agree wholeheartedly, but we must make sure everybody knows precisely what they've got to do before we move this forward.'

The Toadying Toad

✦ Will agree with everything you say, in case you end up being right. But they'll agree with everyone else as well, so they don't make very reliable allies.

The Hare-brained Hare

✦ Will tell you your ideas are 'terrific' and give you a whole load of their 'great ideas' and maybe even rush around telling everyone about the wonderful new plans. But they're not respected, are generally ineffectual and again are not the best of allies.

People may use either one or several of the above tactics to trap you into useless discussion. Some will use one after the other – so just as you think you've dealt with their latest objection, out pops a completely different problem or excuse, sending you scurrying off in yet another direction. Sometimes the above reactions can be genuine and people may really believe what they are saying. But most often these are delaying or diversionary tactics, a bit like a fighter plane spreading chaff to confuse hostile missiles. Unless you see these responses for what they are, you are doomed to become increasingly mired in pointless attempts to deal with apparent objections which are not connected with people's actual concerns. And unless you unearth and deal with their real concerns, you're unlikely to make much progress.

Organizational resistance to change

Organizations, with their collective history, culture, mindset and ways of working, are formidable entities to try to change. And most of them successfully manage to defeat change efforts, until their situation becomes so precarious that only crisis measures are enough to save them – if, of course, it is not already too late. Some of the most common reasons for organizations being so resistant to a change of direction are summarized in Figure 10.3.

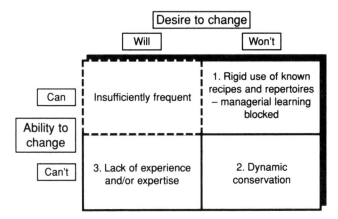

Figure 10.3   Some of the main reasons for organizational immobility

1. Recipes and repertoires

Recipes and repertoires are the ways in which an organization gets used to acting which have led to its past success. However, as market conditions or consumer tastes change, these well-learned patterns of behavior can move from being strengths to developing into handicaps. They prevent the organization from learning new methods of responding to outside pressures. For example:

> IBM and the main American car companies are often quoted as organizations which became phenomenally successful through creating strong, single-minded and perhaps fairly uniform cultures. This meant that, when IBM's market shifted quickly from large mainframes to networked PCs and the car market swung from 'gas-guzzlers' to smaller 'economy' vehicles, these organizations found themselves unable to hear the messages the market was sending them. Their inability to adapt their thinking led them into serious economic crises, resulting in the loss of hundreds of thousands of jobs before they learned how to respond.

Usually those who are at the top of these organizations have risen to their current positions precisely by developing, or at least sticking to, these recipes and repertoires. So they are naturally unwilling to try anything new, even if they are aware of the shortcomings of their approach. This pattern of events has been called the Icarus Paradox (Miller, 1990) – when organizations keep on building success through repeating the same behavior patterns until a crisis halts them in their tracks because the recipe for success is no longer effective and yet they are unable to break free from it. Some, like IBM or the Dutch electronics multinational Philips, do react and survive, although usually as a much diminished version of their former selves. Others, such as the British motorcycle makers or TV manufacturers, all but disappear.

2. Dynamic conservatism

In some ways, this can be seen as similar to sticking to known recipes and repertoires. However, when organizations are caught in dynamic conservatism they don't just continue to repeat known patterns of behavior. When faced by outside threats, they start to 'return to their roots', instead of looking for new ways to counter those threats (Figure 10.4).

Essentially, you have a core in the organization which holds power. This can be finance, engineering, marketing or whomever. Gradually the evidence builds up of a mismatch between the organization's approach and what the changing environment requires. The central power group attributes the organization's declining performance to its having allowed other, 'less reliable', functions to gain too much power or autonomy. Their reaction is therefore to reexert their control.

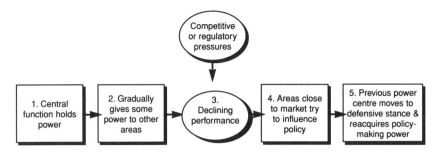

Figure 10.4   Dynamic conservatism in action

Dynamic conservatism can be viewed as a kind of organizational neurosis (Kets de Vries & Miller, 1987). When they come under stress, these organizations shrink back into a very limited set of behaviors, often linked to a powerful founder's or executive's personality. If they were driven by the need to control, this can start to become an obsession. If they have been founded by an entrepreneurial risk taker, they will court disaster by taking one risk too many. If they have a basically distrustful culture, the organization can quickly become paranoid, firing one manager after another as if they were personally responsible for the problems.

It is extremely difficult to help such organizations. Too often, power has been so monopolized by one interest group that they find it impossible to take a balanced view of the challenges they face.

3. Lack of experience

Some organizations simply don't have the experience of implementing change, as they have never before been exposed to a major shift in their environment or intense competitive pressure. Many financial institutions (banks, insurance and pension companies), railways and most airlines are suddenly finding themselves faced by deregulation, new, aggressive competition or being exposed to a market for the first time. The knee-jerk reaction from most of these organizations is to try to hold back the tide of competition. Airlines such as SAS and Air France have used their influence with governments in a bitterly fought attempt to preserve their high-priced quasi-monopolies, while banks and insurance companies have relied on so-called self-regulatory bodies and market power to restrict access to their lucrative hunting grounds.

However, for most of these once sacrosanct institutions, the need for change eventually arrives. There are, of course, always some exceptions – the 'denationalized' utility companies (water, gas and electricity) in Britain, for example, managed initially to retain their unchallenged monopoly power, while at the same time being free to pay their hungry top executives five to ten times the salaries they were apparently worth before these spurious privatizations. Nevertheless, as stated, most of these organizations will eventually have to change. For example, the miserable performance of some British water companies during the 1995 hot summer caused public fury and intense media pressure to improve their service. While restricting water supplies to domestic consumers through claiming shortages, they profitably sold millions of gallons to other water companies which had genuine shortages.

Too many examples of change management have not been particularly promising. Faced for the first time by serious threat, the initial reaction of many of these organizations seems to be widespread cost-cutting. It is not unusual (British Telecom, British Gas, several electricity and water companies) to see 20–30 percent of lower-level staff being thrown out in order to increase dividends for shareholders and, in some cases, bonuses for top executives. These organizations mistake cost-cutting for change. Reducing staff may provide short-term benefits for shareholders and executives, but it seldom improves the way the organization works, nor does it build growth for the future. Unless these organizations can begin to realize that it is through improved focus on the customer, rather than pandering to shareholder and executive greed, which will guarantee their long-term future, life for their staff and often still captive customers will not be particularly pleasant.

Pages 47–54

Summary

When it comes to implementing major organizational change, it doesn't seem to matter how good an intellectual case you have – individuals and the organization will both tend to resist fiercely. So, the first lesson on overcoming resistance to change is to expect it, anticipate it and never underestimate it.

People's reasons for resistance will vary and one of the great skills of a change manager is the ability to look behind what people say and understand their real reasons for opposing you. Only then can you deal with them. A frequent error is an overreliance on rational argument – if people are not resisting for rational reasons, rational argument will obviously be fruitless. Another common mistake is to resort to coercion when rational argument has seemed to fail – but putting pressure on people often leads to an increased push-back, strengthening rather than weakening their resistance.

Trying to cause positive change can be extraordinarily frustrating. You feel you are making huge efforts to improve the lot of the organization as a whole. Yet most people's natural reactions seem to be to oppose you. The only way round this is to try to gather a coalition of like-minded people, then gradually deal with the resisters. This will probably go slowly at first. However, once you start building up a critical mass of people (perhaps 20–30 percent of the key people) who support the changes, many more resisters will begin to fall into line. Some of the most successful change is built up piece by piece – efforts which try to change a whole organization in one go very rarely achieve their targets.

Recommended reading

M.F.R. Kets de Vries & D. Miller (1987) *Unstable at the Top: Inside the Troubled Organization*, New American Library.

N. Martin (1987) *The Manager*, Grafton.

D. Miller (1990) *The Icarus Paradox: How Exceptional Companies Bring About Their Own Downfall*, HarperCollins.

Part Five

Building Effective Teams

11

From Functions to Teams to Networks

Teams are in fashion – no well-dressed organization dares to be seen without them. But if teams are organizational *pret à porter* (off-the-shelf fashion for the masses), networks are definitely the latest in *haute couture*, direct from the catwalks of Paris, Milan and New York (or perhaps that should be Harvard, LBS and Insead).

Ever since *In Search of Excellence* (Peters & Waterman, 1982) correctly identified that we needed simultaneously 'loose/tight' structures, organizations have been experimenting with ways of loosening their joints, which had in many cases become so arthritic that they made all but a limited series of movements either painful or even impossible.

Sometimes there are so many teams that they seem to be treading all over each other – one company had more than five teams all working on redesigning different parts of the new product development process. When you add in all the carefully chosen sponsors, stakeholders and expert resources, you have a substantial, almost self-sustaining industry, using up resources, holding seemingly endless meetings and yet sometimes not contributing directly to providing value to the customer. There has been a rush into teamworking as organizations have seen teams as the latest panacea. And yet, even before most organizations had found out how to manage teams successfully and integrate them into their basic structure, management experts are proclaiming that teams are only part of the solution and that networks are the next step. Managers could have some justification for feeling that the experts keep moving the goal posts.

Teams, of course, have an important role to play, so do networks and so too, perhaps surprisingly, do bureaucratic hierarchies. The key is to establish which is most appropriate to a particular situation (Figure 11.1).

Hierarchies	Teams	Networks	
– What is relatively stable and the organization knows how to do	– What is changing and the organization does not yet know how to react to, but has the capacity to learn	– Internal: for passing information and learning rapidly without the help of formal structures	– External: for learning from and exerting influences over the outside world
– When speed is critical	– When breadth of experience is critical	– When range of capabilities is critical	

Figure 11.1   Appropriate uses of hierarchies, teams and networks

For example, you may arrive at a much more appropriate strategy through involving a number of cross-functional teams with a broad range of experience, technological skills and customer contacts. However, when it comes to taking rapid decisions and implementing them, sometimes a fluid, team-based structure can slow you down and a tighter hierarchy may be much more effective.

One useful model picks up this theme of identifying where hierarchies, teams and networks are most appropriate by showing their use in relation to the rate of change in an organization's operating environment and the existing organizational capability to learn and respond (Figure 11.2a). For stable activities which the organization knows well how to do, a traditional hierarchy is probably the most efficient way of functioning. However, when there is a rapid rate of change and people need to learn new skills to adapt, teams and networks are much more appropriate.

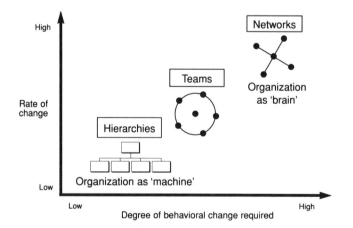

Figure 11.2a   Linking hierarchies, teams and networks to the organization's external and internal situation

The successful organization is, obviously, the one that manages to run the three different types of operating method simultaneously, rather than the one which sticks rigidly to any one of the three.

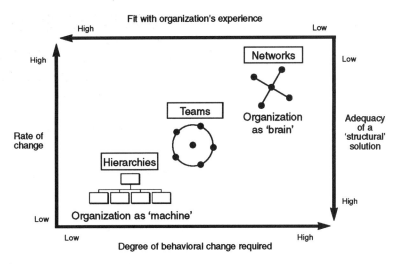

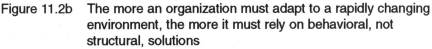

Figure 11.2b   The more an organization must adapt to a rapidly changing environment, the more it must rely on behavioral, not structural, solutions

You can also build an extra dimension on to this model showing the 'adequacy of a structural solution' (Figure 11.2b) What this tries to indicate is that the more an organization needs to be able to adapt quickly to new situations, the less you will be able to ensure you build that flexibility by the design of a new structure. Flexibility and adaptability will have to come from changing behavior, not structure (see Part Nine – Redesigning the Organization).

Pages 283–6

Why teams?

The move towards teams essentially represents a move away from a Taylorist view of people as costs, to be tightly managed and controlled, to a more modern approach of seeing people as resources, whose skills can be harnessed (Figure 11.3).

As discussed in Chapter 7, employees are no longer seen as replaceable cogs in a machine but are considered instead as being parts of an organism that can think and learn – a brain. Many hierarchies seemed to be based on the principle of limiting the spread of knowledge – you're told what you need to know. Teams, in contrast, operate on the basis that the more knowledge is spread and shared, the more people can create value.

Pages 73–85

Hierarchies	Teams/Networks
– Grouping people of similar skills to gain economies of scale	– Building responsiveness and faster throughput time through connecting people with quite different skills
– People as replaceable parts and work organized to minimize the need for communication skills and learning	– People as assets whose value can be increased
– Offer narrow functional career path	– Offer choice of either technical or more general and varied career opportunities
– 'Need to know' approach limits spread of information	– Spreading information helps people create value

Figure 11.3   Comparing hierarchies with teams and networks

The four most common types of teams are:

+ **project** – running a new product development
+ **process** – serving a certain customer group
+ **change** – redesigning a way of working
+ **departmental** – self-managing work teams

When is a team not a team?

Of the many definitions of what a team actually is, one of the most useful is:

> a team is a small number of people with complementary skills who are committed to a common purpose, performance goals, and approach for which they hold themselves mutually accountable. (Katzenbach & Smith, 1993)

This is useful because it starts to distinguish between real teams and groups of people, often called teams, who are anything but. To illustrate the point, we'll take a few of the above criteria and see what can happen in real life:

+ **'small number of people'** – one technically based company set up cross-department project teams to ensure all viewpoints were represented in each key meeting. By defining departments at too low a level, they ended up with between 15 and 20 people on the 'team'. Unless you have very exceptional people, a team this size cannot be effective.

✦ **'complementary skills'** – too many so-called teams are just groups of people who previously worked together in a department (accountants/draughtspeople/systems analysts etc.). To keep up with fashion, management will sometimes like to rechristen them as a team. Another suspect type of team is the board of directors of some old-fashioned companies. Here the members all tend to have the same backgrounds, the same outlook and the same social contacts, and eventually their blinkered and uniform outlook on life will lead to organizational rigidity and failure to respond to critical changes in their environment.

✦ **'common purpose'** – there are too many teams, particularly those made up of people from different areas of an organization, which are really collections of individuals representing their different functions and defending their functional interests, rather than working together towards a common goal.

✦ **'mutually accountable'** – real teams share accountability for their decisions. Committees, on the other hand, whatever the stated aspirations of the group, can seem to be more interested in the diffusion of or avoidance of responsibility. In this case, meetings are 'talking shops', few decisions are taken and action items are seldom followed up on. But, in spite of their ineffectiveness, committees love to meet – going to meetings lets their members demonstrate how busy and important they are.

Making teamwork a reality

The two aspects of running teams which should be simple but appear to be the most complex are:

✦ **Enabling team members to work together effectively**. For many reasons, we find it difficult to reproduce at work the camaraderie, sense of belonging, mutual support and awareness of each person's unique contribution which seem to come so naturally in the teams we participate in to play sport. Until we solve this problem, our teams risk remaining groups of individuals not bound by common purpose and loyalties and whose combined output is less than, rather than more than, the sum of the parts (see Chapter 12 – Building Effective Teams).  Pages 142–53

✦ **When teams and hierarchies try to work alongside each other** organizations find themselves faced by a whole new set of

challenges, mainly caused by the question of who should wield the ultimate decision-making power. The vexed issues of whether functional managers or cross-
functional team managers should own budgets and resources, have the final say
on which activities should be supported and exert control over people's career
progress and compensation (and the political infighting which surround these
issues) have probably killed more team-based programs than any other reason.

Organizations are continually trying ever more complex new solutions to try to
solve this issue of whether power should lie with functions or teams. They have
tried clear lines of authority, balanced matrices, unbalanced matrices, three-
dimensional matrices, managers with two or three 'hats'
and other imaginative schemes. But these structural solu-
 tions seldom prove ideal and a new approach is needed (see
Part Nine – Redesigning the Organization).

Networks – the next phase?

Managers have been told for years that they needed to move from a functional
organization to a team-based approach to meet the demands of a rapidly
changing environment. Many have struggled hard to put teams in place. Those
who have might well feel let down hearing some management experts now
talking of the limitations of teams and the need to move more towards networks (Lipnack & Stamps, 1994). There are two main kinds of networks
which an organization can form – internal and external.

Internal networks

Internal networks have always existed. Everyone in an organization has their
friends, confidants, spies, enemies, moles, power groupings, villains, professional peers, pet hates and so on. Without these, organizations would be lonely
and boring places to work. But what is happening now is a recognition that for
some business activities to be carried out, certain networks need to be formalized. Some business relationships are becoming so multifaceted that any structural solutions will be too complex and unwieldy to be workable.

Take the development of a multinational company. It starts growing in its
home market and wants to expand abroad, so it sets up an international
sales division. Then it decides to set up local operating (manufacturing and
sales) companies in its major markets, while leaving the 'rest of the world'

minor markets to the international sales division. At this point the major country managers become powerful figures, often responsible for thousands of people and sometimes controlling much of their own manufacturing, distribution, sales, marketing etc.

Gradually it becomes clear that the company is not getting the synergies a large international organization should – the organization is not greater than the sum of its parts:

+ There are too many different brands in different countries.
+ Even products which are similar have different specifications, different pack sizes and different market positioning and pricing in different countries.
+ There are many factories spread around the world, with different levels of efficiency. There should be large benefits from centralizing production in just two or three of the most cost-efficient plants.
+ Some key customers operate in several countries and have trouble dealing with a number of country companies selling virtually the same product at different prices and with different specifications.

The multinational company realizes that the next step is to manage manufacturing, distribution, sales and marketing on a regional or even global basis, if real economies of scale are to be achieved – the same product specifications, same pack sizes, similar branding and pricing and centralized manufacturing. Yet each country market still has specific characteristics which cannot be ignored. The issue is how to structure the organization to achieve this.

In the old structure, with local, almost self-contained country companies, the organization structure and responsibilities were clear (Figure 11.4).

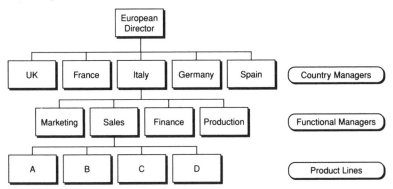

Figure 11.4   Typical organization structure for the European part of a multinational

But now there are a large number of new organizational problems to resolve, for example:

✦ Should all the main functions (manufacturing, sales, marketing, distribution etc.) be managed at a European or even worldwide level?

✦ If so, what role does the country manager now have?

✦ Should country product line managers report to a country marketing manager, a European marketing manager, a worldwide marketing manager, a European product line manager or a worldwide product line manager?

✦ Likewise, should a key plant production manager continue to report to a country manager, or should they have a direct organizational link to a European production manager, a worldwide production manager, a European supply chain manager or even a worldwide supply chain manager?

✦ If country managers no longer 'own' the major functions, how can they be responsible for the results in their country? After all, the major decisions will now be made at European or global level. So who, if anybody, will be accountable for each country's and even the company's performance?

Also, there will be some very difficult trade-offs to be made, for example:

✦ If you close a factory in Italy, you may make gains in France by putting more volume through a facility in France with spare capacity. But, with currency fluctuations and a longer distance to travel, your Italian prices will go up and service level down, making you less competitive. What decision should be made? And who should make it – the European production director, or sales director, or should the Italian country director be allowed to make or buy products in a way that best suits the local Italian market?

✦ What if you are selling your product for a higher price in Germany, with slightly different specifications, but some customers are buying it from you cheaper in France. Do you push up your French price to protect your German market yet risk losing market share in France? Or hit profitability in Germany by harmonizing prices at or near the French level?

Many companies try to deal with this new level of problem by designing extremely complex structures, usually matrices. They may have some limited success. But they are more likely to create such ponderous and Byzantine structures that the organization will spend increasing amounts of its time trying to work through or, more often, around these structures and will be dragged into an internal focus, where energy is used working through the organization rather than working for customers.

At some point, usually when you are unable to explain your organization structure easily to outsiders, you have to freeze your structure, however wonderful or flawed it is, and look for solutions through networking and behavior change (see Part Nine – Redesigning the Organization). There is probably no formal, workable structure which can cope with the complexity of functions/geographies/product lines/market segments. So organizations must look to non-structural solutions (teamwork and networking) to help them adapt to these new levels of market demand.

Pages 277–94

Once you have decided what teams and networks should be in place, you can start designing how these should work – monthly meetings, international teleconference calls, electronic links or whatever. International pharmaceutical product groups, for example, often rely on teleconferencing, whereas automotive engineers would tend to have electronic links to send designs between their different offices.

This process has been called layering. You first fix your basic organization structure, then you put in layers of groups, who will work together, along with the methods they will use to communicate.

External networks

Just as internal networks have always existed, so have external ones. Organizations have always had more or less close relations with suppliers, customers, authorities, competitors, local communities etc. But again, we are moving towards a time when some of these networks may have to become more formalized. For many organizations, close relations with external constituencies may have to go from being an added bonus to becoming a key to survival.

To use an S-curve chart again, we can simplistically trace the kind of development pattern many organizations go through (Figure 11.5). Most large organizations will spend much of their existence based on a clear functional structure (S-curve 1). As competitive pressure builds up, they will probably start to launch a number of project teams – usually around speeding up new product development and/or implementing operational improvement programs (S-curve 2). These teams yield some results, but there is now a feeling that,

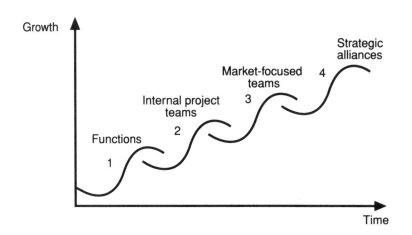

Figure 11.5   Typical development phases for many companies

although the company may have cleaned up some of its internal processes, it is not close enough to its key customers. So next it sets up a number of market-facing teams, either around key accounts or market segments (S-curve 3).

Again, there are significant results. The level of customer service rises, the firm's offering is better tailored towards the individual customer group needs and response times to customer requests improve dramatically. But after a few years, it is felt that the company no longer has the resources (technical, financial or human) to go it alone. Any further progress can only be made by working in partnership with organizations from either the same industry sector or from completely different areas (S-curve 4).

Networks can also be set up with customers and suppliers through electronic data links (EDI) so that orders can be placed directly without passing through a functional bureaucracy. Visits to each other's facilities can be arranged, so line managers and workers can meet and understand how they can work better together. Joint design or marketing teams can be formed, so that organizations can find ways of cooperating in both their interests.

Even quite different organizations can set up mutually advantageous links to exchange ideas, skills or to give mutual support. Some experts have proposed that many Japanese companies gain part of their competitive strength from working in 'clusters'. By setting up cross-shareholdings between banks, insurance companies, industrial concerns and suppliers, each is able to assist the other for their common gain. A Japanese bank may allow a manufacturer to give a low return on investment for some years and this then provides the manufacturer with the financial muscle to take a strategy based on market share (rather than short-term profit) and thus build up its competitive strength over the longer term. It may even turn out that organizations which cannot develop such clusters will always have difficulty maintaining their competitiveness on their own.

Summary

Many organizations reach a point where either they can no longer structure themselves to meet the conflicting demands of a complex marketplace, or else they cannot buy in the skills, technology or market power they need to prosper. Too many fight on creating ever more impossible structures – many multinationals are caught on this track. Or they overreach their resources trying to acquire what they feel they need to control – the frenzied purchasing of estate agents by British banks and building societies in the 1980s, and the buying up of US health-management organizations and each other by drug companies in the 1990s are examples.

There is, however, another solution. Stick with the structure or resource base you are familiar with and you know how to manage. Then look to behavioral solutions such as teams and networks to give you your next competitive advantage.

Recommended reading

J.R. Katzenbach & D.K. Smith (1993) *The Wisdom of Teams: Creating the High Performance Organization*, Harvard Business School Press.

Jessica Lipnack & Jeffrey Stamps (1994) *The Age of the Network: Organizing Principles for the 21st Century*, Oliver Wight (US)/Omneo (UK).

Tom Peters & Robert Waterman Jr. (1982) *In Search of Excellence*, Harper & Row.

12
Building Effective Teams

Some of our most satisfying and exciting experiences at work probably come from having been a member of a high-performing team in which everything just seemed to come together – the right people dealing with the right problem at the right time. But many of our most frustrating disappointments are also probably due to the failure of some team to achieve its potential, as it allowed its internal problems or its relations with the rest of the organization to block its ability to deal with the task it was set up to handle.

The subject of team productivity has proved a fertile hunting ground for experts from a multitude of disciplines. Psychologists came at it from the study of individuals. Behavioral scientists arrived looking at interpersonal interactions. Sociologists were interested in the group as a social entity. And management scientists scoured the terrain in their never-ending search for the perfect organizational form, before moving off again in the direction of networks.

Managers have had a load of theories for improving team productivity thrown at them by academic experts – sociometrics, Johari windows, Homan's theory of group formation, sociotechnical design, interaction analysis, cognitive balance theories, the law of requisite variety and many more. Some have been accessible, but many have been more intellectual exercises than useful contributions which can be employed in our day-to-day work.

Nevertheless, building the ability to work successfully in teams is becoming increasingly important. In the move away from hierarchy to managing cross-functional processes, the team or group is where everything now comes together. It has largely replaced the functional area as the basic driver of work. If we can't make our groups work effectively, our organizations will falter, however brilliant our products or services.

It is fairly obvious that the aim of a team or group is that the output of the group should be greater than the sum of the individuals' input. Otherwise there would be no point in having the group at all.

Yet, as we see executive groups that stumble over personality conflicts, project teams where members from different specialities seem unable to understand each other, and cross-functional teams which use meetings as opportunities to score points off or even decimate each other, we start to get to situations where the sum of the group's work is less than individuals could achieve on their own. So instead of adding value for the customer, the group is actually destroying it.

Internal and external dynamics

Much of the analysis on team performance has concentrated on the team's internal dynamics – how members work together, how conflict is handled, what roles people adopt and so on. But many of the problems which hamper team performance come as much from the relations between the group and the organization as from within the group or team itself. Here the main useful contributions to improving internal group dynamics will be reviewed briefly before moving on to looking at relations between the group and the organization (Figure 12.1).

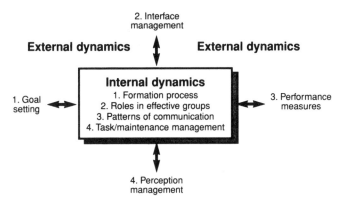

Figure 12.1   We need to manage both the internal and external dynamics of a group or team

Internal dynamics

Group formation

There are four main models of how groups form. Most split the process up into four or five main stages:

Tuckman	Bass & Ryterband	Obert	Glass
Forming	Developing mutual acceptance and membership	Membership	Birth
Storming	Communication and decision making	Subgrouping	Childhood
Norming	Motivation and productivity	Conflict	Adolescence
Performing	Control and organization	Individual differentiation then collaboration	Maturity

Of these, Tuckman's is probably the most well known. All these models give a similar message. We should not expect groups to function well immediately they are formed; they have to go through a development process. The key to building an effective group is to understand this process and manage it.

The four main stages which Tuckman (1965) identified groups as going through are:

+ **Forming** (birth) – the initial formation of the group. People will tend to be polite and careful. Members will be torn between being cautious about expressing any strong views and being anxious to make an impression. They will be testing the water and will probably not make any real progress with the group's main task.
+ **Storming** (childhood) – the group starts to work. As their comfort level rises, members put their views forward much more forcefully. The initial consensus breaks down. There can be disagreements about the task, arrangements made in the initial meetings, operating methods, leadership – everything can quickly be called into question. Conflicts stemming from personality or functional approach break out.

    If this stage persists, some members will become frustrated at the lack of progress and withdraw mentally or physically. If this phase can be controlled, the group can productively redefine its objectives, approach and ways of working.

✦ **Norming** (adolescence) – as members start to resolve style and character differences, they begin to find ways of working together. A new unofficial hierarchy can arise, a set of unwritten codes of behavior gradually forms, norms for managing task and conflict develop.

✦ **Performing** (maturity) – the group is now a cohesive unit, individual members know and accept their roles, they associate with the group's interests rather than their personal agendas, people start to bond and they can now usefully make progress with the task they were formed to address.

Some groups start off with too high expectations for immediate results – when no progress is made at the forming stage, members become frustrated and give up on the group as a lost cause.

Many other groups get stuck at the storming phase – they fail to resolve their internal conflicts. So any time a controversial issue comes up, the personality or style clashes rapidly resurface and the discussion deteriorates as old battles are relived. It is common to see these groups, about to make significant progress, suddenly relapse into storming.

This model can be powerful, because understanding the process can help us to shorten it. Moreover, a group whose members understand the dynamics of group formation are less likely to get irreparably caught at one of the intermediate, less productive stages.

Roles in effective groups – the importance of variety

A great deal of work has been done studying whether groups of similar people are likely to be more productive than groups containing a high degree of diversity. One theory which seems intuitively plausible is called Ashby's law of requisite variety. This proposes that for a system to survive, it needs to be at least as complex as its environment (Buckley, 1968). Thus simple tasks can be accomplished by teams with little variety in membership, whereas more complex cross-functional processes require a diversity of skills.

Managers of groups will often tend towards wanting to work with 'like-minded' people. There tends to be less conflict and so this feels easier and more productive. However, Ashby's law warns against taking the path of least resistance. A number of the failures of British companies over the last 30–40 years can be ascribed to their management groups, which have the same background, even having gone to the same schools and universities, being unable to handle an increasingly complex business environment.

The most quoted study on roles (Belbin, 1981) proposes that the most effective groups are not those containing the 'brightest and the best', but rather those which have a good balance between eight main roles:

+ **Chairman** – leads and coordinates
+ **Shaper** – drives the task forward
+ **Plant** – source of breakthrough ideas
+ **Evaluator** – analytically tests ideas
+ **Company worker** – administrator
+ **Team worker** – manages conflict
+ **Resource investigator** – helps the group by using contacts in the organization
+ **Finisher** – highly conscious of time pressures, pushes group to meet deadlines.

Of course, you're probably never going to get a group with these eight theoretical characters in it. But the model does act as a warning that we should beware of easy similarity and look for diversity, balance and synergies when working in groups.

In general, the message here is to accept and manage diversity in groups, understand that differences and conflict can be positive and not take the easy road of staffing your teams with like-minded clones of yourself or your organization.

Much has been written about self-managed teams, with the leadership position rotating between the members. These may work in some organizations. But usually if a group has a defined task to accomplish within a set time frame and cost, it needs some kind of clear management and role structure to work effectively. For example:

+ **Leader** – gives direction and motivation but also acts as a diplomat, managing relations with key figures outside the group
+ **Task manager** – focuses more on ensuring that the task is accomplished
+ **Resources** – have (or have access to) the necessary knowledge, skills and creativity to achieve the team's goals.

Patterns of communication

The way in which communication flows within your team can be critical to its productivity. For example, if everything seems to pass through the leader, this probably slows down decision making and limits the exchange of ideas. Or else cliques can form, communicating intensively within themselves but infrequently with the rest of the group. Obviously, you're looking for balanced and open communication between all members, although this is often difficult to achieve due to personality and organizational issues (members with similar interests or from one function are likely to stick together). Figure 12.2 suggests some of the communication patterns you might come across. Clearly, the nearer you can move towards the 'open, all-channel' communication pattern, the more productive the group is likely to be.

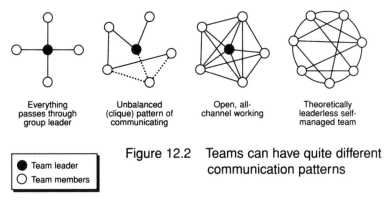

| Everything passes through group leader | Unbalanced (clique) pattern of communicating | Open, all-channel working | Theoretically leaderless self-managed team |

● Team leader
○ Team members

Figure 12.2   Teams can have quite different communication patterns

Task and maintenance management

A basic, but useful, model is to divide a team's activities into 'task' and 'maintenance':

✦ **Task activities** are aimed at problem solving and achieving the team's concrete goals – developing a new product or managing a key customer.
✦ **Maintenance activities** are all about managing how the team works together, its emotional life and the quality of members' interactions. These are focused on resolving conflict, balancing airtime, giving individuals encouragement and support and so on.

If, for example, a team contains a number of technical experts, they may perform brilliantly on the task side but can be abysmal in handling the human interactions. Then, greatly to their surprise, the rest of the group rejects their technical solution, as they feel they were insufficiently involved in its development.

And we've probably all been in groups where most of the time was spent navel gazing (maintenance) around how we were interacting and how we felt about each other – of course, little was ever achieved. It is probably obvious that the more a group uses up emotional energy and time dealing with maintenance activities, the less likely it is to make real progress with the task; although complete concentration on the task is also often unproductive as insufficient effort is given to managing team dynamics. The skill is to find the right balance for each situation (Figure 12.3). Here, as with the other models, an awareness of group dynamics can help us diagnose and deal with problems as they arise, rather than letting them linger on unresolved.

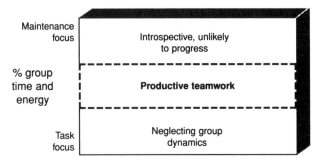

Figure 12.3   We need to find the right balance between task and
maintenance management

External dynamics

Goal setting – ensuring clarity and consistency

All too frequently, there is a mismatch between the goals a team is given and the circumstances in which it has to work.

✦ **Project teams** (for example, developing a marketing campaign or a new product) often start in a flurry of activity. But as daily operational problems occupy people's attention, it becomes increasingly difficult for the team to get access to the required skills or resources – key people are busy, production lines needed for testing new products are fully scheduled with customer orders, managers have other things on their mind and so on. Gradually the team becomes bogged down and is viewed by the organization as a failure.

Another common scenario is when project team members can be only part-time and are still mainly 'owned' and paid by their functions. In this case, functional managers will tend to prioritize functional activities over project work, with the result that projects suffer.

✦ **Business process teams** are set up to manage, for example, supplying a particular customer. Such a team could consist of a production scheduler, a supply chain coordinator, someone from finance, a sales promotion representative and someone from sales. Sometimes these teams are dropped in to a strongly functional organization which has not been prepared for the new, customer-focused, horizontal way of working. When the team members come with their customer group requirements they find that nobody's got the time or interest to help them – production are busy ensuring high plant utilization, distribution are fighting to keep stocks low and marketing are taken up with thinking up their next national campaign. Trying to serve the customer group seems to be more a fight against, rather than a joint venture with, the rest of the organization.

✦ **Operational improvement teams** are formed to sort out some specific operational problem. They usually find out that the source of the problem is not as tightly localized as managers had originally thought – quality problems might be due to design and purchasing as well as production, for example, or low service levels might involve production, finance, sales and marketing and not just be due to some blockage in distribution. At this point, when the issue becomes one of managing a broader cross-functional change, many organizations clamp down on the team, accuse it of overstepping its brief and push it back into the impossible task of solving some problem without allowing it access to the areas at which the problem originates.

One way of trying to avoid these typical situations is to focus the first phase of the team's work consciously on goal redefinition, so both the team and organization are clear about what is expected and the implications. Part of this process can be one-on-one interviews with key executives and stakeholders, finding out their expectations and what would and would not be acceptable. These interviews should include questions such as:

✦ What are your expectations from the team?
✦ What would you like to see change for your area?
✦ What could the team do to overdeliver for you?
✦ What are the main dangers/traps facing the team? How could we avoid these?
✦ How would you measure the team's performance quantitatively?
✦ Is it the right time to launch this team? Why or why not?

A few simple questions such as these can be extraordinarily useful in getting guidance from key influencers in the organization about the expected practical results of the team's work and also the potential political and emotional pitfalls awaiting them. If the team fails to cross-check its goals and also any no-go areas early on, it can easily risk finding itself in conflict with important members of the organization.

Interface management – building a support structure

It is becoming increasingly common for organizations to take a more formal view of how teams should interface with the rest of the organization and to build a series of roles around the team (Figure 12.4).

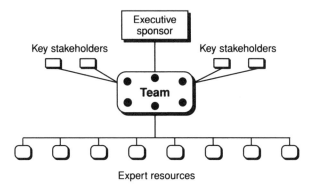

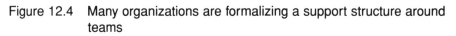

Figure 12.4   Many organizations are formalizing a support structure around teams

+ **The executive sponsor** takes responsibility for guiding and supporting the team through some of the more tricky political situations it encounters. They are also responsible to the executive group for the team's success.
+ **Stakeholders** are people with influence in the organization whose areas will be most affected by the team's work.
+ **Expert resources** are individuals outside the team whose knowledge or skills will be critical to helping the team succeed.

It is usually much easier for a team to think through and set up such a structure early in their lives, when they still have the organization's interest and attention. Doing this can often guarantee the political support, the influencer network and the resource availability which would be much more difficult to arrange later on, when the organization has other things on its mind.

Performance measures to match the team's goals

Setting up a team generally implies a change in the way at least part of an organization operates. It makes sense, therefore, to also change the way in which that part is measured. If you  don't, you risk reaching a situation where the measurement system actively hinders the team from operating effectively. For example:

Pages 22–33

✦ A hospital set up a new operating room management team to improve room utilization levels. But it continued to measure the different medical specialities (cardiac, renal, neurosurgery etc.) on the number of completed cases. To ensure they met their targets, each speciality would keep all its operating room slots in case they could be used, even if it was doubtful whether some would be needed. So the old measurement system led to behaviors that prevented the new team achieving its goals.

✦ A consumer goods manufacturer launched key account teams. However, it kept its old financial reporting system, which emphasized low stock levels and high plant utilization but didn't adequately measure service levels. The team found it difficult to persuade production and distribution to provide the necessary flexibility, as these two critical departments were still focused on their old functional goals.

✦ An engineering company started a multifunctional new product development team for a key new product. But the functions to which the members of the team belonged were measured on their monthly personnel costs and other costs vs budget. So when the team needed essential work done quickly by one heavily loaded department, they found themselves pushed to the end of the line and had to wait weeks for their work. If the functions hadn't still been under the old budget control measurement system, they could have easily outsourced some work and kept the critical project on schedule.

As with its goals and support structure, a team must think through early on exactly how it should be measured and how any existing performance measurement systems might cause people to behave in ways which obstruct the team's work. It is extremely easy to launch teams innocently and optimistically without thinking through the implications of current measurement systems – and it is equally difficult to address the situation once the team has started to flounder.

Management of perceptions

Successful teams rely to some extent on creating their own community within the organization. The members transfer a degree of loyalty to the team and they develop particular ways of working which can be specific to the team. Without this sense of community and local team culture, they would just be collections of individuals. At this point, there can be a risk of the team becoming isolated from the rest of the organization. It can quickly develop common views on where the organization is not performing and start to believe that it is superior to other departments or teams. The organization can rapidly begin to see team members as elitist, excluding people who are not 'on the inside'. Often people think of the team as having the easy option of saying what needs to be done without having to get their hands dirty in the organization's day-to-day operations.

The role of any team is to focus the organization's efforts and skills on accomplishing a task. Too frequently, the team members begin to think that they alone hold the solution to a problem and forget that they're just a method for channeling the organization's resources at the issue. Teams should usually be catalysts to the organization achieving something, rather than trying to 'go it alone'.

It is easy for a team to slip out of sync with the organization. When it does so, the emotions, suspicion and hostility that are generated can quickly destroy any concrete progress the team is making. Team members need to be constantly vigilant in managing how they perceive the organization and how they are perceived by it. Ideally, the team should set up influencer charts – organizational charts with all the key figures highlighted – and establish a regular update schedule to keep these people informed of progress and test the water for the organization's response. The greatest ideas developed in isolation by a team will seldom be accepted, however wonderful they are, unless the team has worked carefully on managing the organization's perception of its methods and progress.

There are three main dimensions along which the organization will judge a team – rational, political and emotional (Figure 12.5).

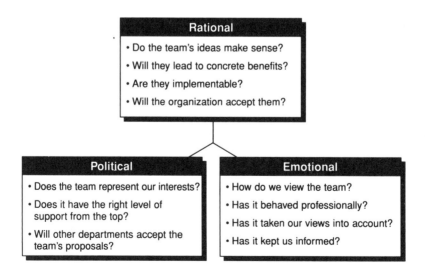

Rational
- Do the team's ideas make sense?
- Will they lead to concrete benefits?
- Are they implementable?
- Will the organization accept them?

Political
- Does the team represent our interests?
- Does it have the right level of support from the top?
- Will other departments accept the team's proposals?

Emotional
- How do we view the team?
- Has it behaved professionally?
- Has it taken our views into account?
- Has it kept us informed?

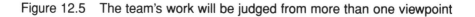

Figure 12.5   The team's work will be judged from more than one viewpoint

Unless all of these three aspects are carefully balanced and managed, the team risks ending up with its proposals being rejected by the very organization it thought it was helping.

Summary

Most people find it much more satisfying and rewarding to work as a member of a team than on their own. Teams can provide social contacts, new experiences and learning. But too often, when teams have worked well, it has been due more to the coincidence of compatible people coming together at a critical moment to achieve an important, but digestible, task. Essentially, success has been a result of serendipity rather than planning.

The 'hit rate' for success with teams is not particularly high in many organizations. By building a deeper understanding of the dynamics of group formation and of ways of managing the team's interactions with its external environment, we can start to work actively on improving team effectiveness and not continually rely on luck to make our teams productive.

Recommended reading

R.M. Belbin (1981) *Management Teams: Why They Succeed or Fail*, Butterworth-Heinemann.

W. Buckley (ed.) (1968) *Variety, Constraint and the Law of Requisite Variety: Modern Systems Research for the Behavioral Scientist*, Aldine.

C. Hastings, P. Bixby & R. Chaudhry-Lawton (1986) *Superteams: A Blueprint for Organisational Success*, Gower.

B.W. Tuckman (1965) 'Development sequence in small groups', *Psychological Bulletin*, Vol. 63.

R. Wellins, W. Byham & J. Wilson (1991) *Empowered Teams*, Jossey-Bass.

13
The Art of Meetings

It's easy to be cynical about meetings. In fact, it's easy to be cynical about most aspects of organizational life. But meetings seem to attract particularly high levels of satire and derision. Given the increasing frequency, poor quality and inconclusiveness of most meetings we attend, it's not surprising that we so openly ridicule them. Yet in spite of our scorn, we can still occasionally be caught trying to impress colleagues with our packed diaries as we moan about the fact that the many meetings we 'have to' attend prevent us getting on with 'real work'.

But if they found a way of stopping all meetings tomorrow, many of us would be hard pressed to find ways of usefully filling our working days. And should a naive co-worker take our theatricals at face value and not invite us to some important meeting, then there would be trouble. We would be insulted and outraged. It would be a snub to our sense of our own indispensability. And, in addition, we would be deprived of the opportunity to display our knowledge, experience and ideas once more. There's no sadder sight than a manager with an empty diary because nobody considers he or she has any contribution to make to their meetings.

The changing role of meetings

Meetings reflect the organizational environment in which they are held. In top-down, command-and-control organizations, meetings with subordinates are one means of exercising that control. Usually such meetings are based around one-way communication – managers informing employees what they want to be done.

Meetings can play many other roles – in risk-averse bureaucracies, for example, they are excellent devices for the avoidance of decision making and any attendant responsibility.

As we move to flatter structures, within which work is increasingly centered around cross-functional, multiskilled teams, meetings become more critical. From being just one of the ways in which an organization operates, they become a key method for achieving the organization's goals. Twenty or even ten years ago, many meetings might have been aimed at managing unanimity within a single function or at least between several closely related areas. Now they're mostly built on productively managing a diversity of skills and functional backgrounds to achieve better solutions than any individual or single department could have come up with alone.

Yet despite their increasingly critical role, many meetings are still poorly prepared, badly managed and ineffectively concluded. To build on Parkinson's Law, one could reasonably claim that 'meetings always expand to fill more than the time available in the most unproductive way possible'.

Moreover, meetings will become increasingly important and more difficult to manage effectively as they are applied to complex multifunctional and multinational issues:

+ When you bring a three-continent marketing development group together for two days to build the next year's campaign, they have only a small time window to get it right. Once they've split up again, it can be very difficult to make major changes.
+ When you fly in four engineers from a major customer to work with your designers on improving the manufacturability of parts, the last thing you want is for a couple of vociferous participants to hog all the airtime blabbing about past problems, so that by the end of a potentially useful day you've achieved less than the square root of zero and you've created a poor impression of your organization's capabilities as well.

It is vital that the meeting moves quickly from a cold start to a high level of productivity, otherwise an important opportunity is lost.

Power and influence in organizations used mostly to be expressed through hierarchical position. As hierarchies have reduced, people are spending less time in their functions (where they are well known) and have been pushed more to work in cross-functional groups with others who may not appreciate their background, position or technical standing. The meeting has to some extent replaced the hierarchy as the main forum for making progress. So when coming to meetings, many people will feel a strong need to project themselves to establish their technical, positional and/or intellectual qualifications. Achieving the right balance between people's personal needs at the meeting and the requirement to make concrete progress can in some cases be extremely challenging.

Although most of us feel we have been exposed to enough 'meeting effectiveness' training courses to last several lifetimes, it is still worth reviewing some ways to improve our meeting management significantly, both as 'owners' of and as participants in meetings.

This chapter is mainly about significant meetings and honest meetings. A significant meeting is one controlling an important project or where some major proposals are to be developed or decisions made. There are many other kinds of meetings – regular daily or weekly department meetings – which generally follow a well-worn routine, people know each other and they can be quite efficient.

Honest meetings are those where most participants genuinely want to make progress. Other meetings are called to diffuse responsibility, to sabotage projects, to score political points over opponents, to give old-fashioned autocratic managers the satisfaction of publicly humiliating subordinates and so on. There's no point in trying to improve such meetings – they should never exist in the first place.

Going beyond the basics

Most general management books have a section on meetings. And most cover the basic dos and don'ts in the three main phases of running a productive meeting (Figure 13.1):

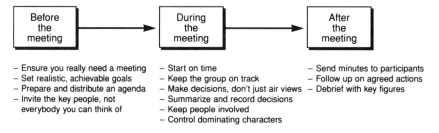

Before the meeting	During the meeting	After the meeting
– Ensure you really need a meeting	– Start on time	– Send minutes to participants
– Set realistic, achievable goals	– Keep the group on track	– Follow up on agreed actions
– Prepare and distribute an agenda	– Make decisions, don't just air views	– Debrief with key figures
– Invite the key people, not everybody you can think of	– Summarize and record decisions	
	– Keep people involved	
	– Control dominating characters	

Figure 13.1   The basics of meeting management are mostly obvious

There are also more advanced ways of cranking up the quality of meetings.

Separating process and content

Too frequently, meetings fail because we don't distinguish the content (what we want to achieve) from the process (how we manage the participants) (Figure 13.2).

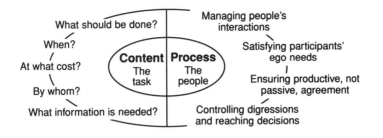

Figure 13.2   Any meeting operates at two levels

Failure to manage both the content and the process can lead to a poor process destroying the meeting's effectiveness. Personality battles or dominating characters can kill off good ideas. Poor time management allows the meeting to drift on so that it doesn't have time to achieve its goals.

People close down and stop contributing when their ideas are passed over, or when participants' hidden agendas keep derailing the meeting's flow.

One way of trying to separate what you want to achieve from the minefield of human interactions is to split the chairperson's position between two people. A commonly used meeting structure is to have three main roles:

+ **Facilitator** – manages the process of the meeting, controls the agenda, keeps it on track, balances all the participants' contributions, deals with diversions.
+ **Client/manager/team leader** – is responsible for achieving the content goals, states the objectives, assigns actions, makes any necessary decisions.
+ **Resources/participants** – bring information, expertise and ideas, help solve problems, complete whatever assignments they are given.

You don't need to split the chairperson's role like this, but unless you consciously set out to manage the process as well as the content, you will often be surprised at how easily your meeting is diverted from its goals. Usually, it is the process side of the meeting that fails – the human interactions.

If you can't achieve the content (the decisions you need to take) for technical reasons – lack of information, the right people not being present, special equipment not working or whatever – it's not that difficult to call another meeting when you can assemble the needed components. But if your meeting bombs because participants are at each other's throats, because someone pulls rank or monopolizes the time or because a subgroup hijacks it for their own purposes, it can be very difficult to repair the damage. Once people have assumed certain positions, they can be impossible to shift.

Managing the process

Frequently, we put a great deal of thought into the technical content of our meetings. Energy is spent assembling statistics, writing and circulating reports, polishing up presentations. But few people ever put much effort into preparing for management of the human interactions. We assume that they will take care of themselves. Yet we know from experience that it is precisely in this area that we are likely to get bogged down.

There is a contradiction in our attitude to people's behavior in meetings – we expect people to behave logically, yet if they did we almost wouldn't need the meeting. We could just send round some relevant data and presumably everyone would agree with our proposals. Yet when people do react more on emotional and political levels in meetings, we are often surprised and even disappointed.

There are many reasons for the human side letting us down. For example:

✦ **Personal agendas** – participants are out to prove something, maybe a technical point or possibly they're trying to gain some advantage for their functional area or country.

✦ **Ego needs** – some people feel a need to prove their own competence and worth.

✦ **Personalities** – a clash between someone who enthusiastically wants to move ahead with a proposal and a detail-oriented, steady-as-we-go person has sunk many near decisions.

✦ **Ideas linked too closely with the person** – when people propose ideas, they frequently see any comment on the idea as a comment on them personally. It's a bit like thinking, 'if you don't like my idea, you don't like me'. This can lead to their using large amounts of time and energy defending suggestions about which even they, deep down, may not be that sure.

✦ **Hierarchies** – usually meetings are aimed at making decisions. This may mean changing something in the way things are done and thus may imply some criticism of the *status quo*. If different hierarchical levels are present, this may inhibit some more junior people from speaking out.

✦ **WIIFM (what's in it for me?)** – everybody will want something out of the meetings they attend: prestige, decisions, recognition, social contact, information, power. Unless you can anticipate people's WIIFMs and try to satisfy them, they will often wreak havoc with your meeting planning.

✦ **Groupthink** – many groups made up of similar types of people will quickly fall into easy unanimity, comfortably reinforcing each other's views and clubbing together to dismiss any possible criticism of the actions they propose.

These cosy, mutual back-scratching committees seldom come up with useful proposals, generally ignore or discount changes in their environment and in many cases lead their organizations into disaster because they are unable to find new ways to deal with changing situations.

✦ **Satisficing** – a mixture of the words 'satisfactory' and 'sufficient', this describes how, when under pressure to move forward, many groups will jump on the first reasonable suggestion that crops up and will not try to find alternative and possibly better or more ambitious proposals.

✦ **Dialexia** – this is discussion for the sake of discussion, because people enjoy the dialectics of exchanging opinions. While this may be intellectually stimulating, it seldom leads to action

To manage the human side of the meeting, you need to look out constantly for these behaviors and counteract them. You must create a safe area for all participants to speak their mind, deal firmly with ego-based interruptions, encourage positive ideas, balance participants' contribution and so on. Failure to manage the process actively will normally lead to failure in achieving the content.

Building a decision-making process, not an event

Most of us see meetings as one-off events. We know there's a bit of preparation and some follow-up, but the main work for us occurs at the meeting itself. Our mental model would be similar to Figure 13.3.

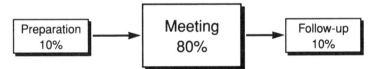

Figure 13.3   Most of us see meetings as events with almost all the effort concentrated on the meeting itself

However, if we want to improve our meeting productivity, particularly for more difficult or more significant meetings, we probably need to move to a model where much more work is done before and after the meeting (Figure 13.4).

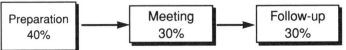

Figure 13.4   For key meetings, much more work needs to be put into preparation and follow-up

For example, with a meeting where you wanted some reasonably major proposals developed or decisions made, the following would not be unusual:

✦ **Preparation** – hold one-on-one meetings with all participants to brief them on objectives, discuss their points of view and possible objections, review with them the likely reactions of other participants and how they can help deal with the others, and enlist their help in presenting any key figures in their area with the aims of the meeting in advance.

✦ **Meeting** – the aim here is not so much to open up the discussion to any kind of contribution, but rather to build on the extensive preparation work to move towards a constructive consensus on a way forward. The challenge is to try to anticipate any really good or disastrous ideas before the meeting so that you can build on the good ones and prevent the disastrous ones from knocking your meeting off course.

✦ **Follow-up** – again, if it was a significant meeting you should meet individually with all participants, debrief them, get their opinion on what went well or badly, ask whether the decisions were clearly understood or not, solicit their help in pushing forward the decisions and, of course, establish whether they were satisfied with their roles and the outcome.

Exploiting the productive lifecycle

Meetings are not consistently productive all the way through. People often arrive with other things on their mind and take time to switch over to the meeting's wavelength. There's then a period of potentially energetic activity as people concentrate on the matter in hand. After 20 minutes or so (or much earlier if you're boring them) people's attention starts to wander. Gradually participants' energy levels will wind down unless something particularly interests them. This energy curve can be called the meeting's productive lifecycle (Figure 13.5).

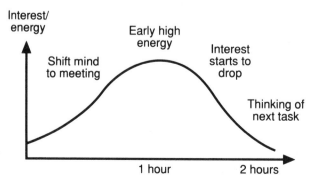

Figure 13.5   The productive lifecycle of a meeting

This concept is probably common sense. Yet time and again, meeting agendas are set in direct contradiction to this energy/interest curve:

+ Many meetings start with a tedious review of all the points from a previous meeting or with some long-winded presentation by someone enamored with the sound of their own voice or by a younger employee anxious to make a good impression. Either way, you can waste the most productive part of your meeting achieving nothing and, worse, switch people off so that when you come to the main topic you've lost their hearts and minds.
+ It may be necessary to review the action points from a previous meeting, but this should be carefully controlled. It should take no more than 10–15 minutes. Moreover, if you allow participants to report back, you risk losing control – once someone's started talking, they usually like to continue. The best solution is to have contacted the relevant people before the meeting, so you can summarize their progress and look to them for brief confirmation. If you let this review of action points from previous meetings run for more than 20 minutes you've probably lost much of the productive energy for the current meeting and your meeting will turn into an unproductive continuation of the previous one.
+ Often the most difficult issue to solve is the first item on the agenda. There's a certain logic in this, as you can argue that the toughest subject should be handled when people are at their most productive. But there's a counter-argument that says you should knock off a few easier items in quick succession to get some momentum going and this will help prolong the productive period.
+ When structuring the agenda, you should try to schedule the issues to get some momentum going, then deal with harder problems. It can also be useful to plan some high-interest item for the last hour. This can help rekindle participants' interest and energy just as they are starting to flag.

Applying other tools and techniques

Pre-meeting preparation

In no particular order, some issues you should have thought about include:

+ **Agenda** – match to the productive lifecycle, put times on each item, distribute with at least some explanation to attendees before the event. Try to get their opinions on the agenda before the meeting – you don't want to be waylaid by someone in the first couple of minutes asking why an issue, important to them, is not included.

✦ **Present key players with vital information in advance** – you can save yourself a lot of grief if you know where your key players are coming from and you've already got them on your side by showing interest in their views prior to the meeting. Ensure you get their opinions on the agenda – is it right? Should something be added or something taken out?

✦ **Duration and time** – obviously different subjects will require different amounts of time. In general, anything longer than two hours starts to become unproductive. And only the most exceptional all-day meeting achieves a lot more than half a day would have done – there's nothing worse than drifting back to an untidy meeting room after lunch to continue discussions that a tighter agenda and better preparation could have completed in the morning. As for timing, most people are much more productive in the morning. If you want creativity go for the morning, if you're after somnolent acquiescence straight after lunch is best.

✦ **Review alternatives** – in too many organizations, calling a meeting is a knee-jerk reaction. Before you convene your meeting, think through if there are other more efficient and/or less risky ways of achieving your goals.

✦ **Invitees** – for a fully participative meeting anything over 8–10 people is probably too many. Some say 6–8 is ideal. When you're up at 15+, most participants won't be participating for most of the time, and someone who's not actively involved can frequently derail a meeting just out of boredom. Also think through whether everyone needs to be there all the time.

✦ **Alternative strategies** – sometimes your meetings won't go as well as expected, sometimes they'll go better. Either way, it can be useful to have thought through your next move if you're confronted by glittering success or abject failure. This can prevent you from getting publicly hemmed into a situation from which you can't escape with ease.

✦ **Roles and responsibilities** – you may want to give different participants specific roles to play, or encourage them to put forward certain information or ideas, or even advise them against bringing up issues which will cause them problems.

✦ **Airtime planning** – a two-and-a-half-hour meeting can sound like a reasonable time. But once you start dividing up the time between the different participants, each person actually has very little opportunity to speak. Say, for example, the chairperson talked for about 25 percent of the time (just under 40 minutes) – that leaves eight other participants less than 14 minutes each. Allowing for delays and interruptions, most participants won't talk for much more than 10 minutes each. Again, you should ask yourself whether the meeting is the most productive way of using people's time and achieving your goals.

Starting up – the first few minutes

You should have some very good reasons for deviating from the following series of steps:

Opening up	3–5 mins	Brief outline of purpose, time and expected outcomes. Make it clear where you expect decisions, proposals or just information.
Introductions	3 mins	For groups who don't meet regularly, ensure that everyone knows who everyone else is.
Agenda review and meeting ground rules	5–10 mins	Run through the agenda in sufficient depth so that everyone's up to speed, but don't bore them with too much detail. You may also want to set some meeting ground rules – how you expect people to behave, for example not digressing with 'war stories' about the past, not shooting down other people's ideas, giving brief headlines first before launching into detailed explanations, not interrupting and so on.
Expectations exchange	5–10 mins	Ask if anyone has anything they feel should be added to the agenda or any other expectations from the meeting. This can be very useful in surfacing personal agendas and also involving participants who have something burning they want to say and won't be listening until they've got it off their chest.

On this list of start-up activities, the one that is most frequently not used is the expectations exchange. Yet it can be very risky going into a key meeting focused only on your objectives. You can derisk the situation by pausing and checking whether any of the participants is concerned that some other issue should be addressed.

One other very useful item is agreeing some meeting ground rules. People seldom think about whether their behavior at meetings is productive or disruptive. By setting some basic agreed rules you can often avoid many of the distracting behaviors in which participants would normally indulge.

The first agenda item

As discussed above, you have to take some care choosing your first agenda topic. Long reviews of the last meeting's minutes, lengthy presentations, really difficult subjects are all to be avoided. They can ruin what is potentially the most productive period of your meeting.

The chairperson's style is critical during this first item. People are watching to see what is going to be encouraged and what will be unacceptable:

◆ **On the positive side** – Will the chairperson protect them if they express original but iconoclastic ideas or are people expected to toe the line? Are off-the-cuff suggestions acceptable or does everything have to be rigorously supported with reams of evidence? Is the meeting about breaking new ground or just rubberstamping a foregone conclusion?

◆ **On the negative side** – Can they digress endlessly, bring up pet topics, tell loads of stories about how things used to be, blame other areas, interrupt, use hierarchical authority to dominate the discussion and so on?

How the chairperson handles these kinds of subcurrents will set the tone for the rest of the meeting.

Closing the meeting

At the end of each topic, the chairperson should sum up what has been agreed to ensure everybody has the same understanding. In particular, any action points should be repeated, along with the responsible person and the expected completion date.

If the meeting is running late, you should not assume everybody is delighted to stay until you have completed your objectives. Take a temperature check about 20 minutes before the planned end time and see if people want to stay and complete the agenda or reconvene at another time.

On the other hand, if things are moving well and you can finish early, don't drag out the meeting, close it off. Most people will appreciate a few extra minutes freed up in their timetables.

If there is time, it can be useful to ask the participants if they have any major outstanding concerns about any of the items dealt with. Don't try to cover these immediately unless something is shared by most of the group. Instead, note the details and promise to get back to the individual with an answer.

Following up

You can do yourself a great favor by meeting one-on-one with all the participants to get their reactions, suggestions and help in moving any action items forward.

Summary

For many people, meetings are a kind of blind spot – they know that many are not effective, but don't really feel able to change this situation. Frequently, an enormous amount of well-intentioned work goes into taking a project or product to a certain stage, then the whole thing seems to fall apart at some critical and disastrously managed meeting – some key executive seems unable to understand what the group is proposing or else hijacks the meeting to expound on a subject of great personal interest. This is an extraordinary waste of effort. It's like beating the defense and goalkeeper in soccer and then forgetting to kick the ball into the net. By failing to manage these meetings properly, we are letting down both ourselves and all those who have worked with us.

We tend to see meetings as out of our control. We ascribe poor meetings to the unpredictability of human nature and good meetings to luck. However, excellent meetings seldom just happen. They are normally a result of careful planning and preparation. And there are a whole range of tools and techniques we can use to help us improve meeting productivity. Meetings can and should become controlled events – not tedious talking shops or quite unpleasant, unexpected surprises.

Recommended reading

Antony Jay (1976) 'How to run a meeting', *Harvard Business Review*, March–April.
Andrew Leigh & Michael Maynard (1995) *Leading Your Team: How to Involve and Inspire Teams*, Nicholas Brealey.

Part Six

Enhancing Personal Performance

14

Motivation: Bringing Out the Best in People

You can usually get subordinates to carry out instructions one way or another.

Threats of punishment or offers of reward are probably the most frequent means which organizations use to encourage employees to carry out their wishes. Normally these threats or offers are not made openly – they remain unspoken. But people know that if they act in certain ways, rewards will follow; and if they are seen as uncooperative, sanctions will result. Many organizations publish fine-sounding values statements and talk about their people as 'their most important resource'; but just try refusing a few work assignments that don't interest you, or openly criticize some management decision you're convinced is wrong, and see how long you survive in your current position.

According to the principles of scientific management, people were sources of potential error, inefficiency and lost time. So to control them, organizations were advised to split jobs into small, repetitive, easily measurable actions. There was less chance of mistakes and productivity could be tightly managed. More money could be offered to better workers and poor performers disciplined or fired. Up to the 1950s and even 1960s, this was the way many large industrial companies worked.

Most people's reaction will probably be that we've all come a long way since the days of treating employees as disposable parts of a machine. But even today, when times get tough, many organizations still revert to this kind of behavior.

A major service organization, which preaches caring values, teamwork, being 'part of the family' and employee involvement, experienced a downturn in business. The immediate management response was a series of waves of staff reductions taking out 10–20 percent of its people. At the same time, top executives were guaranteed a minimum of 80 percent of their annual bonuses if they stayed with the company.

One suspects that if this had been a Japanese company, top executives might have agreed to a self-imposed salary reduction until the situation improved. But in the west, we always seem to end back at the 'protecting the people at the top' and 'carrot and stick' method of motivation for the rest, however pompously we proclaim our 'people first' values.

When people work in functionally based groups doing repetitive tasks, where you're mainly interested in maintaining productivity or efficiency, the carrot and stick approach can appear sufficient to ensure a reasonable level of work performance. This is despite various studies which have shown that employees on production lines and in administration have innumerable ingenious, but virtually undetectable, ways of obstructing work – and the more demotivated they are, the more they'll use them.

But as we move to employees participating in local functional teams or cross-functional groups, we're going to require people to be committed to performing well, rather than just participating because they have no other choice. And as we change from viewing people as cogs in a usually not very smoothly running machine to believing that they are productive resources to be developed and challenged, we're going to have to change radically the way we go about motivating them:

FROM	TO
Cogs in a machine	Valuable resources
Sources of error	Sources of ideas
Productivity targets	Wanting to perform well
Impersonal control	Development of individuals
Obedience	Enthusiasm
Physical effort	Creativity and flexibility
Coercion	Commitment

Before moving on to some more productive approaches to bringing out the best in people, it might be worth quickly reviewing some of the building blocks of modern views of motivation. These fall into two main groups:

+ **Needs theories** – why we work and put in varying degrees of effort: Maslow's hierarchy of needs, Alderfer's three needs model and Herzberg's two factor theory.
+ **Individual perception models** – how we view ourselves and our relations with organizations and how this influences our performance at work: self-concept, life positions and informal contracts.

Needs theories

Maslow's hierarchy of needs

In the 1940s an American, Professor Abraham Maslow, identified five types of human need, which he rated on an ascending scale.

At the time the model was proposed, most organizations were heavy hierarchical bureaucracies, in which the main means used for motivating staff were money, fear about job security, promotion or demotion. The breakthrough which Maslow's model provided was that it showed the motivating power of satisfying people's needs for self-respect and personal development at work. It proposed a shift from 'extrinsic' motivators (money, fear, discipline) to 'intrinsic' motivators (desire to perform well, wish to develop our abilities, wanting to be part of a social group).

Maslow argued that unless people could achieve a degree of self-actualization, both they and the organizations they work for would underperform. The main characteristics of the five needs are shown in Figure 14.1.

Maslow's theory was that only when each lower need is satisfied does the next higher need become important to us. If we are anxious about job security, we will not worry about how satisfying the job is. However, if we feel we have that security, then we will look to satisfaction of our social and self-esteem needs and will be frustrated if these are not catered for, at least in part.

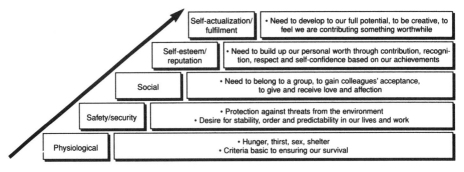

Figure 14.1   Characteristics of the five needs

Alderfer and Herzberg

Alderfer (1972) proposed three needs:

✦ **Existence** – similar to Maslow's first two needs, physiological and safety.
✦ **Relatedness** – our urge to belong to a family, a community, a work group and to be respected by them.
✦ **Growth** – developing our own potential and achieving our perception of our own abilities.

Like Maslow, he argued that people will tend to want to satisfy the higher needs like relatedness and growth only once their existence needs are met.

Herzberg (1974) split motivation factors into 'hygiene' and 'motivators':

✦ **Hygiene** factors tend to be external, such as salary, job security, interpersonal relations, working conditions. These cannot motivate us, but they can make us dissatisfied if we do not reach a certain minimum level.
✦ **Motivators** are usually more internal, such as sense of achievement, recognition, personal growth.

He believed that if we really want employees to contribute, then we have to minimize any dissatisfaction caused by problems with the hygiene factors. But the real root of high performance will come from focusing management effort on the motivating factors.

Using these models

The relevance of these theories to managers is that they can help them understand how to get the best from their people.

First, they highlight the important, but still limited, power of money to achieve improved performance. Once staff are earning what they believe to be reasonable pay, they will start to look for other things at work such as job interest and satisfaction, social respect and self-development. Too often, managers fail to notice this change in their people's priorities. When people are frustrated by uninteresting work, managers try to deal with performance problems by inventing ever more complex, unwieldy and expensive bonus schemes. They fail to address the real issues which may be boredom, desire for more responsibility or dissatisfaction with work conditions.

Many implementations of new manufacturing or information technology, for example, fail to give the desired results because they split up work groups and isolate people, forcing them to work for several hours at a time without any human contact. It is critical, when thinking through such methods for productivity or service improvement, to assess the effect that they will have on employees' social relations at work.

People in the west are good at expressing lower order needs – for food, money, security – but poor at articulating the higher needs. If we cannot get what we want from a job, we tend to ask for what we think we can get. Frequently, workers who are dissatisfied with conditions, management's attitudes or their job structures will react by demanding more money, even though money is not the root of the problem. A process of conflict or bargaining then follows. But a truly satisfactory solution is never found, as money was not the issue in the first place. Seldom, if ever, does a trade union ask for more responsibility for members, replacement of incompetent management or more interesting jobs. Yet too frequently, these are precisely the causes of dissatisfaction which misleadingly and destructively find expression in demands for more pay.

Individual perception models

Self-image/concept

This is a simple idea which can help us understand how better to interact with other people.

Each of us has an image of ourselves. This is formed by our childhood, education, character and experiences. Our self-image is our own view of our abilities and our rightful place in society. However, often at work there is a gap or conflict between our perception of ourselves and the position we actually occupy. The greater this gap, the greater will be our dissatisfaction, frustration and even anger. Many employees who have an authoritarian boss, for example, experience this conflict between their self-image and the way they are treated at work (Figure 14.2):

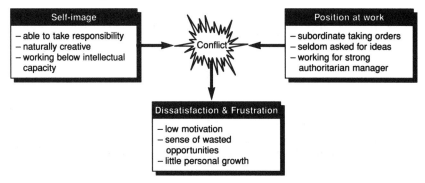

Figure 14.2   Many people working for an authoritarian manager feel underutilized and dissatisfied

The opposite can also be true – if people feel they go to work just to earn money to support their family and outside interests, they may become increasingly frustrated with the kind of modern manager who is always trying to give them new responsibilities and development challenges.

Using the model

If there is a gap between a person's self-image and the reality at work, a manager has to try to narrow the gap if they are to get the best from that person. This can be done by helping create the necessary conditions for the person to move closer to their self-image or by helping them understand the unreality of their self-image.

If a person is performing poorly due to the tension between their role and their self-image, offering more money, appealing to their loyalty or making open or veiled threats will not solve the performance problem. In fact, it will probably be counterproductive and increase their frustration.

Too often, we mismanage people by attributing our own self-images to them when they have quite different motivations. A typical example would be when a manager decides to decentralize an operation and give more responsibility to subordinates. This the manager sees as a positive move as he or she values, and is paid to deal with, challenges and uncertainty. The staff, on the other hand, may have different ambitions and see the new responsibilities as unwanted, as managers avoiding their responsibilities and as a burden they are not paid enough to take on.

Four life positions

One useful classification of people's self-image is into four life positions (Berne, 1972):

I'M OK, YOU'RE OK	I'M OK, YOU'RE NOT OK
Usually optimistic people who relate well to others and assume a positive attitude to their life and work.	Generally distrusting and suspicious people. May be competitive and ambitious. Feel they can only satisfy their needs at others' expense.

I'M NOT OK, YOU'RE OK	I'M NOT OK, YOU'RE NOT OK
Often people believe they are the victims of circumstances and are envious of others' luck. They may feel inadequate compared to others and may blame others for their own lack of achievement.	There is a group of people who see little value in themselves or others. They are usually cynical, negative in their relations with others and often resistant to any form of change.

Figure 14.3 The four life positions

Nobody will ever fall completely into any one of these four categories and people will change according to their circumstances. However, by trying to picture a person's self-image as being nearer one or other of these life positions, we can move nearer to understanding how they think and how we should most successfully deal with them.

Formal and informal contracts

Another idea which helps understand how better to motivate people is the concept of formal and informal (or psychological) contracts. Most people have a written contract with their employer covering salary, hours at work and duties. But there is also an unwritten, 'informal' contract, which is much broader in scope (Figure 14.4).

This informal contract covers both our and our employer's expectations:

✦ employees may expect to be treated with respect, to have their opinions taken seriously, to be given challenging or maybe unchallenging tasks, to have work which is interesting and time consuming, or else which is repetitive and leaves them free to concentrate on their personal lives
✦ the organization may expect us to be loyal, to accept management's authority unquestioningly or else to be free with criticism and ideas, to respect age and authority or to contribute new thoughts and methods.

FORMAL CONTRACT	INFORMAL CONTRACT
Salary	Behavior expectations
Responsibilities	Degree of personal freedom
Holiday entitlement	Level of obedience required
Benefits	Permission to criticize decisions
Disciplinary procedures	Speed of promotion

Figure 14.4   Formal and informal contracts

If the unwritten, informal contracts of employees and organizations are not in harmony, then misunderstanding, conflict, dissatisfaction and low performance usually result. Some common mismatches in informal contracts are suggested in Figure 14.5.

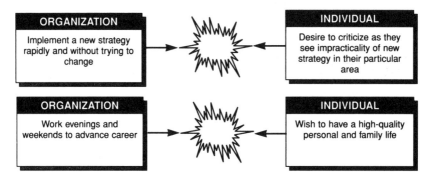

Figure 14.5   There are frequently conflicts between informal contracts

Managers need to be aware of the wide range of informal contracts which their people may have when judging how to deal with them. In particular, organizations need to be realistic about the expectations they include in their informal contracts. If they offer interesting, stimulating work with a great deal of freedom, responsibility and opportunities for employees to improve their skills, then they can reasonably expect loyalty, dedication and a certain level of self-sacrifice. But if the job is selling hamburgers or working on a production line, then they can hardly expect employees to find self-fulfilment at work and so must allow them freedom to have a life outside their jobs.

Too often, employers misguidedly try to motivate staff doing menial, boring and poorly paid tasks with expensive internal public relations campaigns, often based around calling them teams or members of a family. Usually these just lead to cynicism and alienation, as employees are exhorted to make sacrifices for a company which would rather throw money at costly motivation programs than improve work conditions or pay.

Performance through development, not control

Most people want to feel they are doing something useful at work, are respected for it, are learning new skills and are offered new experiences. There are a number of methods which we can use to go some way towards satisfying these needs (Figure 14.6).

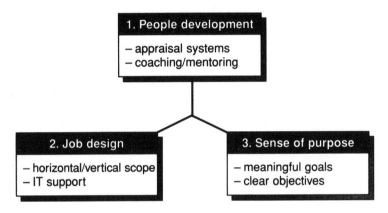

Figure 14.6   Three main areas for building motivation

1. People development

Appraisal systems

Whether they're given fancy names like personal development plans or more straightforwardly called performance reviews, most appraisal systems are judgmental. They look backwards and assess employees' past performance against more or less well-defined targets. Occasionally they will contain a 'development needs' section, but this tends to be a minor part of the exercise. Most of the time will be spent on evaluating the past.

When you add in the fact that most managers feel uncomfortable in doing appraisals, most employees dislike the process and few criteria are concrete, the result is a fairly unsatisfactory process in which the unprepared (managers) evaluate the unwilling (subordinates) against the unmeasurable (loosely expressed targets).

It is difficult to develop people if the goal of your appraisal process is to judge and score them on what they did three, six, nine or even twelve months previously. The events you're discussing will be history, memories will be inaccurate and it will be too late to change anything in any case. In a sense, many appraisal systems push people into a corner because there is nothing concrete which either appraiser or appraisee can do to change things.

To develop people we need to move from appraisal systems to genuine development plans. This means a shift from evaluating how things went in the past to preparing people to do well in the future. We have to go from a judgmental, backward-looking process like Figure 14.7a to a constructive, forward-looking process like Figure 14.7b:

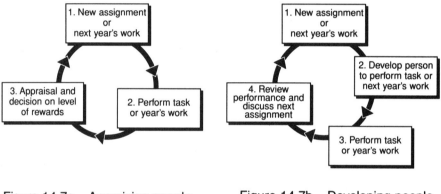

Figure 14.7a   Appraising people
on past performance

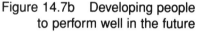

Figure 14.7b   Developing people
to perform well in the future

As long as appraisal systems and financial rewards are inseparably linked, most attention will be focused on this link and the outcome. If there are disputes, they will tend to become quite emotional because of this link. If there was some way – team or work group bonuses, for example – of breaking this link between evaluation and reward, appraisal systems could start becoming people development systems and they could move their spotlight away from how we did in the past and how much bonus or salary increase we're going to get for it, to helping us develop a joint action plan for doing better in the future.

Coaching/mentoring

Linked to the concept of trying to develop rather than just evaluate employees is the idea of formalizing a system of mentors or coaches. Many people have informal mentors during parts of their careers, who help them deal with technical or political issues. By making this process official, many more people can gain from it.

It could be claimed that an employee's manager is responsible for their development and so having yet another person (a mentor) involved just muddies decision making and duplicates an important part of the manager's role. However, a mentor can fulfil two important roles which a manager can't normally cover – being a more experienced confidant/partner to an employee and a breaker of deadlocks between manager and employee:

+ **More experienced confidant/partner** – given the fact that they will have a hierarchical relationship, it is often difficult for employees and managers to be totally open with each other. They may be colleagues, but there will always be a distance between them. The mentor can act as a much closer contact to the employee and, by having more experience in the organization, help them solve any difficulties they have, in a way that a manager could not.
+ **Breaker of deadlocks** – when a manager feels an employee is not performing satisfactorily, negative feedback to the employee is often met with resistance. The employee will often claim that the manager only knows part of the story or that there were exceptional circumstances which were outside of the employee's control or whatever. A deadlock can be reached quite quickly. At this point a mentor can step in, hear both sides of the story and defuse the situation by working through it with the employee as their friend, rather than the manager, who starts being seen as a tormentor, handling it alone.

2. Job design

From micro-activities to business processes

Instead of splitting jobs up into micro-activities, as under scientific management, organizations today are trying to reassemble micro-activities into meaningful units of work:

+ issuing a whole insurance policy, not just handling a small part of the process
+ running a project for its life, not just managing limited portions of it
+ managing a whole supply chain, not just deliveries or invoicing
+ providing total administrative support for one construction project instead of just doing invoicing for a large group of projects.

Job design is a key way of creating intellectually rewarding activities for employees so they feel in control of their destiny and that they're doing something useful.

Horizontal and vertical scope

The potential for redesigning jobs is normally shown along two axes:

+ **horizontal** – adding activities that happen either before or after the job being looked at such as quality control and customer contacts
+ **vertical** – adding activities that are normally done by a higher level in the hierarchy such as planning and budgeting.

Pages 295–304

The major event in increasing horizontal scope has been business process reengineering (BPR) (see Part Nine – Redesigning the Organization). By switching an organization's focus from internal functional activities to cross-functional customer-facing processes, BPR has greatly expanded the horizontal scope of previously isolated tasks, making jobs more varied and meaningful. However, it also tends to cut out process inefficiencies and this can allow up to 30–40 percent of employees' time to be released for other activities, if these exist – or it may result in staff cuts. So while the survivors of a BPR exercise may have more fulfilling jobs once the dust has settled, there may be a period of great disillusionment and low motivation while the operation is underway. You may even find that your best people leave voluntarily during the turbulence as they can most easily find other jobs.

The move from hierarchical organizations to flatter structures and from supervisors and workers to self-managed teams is providing vertical job growth. A whole series of activities which were previously the responsibility of multiple levels of management are now being passed down to front-line workers. Planning their work, budgeting, recruiting and training team members, management reporting, dealing with disciplinary matters – all of these are being carried out at much lower levels of the organization than previously.

The role of IT

Information technology can be a either a powerful enabler or a implacable enemy of job redesign. IT is theoretically neutral, but as most IT systems are unfortunately built to serve an existing and known, rather than planned, future situation, they tend to support previous methods. For example:

✦ A major multinational spent millions installing a new computer system that reflected its previous system by being able to tell top management exactly how much stock they had in fourteen countries, how much each of their hundreds of sales people were selling and which of their thousands of accounts were in arrears. But the system couldn't satisfy new requirements like telling key account managers which accounts were most profitable or the current status of all their customer deliveries.

✦ Different departments in an engineering company had invested large sums of money over the years in building up their local functional computer systems, none of which would talk to each other. So the new generation of cross-functional project managers had extreme difficulty finding out the schedule and cost adherence to plan of the thousands of activities which made up their projects.

✦ Many pharmaceutical companies have different software in the different departments which have to contribute to the regulatory submissions of more than 100,000 pages which every new drug must have. This makes it difficult to access and assemble the necessary data easily. Too much of key experts' time can be spent on semi-clerical tasks of finding information and checking copied information, instead of adding value to it.

In all these cases, the IT systems could have helped tremendously in breaking down hierarchical and functional barriers and in underpinning redesigned and enriched jobs. Instead, the systems were designed around the previous methods and so turned out to be a major impediment to people functioning effectively in their new roles.

3. Sense of purpose

Providing meaningful goals

As hierarchical control reduces, employees are expected to show greater flexibility and inventiveness in adapting to changes in their operating environment. To avoid greater freedom turning into limited, or even unlimited, anarchy, many organizations are finding a need to replace control and stability with a strongly shared common sense of purpose.

It is no longer sufficient to inform employees that next year's goal is x percent increase in dividends to shareholders. That's not going to incentivize anybody, except of course the few top executives who happen to have their bonuses linked to share price.

To try to provide this sense of common direction, it has become fashionable for organizations to pay thousands of pounds to consultants to develop vision statements. This can be very positive, providing managers' actions don't contradict the spirit of the vision. When this happens employees quickly realize that it is only for public consumption and not for practical direction.

Certain organizations do, however, manage to create a sense of shared purpose which acts as a guiding principle for the new breed of enlightened and empowered employees. Apple, Microsoft, Sony, Honda, Johnson & Johnson, Canon all operate in turbulent fast-changing industries and all have successfully imbued their workforce with a set of common goals that ensure people's efforts are harnessed in the same direction and not dissipated in fighting interfunctional battles.

Giving clear objectives to reduce conflicting demands and stress

Top executives like to think that they've got the most stressful jobs in the organization. They take the big 'life and death' decisions, don't they? Isn't that why they get paid so much more than other employees?

In fact, stress and thus demotivation at work are caused less by the importance of the decisions to be made and more by the level of conflicting demands a person has to handle:

+ A project manager caught between a tight schedule, difficult technical issues to resolve and a group of uncooperative functional managers who are hoarding key resources is much more likely to experience stress than their manager or manager's manager.

+ A key account manager trapped between a demanding customer, an internally focused production department, a marketing department more interested in the next great campaign than some menial customer or other and a distribution department that has 'unalterable' set times and schedules will tend to have a higher level of stress than, for example, a sales director responsible for all the key account managers.

+ A facilities (restaurant, leisure, sport) manager struggling to meet high turnover figures, yet restricted from adapting the service to meet local needs by volumes of corporate rules, will usually have more sleepless nights than area managers, wandering around their sites and enforcing both the targets and the rules.

+ A hospital ward sister caught between unhelpful functional areas (imaging, phlebotomy, pharmacy, physiotherapy etc.) each with its own way of working, timetable and systems can have a tougher day trying to coordinate patient care than do some doctors and surgeons.

Stress tends to occur mostly 'at the coal face', because this is where the problems surface which are inherent in conflicting demands being placed on the limited resources which most organizations have. If not managed carefully, this can result in excessive levels of demotivating stress being placed on the key middle managers, who have the power to make or break the organization. When attempting some kind of restructuring or job redesign, it is important to evaluate the level of conflicting demands each position will have to manage.

If we really believe that most of our employees are, by and large, mature, intelligent and self-motivated, the management task moves from motivating through performance measures and control towards helping them perform through removing the barriers and conflicts which prevent them being effective. To take the four examples above:

+ The project manager's boss should be helping by negotiating resource availability with functional managers, not criticizing schedule slippages.
+ The sales director should be assisting key account managers by helping other departments focus on customer rather than internal functional needs.
+ The area manager should be active in supporting facilities managers in customizing their product offering instead of hiding behind performance targets and the corporate rulebook.
+ Hospital administration should be looking at ways of better coordinating the different functional areas instead of their usual preoccupation with bean counting.

One of the main intellectual breakthroughs of the total quality movement was that 70 percent or more of quality problems stem not from the work done directly by employees, but from the systems and procedures within which they have to work. And many total quality programs failed when it became clear that practices beyond direct production work would have to be changed and this was resisted by the affected functions. If we want to motivate our employees we can give them demanding tasks, but we must also help them achieve those tasks by clearing away organizational barriers which other parts of the organization put up to protect their local functional interests.

Summary – from transactional to transformational management

Most managers would probably admit that their organizations could do much more to motivate their staff. Of course, if you give them more freedom and discretion, some people will abuse this. However, experience suggests that the majority of employees will respond positively and productively to any attempts to improve their contribution through enriching their life within the organization. This may mean that we have to change the way we manage staff. A distinction has been between two types of leaders: 'transactional' and 'transformational':

+ **transactional** leaders are good at looking at financial reports, sales figures, production data and intervening to deal with problem areas. Mostly they have a reactive response to events – they wait for something to happen (a downturn in the market, a new technology, aggressive moves by a competitor) and then they react. With transactional leaders employees are motivated mainly by the knowledge that someone is always monitoring their performance and will hold them responsible for any problems.
+ **transformational** leaders motivate their staff by communicating an ambition or dream of what an organization can become. They engage the whole person in a joint effort to achieve more than any individual thought possible.

Transactional leaders can command respect and even loyalty – but transformational leaders inspire commitment and involvement. As organizations flatten, more workers become knowledge workers and responsibility spreads out to more people, there may have to be an increasing move from a transactional to a more transformational leadership style to ensure motivation and common direction.

Recommended reading

C.P. Alderfer (1972) *Existence, Relatedness and Growth*, Collier Macmillan.

Eric Berne (1972) *What Do You Say After You Say Hello?*, Bantam (US)/Grove (UK).

D. Buchanan & A. Huczynski (1985) *Organizational Behaviour*, Prentice-Hall.

Charles Handy (1976) *Understanding Organizations*, Oxford University Press (US)/Penguin (UK).

F. Herzberg (1974) *Work and the Nature of Man*, World Publishing (US)/Granada (UK).

A.H. Maslow (1943) 'A theory of psychological motivation', *Psychological Review*, July.

Victor Vroom & Edward Deci (eds) (1989) *Management and Motivation*, Viking Penguin.

15

Culture, Power and Politics

You can flatten your hierarchies, build your networks, reengineer your processes, empower your people, set your strategic intent, focus single-mindedly on your customer and do all the other fine things the business gurus tell us we should...

But say you have two project managers:

✦ Project manager A is technically brilliant and can solve problems which would make even the best of his colleagues tremble in their rubber-soled suede shoes, but is not very good at handling organizational politics or at motivating staff.
✦ Project manager B is technically OK but certainly not as good as A, but she can play the organizational structure like a Stradivarius, making it do exactly what she wants. Getting the best resources, the right facilities, executives' agreement is second nature to project manager B.

Which one would you give your key project to?

And if you have two key account managers:

✦ Key account manager A is a dream with clients. They love him. However awful delivery and quality problems are, manager A can smooth them over and almost make your clients feel grateful to him for doing it. However, he has a weakness. He loathes organizational politics and can't understand why people cause so much trouble with customers through focusing on their narrow functional needs. When someone makes a mistake, manager A tells them in no uncertain terms – and he's made a lot of enemies that way.
✦ Key account manager B is OK with clients, but is an absolute genius at getting things done in the organization for her clients. Her personal relations with clients are not that hot, but the service she gets for them is superb.

Which one do you give your most important customer to?

And finally, there are two ambitious executives vying for the top slot when the CEO retires:

◆ Executive A is a wizard with the figures, can spot an error a mile off, thinks of the smartest strategies and seems able to grab market opportunities before competitors have a clue they're there. Unfortunately she can be a bit abrasive, doesn't easily command loyalty and tends to walk over people, disregarding their opinions. After all, she thinks, if a course of action is right, why waste time endlessly discussing it – get on and do something!

◆ Executive B is no great genius. He couldn't tell a discounted cash flow from a net present value to save his soul. He's not that quick on his feet either. But he has a way of commanding the most incredible loyalty and respect from employees and always has time to listen to people's ideas or problems. The staff would follow him to the ends of the earth and back again.

Which one gets the big job?

What really counts, when push comes to shove? Do you put your money on the person who is technically superior or do you bet on the one who is best at playing the organizational games? Most probably, you'd go for the latter.

Which brings us to what perhaps really matters in an organization – not the incredible structure, the thousands of high impact teams, the self-motivated empowered people etc., but the ability to play the culture and the political networks to transform ideas into concrete action.

One organization has the best, flattest structure, wonderful teamwork and superb information systems, but a leadership group who are distant, anaemic and politically inept. And a competitor is a bit disorganized, still has an inherited hierarchical horror story of a structure, but has imported a management team who can make things happen. Which is likely to be the most successful?

Good structures, teamwork, information systems can help an organization – no doubt about that. But in the final count it must be the ability to cause action which distinguishes the good from the also-rans. And making things happen is all about knowing how to play the cultural, power and political games which are such an intrinsic part of how organizations really function.

The basics

There has been plenty of research into organizational culture, power and politics. Before going on to look at an example of how we might manage the cultural, power and political aspects to influence an organization to take a major decision, it might be worth running quickly through some of the key ideas in this area.

Culture – the way we do things round here

The idea of culture being a major contributory factor to an organization's success or failure has been in vogue for the last 10–15 years; although attributing success to a particular culture might be a little simplistic, another result of people in the west always seeking an easy, one-dimensional answer to every problem. There may also be a bit of a chicken-and-egg problem here – are organizations successful (or catastrophic) because they have the right (or wrong) culture? Or do they develop the right (or wrong) culture because they're successful (or walking disasters)?

The answer, of course, is probably that certain cultures suit certain environments and the organizations with those cultures thrive. Then the environment changes. The culture is no longer appropriate. A few organizations manage to adapt, but most struggle boldly on with their tried and tested methods until disaster strikes and only a major shake-up can put them back on track – usually with a significantly changed culture and a different cast of leading characters.

We all know how deep and all pervading an organization's culture can be. Each organization feels different. The physical surroundings – buildings, offices, furniture, decorations and so on. The way people behave – polite, helpful or condescending, busy, stressed or at ease, interested, open-minded or closed and bureaucratic. And the way they think – proactively problem solving, pedantically sticking to the rules or overcome by each situation with a kind of hopeless victim mentality, informal and constructive, or anally retentive and hierarchical, or blasé and cynical. And we've probably all been in some organizations where we felt at home with the culture and in others where the mismatch between us and them was so great that it was almost painful to come to work each day.

Roger Harrison proposed that there were four main types of organizational culture. What seems to distinguish the four cultures are whether power is centralized or decentralized, and whether political processes are based around key individuals or the function/task to be accomplished (Figure 15.1).

The four cultural types Harrison identified were:

✦ **Power** (autocracy) – a single person or small group leads the organization. Often the organization is entrepreneurial, has little respect for formal structures and procedures and high loyalty to the leaders. As it grows in size, it often has trouble in adapting and can start to fall apart. It also risks a high level of political activity as the leaders become surrounded by courtiers eager to attract their attention and cut rivals out.

+ **Role** (bureaucracy) – here it's not who you are but what position you hold that's important. Things are done by the rules; slow, steady loyalty is appreciated; individualism and dynamism are seen as threatening. Role cultures appear to offer security and stability, but they are unable to adapt to changes in their environment and are prone to massive trauma when forced to turn around or perish. Political success comes from knowing how to play the system, using the vast number of committees, rules and regulations to your advantage.

+ **Task** (adhocracy) – describes an organization built around temporary project teams. People form a team, carry out a task and then disband to form different teams for the next task. Consultancies, engineering firms and advertising agencies are prime examples. This has become one of the ideal models for several management gurus. But it relies very much on people 'playing fairly' and can easily break down into vicious political infighting as different groups fight over key resources or the high-profile projects.

+ **Person** (democracy) – generally associated with academic institutions, small architects' practices, new advertising agencies or law firms. This allows each individual to follow their own interests, while maintaining mutually beneficial links to the others. Here the organization is theoretically subordinate to the individuals' wishes.

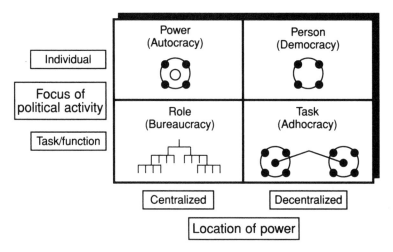

Figure 15.1   Culture depends on who holds power and whether political activity is focused on individuals or the task/role to be done

Few organizations will fall clearly into any one of these four models. And within each organization there are local cultures – finance is different from production, marketing from sales and so on. Different offices will have their own cultures – one might be go-ahead and dynamic, another heavy and bureaucratic. And finally, different countries will have local cultures, which will interact with the organization's culture.

Nevertheless, these four categories – power (autocracy), role (bureaucracy), task (adhocracy) and person (democracy) – can serve as a useful starting point for thinking about how an organization's power and political processes function.

Power – the dirty word

In an age when we like to think of ourselves as free and living in a democratic society, people don't like to talk about power. Power is associated with fascism and other oppressive political systems. However, power is also the basis on which most organizations function. Those who understand the uses of power will tend to prosper, while those who disregard them will be continually surprised as their proposals are sidelined in favor of suggestions coming from people who succeed in acquiring some form of power.

There are obviously many sources of power in an organization. One way of classing them might be on a continuum from open to latent (Figure 15.2):

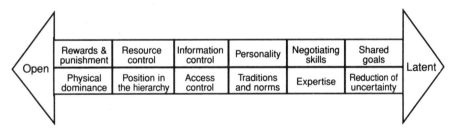

Figure 15.2   Power can derive from a wide variety of sources

Unsophisticated operators will usually be limited to the left-hand side, using their position and their authority to deal out punishments and rewards as ways of having their policies implemented. Hierarchical, authoritarian and bureaucratic organizations obviously tend to function on the left of the continuum. In them, people mostly resort to techniques such as positional authority, access to information and rules and procedures to gain influence over others. In more open, flatter, team-based organizations people generally have to use more subtle methods to influence events, such as personal ability, meeting-management skills, negotiating and convincing others that certain actions are in their interest.

The fewer the sources of power someone uses, the less effective he or she will tend to be. Organizations are strewn with technical experts of all types who, however brilliant they may be, are marginalized because they've failed to understand that it requires more than having the right answer to get an idea taken up.

'Politics? – We don't play politics round here'

If power is a dirty word, politics (the acquisition and use of power) are almost a taboo. People pride themselves on not 'playing politics'. Of course, they're fooling themselves if they believe what they say. We all play organizational politics – you have to in order to survive. We're all members of certain formal and informal power groupings and we all have our informants, enemies, rivals, pet hates, leaders, coalitions, cabals, gatekeepers and dependants. Power and influence are constantly changing in many organizations as key individuals or groups rise and fall. And most of us are reasonably attuned to the latest seismic shift and play all kinds of games so we can win from each upheaval.

You can make a (fairly nauseating) list of political techniques which people who have less of a sense of moral values than we have might use (Figure 15.3):

Building connections	Spreading rumors	Playing on people's fear	Claiming unearned credit	Sliding the knife into a rival's back
	Entertaining the influential	Direct sabotage	Pushing oneself physically close to the powerful	
Concealing information	Attaching oneself to someone's coat-tails	Stroking the egos of the powerful	Exaggerating	Insinuations of lacking competence
	Exuding self-confidence	Borrowing ideas	Stepping over the more deserving	
Disregarding the powerless	Pleasing powerful figures	Saying what is expected	Making oneself acceptable	Unadulterated sycophancy

Figure 15.3   There are many political tactics available – of course, most of us are far too virtuous to stoop to using them

There is, of course, another series of ways of managing the political networks which are less morally questionable than some of the methods above. These would include always keeping key figures informed, pre-presenting all proposals to avoid people getting unexpected surprises and working through both the formal and the informal hierarchy. The discussion below tries to show how some of these might be applied.

'Orchestrating' major decisions

Rather than trying to give pointers about how to improve our political micro-performance (our day-to-day working of the cultural/political system) which is so dependent on individual circumstances, it is more useful to discuss how one might approach trying to orchestrate a major decision (new product development, new marketing campaign, different way of working etc.). The word 'orchestrate' is used deliberately, as the process resembles more an orchestration or choreography of key figures and their attitudes than it does a logical managerial process.

Supposing you, or a group of which you are part, want to have your organization make some significant operational or strategic decision. You could, of course, just try explaining to the key people the logic of your case. You may even be successful with this. But you are more likely to need a more thought-through approach, which takes account of the political and cultural realities.

One way of planning the organization's progress from its existing view to accepting your proposed policy is to lay out a deliberately sequential five-step process (Figure 15.4):

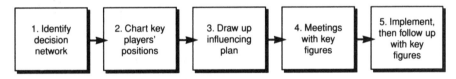

Figure 15.4   Orchestrating a major decision can be seen as a five-step process

1. Identify the decision network

Authorizers, owners, technical buyers, key influencers, cultural guardians, dragons, gatekeepers – for any major decision, there will normally be a whole host of people who must be involved in the process. And each will play a different role, have a different point of view and see different threats or opportunities arising from the decision. Someone will hold the budget, someone else may control access to key figures and so on. Someone may gain power and influence from the decision you want taken, someone else may fear a reduction in budget, staff or prestige. So the first step in orchestrating the decision is to identify the decision network – all the people who can encourage, influence, pay for or block the decision you want made.

You should take your organization chart and start classifying the various people and the main roles they might play in the process (Figure 15.5). Here it is proposed to split key people into six main categories – you may think only some of these are relevant in your particular case. If so, look a little deeper – it's far too easy to underestimate all the constituencies who can influence a major decision and to assume that only two to three key people need to be consulted. You can do little harm to your cause by involving slightly too many people – you can damage it irreparably by overlooking an individual who is apparently peripheral but powerful in reality.

+ **Authorizer (A)** – not directly involved in making the decision, but has the power to sign off or veto it.
+ **Owner (O)** – will take the decision (or be responsible for presenting it to the management group). Their area is the one which will be most affected by the decision.
+ **Gatekeeper (GK)** – can control access to key figures or resources. They can also control what message reaches the management group by offering to carry it for you. These can be very helpful or extremely dangerous figures.
+ **Key influencers (KI)** – people to whom the owner might look for support or who have influence over the authorizer.
+ **Influencers (I)** – as above, but have less say in the matter than do the key influencers.
+ **Technical buyer (TB)** – decision makers will turn to them to find out if the technical part of the proposal stands up to an expert's critical eye.

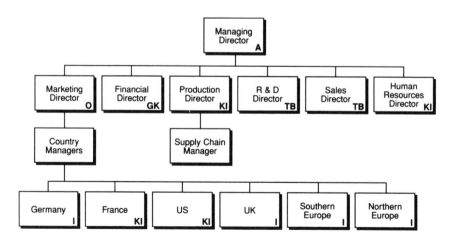

Figure 15.5   A decision network identifies the key figures and their roles in the decision-making process

All these people will be involved in the decision. A lack of knowledge about the details of your proposal, hurt pride at not being consulted, belief that their power base is under threat or genuine fear that you are on the wrong track could cause any of these people to start lobbying against you. So it's important to have identified them, their likely roles and their attitudes towards you.

2. Chart key players' positions

Enthusiasm, ignorance, greed, honest conviction, power grabbing, moral rectitude, revenge, genuine concern, fear, indecision, political advantage – these are just a few of the reasons for people supporting or opposing your proposal. The aim of this step is to clarify the key figures' motivation and to start thinking through how you might both influence and/or upset them (Figure 15.6).

NAME	POSITION	ATTITUDE	GREEN LIGHTS	RED FLAGS	IWIK	WIIFM	MEETINGS		
							1	2	3
AG	MD A	Neutral	Fits in with my existing strategy	More 'change for change's sake'	Bottom-line cashflow effects	Retire with honor	4/8	N/A	5/18
HK	Marketing Director O	Positive	Developing new products	Sticking to existing market segments	Launch plans and costs	Establish my credibility	3/15	4/12	5/15
FR	Sales Director TB	Opposed for political reasons	Being close to customers	Marketing think they have all the answers	Does this differ from last marketing disaster?	Threat to my position as market expert	3/25	5/12	N/A
PL	General Manager UK KI	Opposed: sees as threat to local power	Adapting to the special needs of my country	Another HQ project not linked to real market needs	Will I have to use my budgets for this?	We need to improve our product range	4/19	N/A	N/A

Figure 15.6   You need to understand the motivation of the main figures in order to start planning how to influence them

Some of the sections on your position chart might be:

+ **Attitude** – their current view of your proposal.
+ **Green lights** – the things you could say which would lead them to support the proposal.
+ **Red flags** – things which might upset them or go against their basic positions or beliefs.
+ **IWIK (I Wish I Knew)** – the information about your proposal you think they would like to know.
+ **WIIFM (What's In It For Me)** – what personal benefit (or loss) will be theirs if they support the proposal.
+ **Meetings** – what meetings you can set with them to influence them before the decision is taken, and what you want to achieve in each of those meetings.

3. Draw up an influencing plan

Once you've laid out the main players and their attitudes, you're obviously now in a position to think through what approach you must take to influence each of them. Just from the four simplified descriptions of the individuals in Figure 15.6 it should be clear that you're going to have to adopt quite different approaches for each of the characters:

✦ The **authorizer** (A) – they may not be directly involved in the discussions about the decision, but may still have the power of veto or approval of budget. Maybe you have access to the authorizer, but sometimes this is not possible because of their schedule.

   Here it seems that the authorizer is preparing for retirement, wants to hand over a healthy business, but doesn't want any policies adopted which might be interpreted as suggesting that the wrong policies had been pursued in the past. So obviously your proposal must be presented to them within the context of being a continuation, rather than reversal of previous policies. Also, it looks as if there is a need for quite quick results, so the fastest benefits of your proposal should be played up. However wonderful the long-term implications are, it's possible that the authorizer will be less interested in them as they won't be around to see them.

✦ The **owner** (O) – appears to be a freshly appointed marketing director, in an organization where marketing are resented by sales for treading on their 'close to the market' source of power, and resented by country managers as they represent HQ taking away the decision-making power of the local organizations. Also there appear to have been a number of marketing-driven disasters in the past, so marketing will be eager to build their credibility.

   There's quite a lot you can offer the owner – a new product to establish their credibility and a bridge to cross the gulf between them on the one side and sales and the local country managers on the other.

✦ The **technical buyer** (TB) – the sales director's people will have to sell your great new product idea. So she will be consulted by the organization about your project's feasibility. As you come from marketing, who have lost much of their credibility, you clearly have to take this past history into account when trying to convince her to go along with your idea.

✦ The **key influencer** (KI) – country general managers tend to form quite a tight, informal network in international companies. If a few influential country managers reject your plans as unworkable, then the rest will tend to fall into line – lose one and you've lost them all.

   Here you face a double problem – you come from marketing, who have low credibility, and also from HQ, which can quickly be seen as encroaching on country managers' independence. Somehow you have to deal with both these issues to make your proposal acceptable. Moreover, in this example, you only have one meeting set with the KI – they claim they cannot see you until April (long after your other first meetings) and then that they are too busy to meet you again. This is probably just a defensive stance – but you need to make some major breakthroughs in your first meeting so that they will loosen up their calendar for you.

4. Meetings with key figures – the importance of 'one-on-ones'

In a situation like the one we're describing here, don't ever (unless you have the persuasive powers of a Billy Graham) try to set up a formal presentation with the key influencers. This may, at first, seem the most efficient way to approach selling your ideas. And you may strike lucky – it could work. But, given all the political, emotional and cultural undercurrents in this case, it's likely that a small war will break out in the middle of your presentation and you'll have great difficulty recovering the situation.

Different figures have to go through different logical and emotional processes to come round to supporting your proposal. So, you should try to meet with each of them separately and work individually on moving them from their current positions to where you need them to be:

✦ The marketing director should probably be slowed down as they need to understand the need for careful handling of a politically tense situation. If they just go blundering enthusiastically ahead with your proposal, they'll be shot to pieces by sales and the country managers.

✦ The sales director will probably require 2–3 meetings to convince them that this proposal is genuinely different from the previous marketing director's unimpressive efforts.

✦ The UK country general manager likewise will need a lot of convincing. So you should not necessarily plan to convince them in one single meeting, even though that is all you've been able to set up for the moment. Use your one meeting to open the door – if they are interested, they'll see you again.

5. Implement and follow up

When you've finally manoeuvered all the players into place, got agreement, developed and launched your new product, you should obviously keep in touch with the major players to check if they're satisfied with the result and how it rated against their expectations, if they have any ideas on how to improve the results and if there's anything they think you should have done differently, so you can manage the process better the next time.

And make sure you leave the door open, in case there *is* a next time.

Summary

Management is not a science. Most quantitative techniques which managers learn will never be put to use. Moreover, an excessive emphasis on the 'scientific' aspects of management can distract managers from the real issue – how to turn policy into effective and appropriate action given all the cultural, personal and political aspects involved.

Britain and the US have probably suffered more than most countries from a search for quick and easy management solutions, perhaps because with them, more than most countries, those who control organizations are financiers, marketers and lawyers – people divorced from the real process of creating wealth. In 'engineering' cultures like Germany, Sweden and Japan, where managers have been close to the act of production, where there is less obsession with quick monetary gain and where people feel a greater sense of belonging to their organizations, culture and politics seem to be less of a barrier to effective action.

Managers will always have to deal with political, cultural and power issues. But they will experience many fewer problems if they learn to empathize with those they work with. This may require abandonment of some of the theoretical models which they feel give them the answers to problems, and paying more attention to the ideas of subordinates and colleagues.

Recommended reading

Terrence Deal & Allen Kennedy (1988) *Corporate Cultures: The Rites and Rituals of Corporate Life*, Addison-Wesley (US)/Penguin (UK).

Neil Glass (1991) *Pro-Active Management*, Cassell.

Charles Hampden-Turner & Fons Trompenaars (1993) *The Seven Cultures of Capitalism*, Doubleday (US)/Piatkus (UK).

Roger Harrison (1972) 'How to describe your organization', *Harvard Business Review*, Sept–Oct.

Robert Miller, Stephen Heiman & Tad Tujela (1985) *Strategic Selling*, Warner Books (US)/Kogan Page (UK).

Fons Trompenaars (1993) *Riding the Waves of Culture*, Nicholas Brealey.

16

Improving Personal Effectiveness

A changing business and social environment is demanding quite different skills. Many organizations have moved from valuing stability, loyalty and efficiency to demanding greater flexibility, creativity and entrepreneurism. And our social relationships are probably much more complex and multifaceted than were those of our parents.

The basic skills of personal effectiveness are fairly well known – time management, ability to communicate, good teamwork, stress management, meeting management, planning and so on. In addition, there are a number of useful models that suggest the newer kinds of skills we will need to develop if we are to prosper in the future (Figure 16.1)

Pages 142–65

There are several common elements in the many different models – personal motivation, the ability to understand and influence others, building effective networks and so on. Rather than provide yet another shopping list of skills for survival, I propose to look at three aspects of how we operate – how we think, act and interact – and to touch on some skills that are not dealt with in other parts of this book and that have perhaps received less attention in the many books about personal effectiveness.

How we think

As we are forced to become more self-reliant, critical to our survival will be our internal motivation to have a lasting impact on our world and our ability to view our rapidly changing environment in new ways (Figure 16.2).

Figure 16.1   Four views of the new skills we need

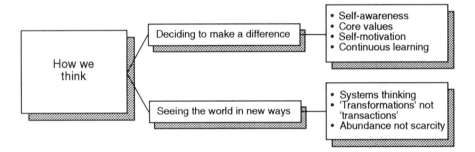

Figure 16.2   How we think

Deciding to make a difference

The most fundamental attribute we will require is the inner motivation to improve. In whatever field we work, most of us probably want to feel that we have contributed in some way. Of course, there will always be a minority who are only interested (or *think* they are only interested) in their own personal comfort and gain. After all, we live in a competitive world – if we don't perform, there's always someone to take our place. And some people believe that the only way to prosper is at the expense of others. However, most of us have a deeply ingrained set of values that make us want to have some positive influence during our lives. Our greatest frustrations in life come when we are prevented from contributing or are pushed into acting against these values.

Borrowing a basic business tool, the two-by-two matrix (Figure 16.3), we can quickly start to assess to what extent we spend our time acting according to or

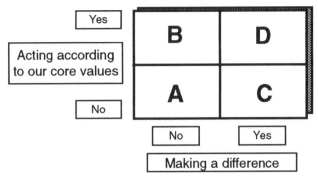

Figure 16.3   Making a difference

against our values and making positive change or having a negative influence.

Clearly, most of us would like to spend most of our efforts in quadrant D – making a positive difference while acting according to our core values. But too often economic, social or other pressures push us into the other three quadrants:

✦ A – many of us will find at some time that, in order to keep our jobs, we feel forced to behave both unproductively and in a way which we consider ethically questionable.

✦ B – other people will feel that while they behave quite ethically, they are somehow trapped in a repetitive pattern and have difficulty causing positive change; for example teachers working in underfunded inner-city schools.

✦ C – too many of us feel coerced into actions which have a significant influence on others but which go against what we believe is right. Salespeople, typically, can easily fall into this trap to meet targets or earn bonuses.

✦ D – this is obviously ideal territory where most of would like to live our lives. Time spent outside D is time during which we become alienated from ourselves. In D we are being ourselves and are contributing positively.

Try to examine your work, family and social lives using this matrix. If you are investing too little of yourself in D, identify what is holding you back – economic situation, family pressures, your skill or education level, aversion to risk or whatever. Only by actively analysing your situation and its causes can you start to develop appropriate solutions.

Seeing the world in new ways

Many of our traditional models for interpreting the world are proving inadequate in the face of a more complex, more integrated reality. Time and again we have seen simplistic cause-and-effect reasoning fail us:

✦ A new road is built because of traffic jams and has the expected outcome of easing congestion. But more people are encouraged to use their cars because of this and there is therefore yet more congestion.

✦ Stock levels are increased and this has the expected outcome of improving delivery performance. But increased stock leads to more difficulty in tracing products in the warehouse, so costs increase and delivery performance declines again.

Pages 34–45

We need to try to move beyond this binary logic and replace it with an understanding of systems thinking, virtuous and vicious spirals and complexity theory.

As part of this systems thinking, we must move from seeing our actions as one-offs – what we can call transactions. Instead, we should understand that each of our actions is part of a system and will have an effect on our environment and back on ourselves – each action is in a sense a transformation – and we must become better at anticipating the results of our interventions.

Furthermore, we can benefit from abandoning 'scarcity' thinking, where we believe that one person's gain will usually lead to another person's loss. In its place we should adopt 'abundance' thinking, the belief that helping others will normally be to the advantage of us all.

In a scarcity thinking organization people hoard information or resources, believing that this will somehow help them maintain their positions and power bases. In an abundance thinking environment, people and groups actively seek to share information and resources as they know this will benefit everyone.

For example, one 200-person research and development organization published a skills and projects matrix (a kind of *Yellow Pages*) showing who was working on what and who had particular kinds of experience. This allowed anybody to know where to go to ask for advice. This particular company is more the exception than the rule. There are too many R&D groups where the greatest experts fail to make progress because of the barriers they erect between themselves through scarcity thinking.

How we act

The information revolution and the loosening of organizational hierarchies should have made decision making easier. Instead, many people and organizations seem almost paralysed by the vast amounts of data they produce and the endless internal meetings that are 'necessary' to coordinate all the groups and teams affected by any decision. We must regain the ability to turn our intentions into decisive and imaginative action (Figure 16.4).

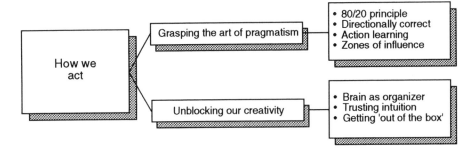

Figure 16.4   How we act

Grasping the art of pragmatism

Time and again we see the 80/20 principle at work in people's daily lives – 80 percent of volume is bought by 20 percent of customers, 80 percent of activity is generated by 20 percent of people using a service, 80 percent of problems are caused by only 20 percent of equipment. This should allow us to focus our energies on gaining maximum leverage from our efforts – really delight the key 20 percent of customers, customize parts of the service to the 20 percent using it most, allocate a taskforce to the troublesome 20 percent of our equipment. Intuitively most of us understand this, but how often do we and our organizations act decisively in the light of this knowledge? Instead many projects and initiatives seem to get bogged down as they try to cope with every aspect of an issue, rather than focusing on the critical 20 percent.

Another classic barrier to action is people and teams never getting beyond analysis of an issue and perhaps a few ideas for solutions about which they can't agree. You don't have to know everything in detail and have total agreement before you start implementing solutions. You only have to know that your general direction is right (that you are 'directionally correct') and you can learn as you do (action learning).

A manufacturer knew that his business was reasonably concentrated around a few key customers (actually he had an exact 80/20 relationship – 80 percent of volume and profits from 20 percent of customers). For over two years various task groups agonized about exactly how these special customers should be served. But unfortunately the groups had difficulty reaching agreement and when they did agree on something, they usually found that computer systems, work processes, organizational structure or whatever prevented their ideas being implemented.

It never occurred to this company to start reducing leadtimes for a couple of customers, to offer to hold stock for some others, to test more frequent shipments for others, to set up a joint supply team with one or two others and so on. They could have just tried out some simple actions and gradually learnt and improved as they went along. But the simple approach of moving in the right direction and using action learning went against the whole way this engineering-oriented organization thought. Its staff's education had taught them that you should not move until you had a full design and detailed specifications of the future way of working. Many organizations are caught in a similar trap

Another way people and organizations hold themselves back from acting is by spending time and effort speculating over things that they cannot influence. We can split our world into three zones of influence:

+ what we can directly influence
+ what we can influence through others
+ what we are unable to influence.

We should, of course, be aware of what we cannot influence. But to be effective, we must focus our effort and time only on those things over which we can have some influence.

Unblocking our creativity

Page 86–103

A number of well-known techniques have been developed to help us break free from the limitations we and our environment impose on our thinking. These include brainstorming, mind-mapping, structured problem solving, idea generation and associative thinking.

There are also a couple of basic principles that could help us all, but that we often overlook:

+ **The brain is a natural organizer and problem solver.** When faced with a tough problem (decision to be made, report to be written, presentation to be prepared) too many of us agonize for hours to develop the best solution. However, we frequently begin to hit the law of diminishing returns – the more effort we put in, the less productive we are. Another approach is to understand that even when we stop working on a problem, our brain does not. Often it is more effective to load your brain with a sufficient amount of information about the issue at hand and then to go off and do something else – walk the dog, listen to music, play with your children or whatever. In the meantime, your brain will carry on thinking about the issue and start generating possible solutions. Using this technique you will find that answers seem to materialize when you are involved in another activity and are not expecting them.

✦ **You have to get right 'out of the box'.** Many organizations work on the same problems year after year – how to improve deliveries, get more consistent quality, reduce costs, improve communication. And often variants of the same solution are applied, usually with little effect. One way to break out of this trap is to consider applying the *exact opposite* of the 'tried-and-tested' answer. If you are hoping to improve deliveries by increasing stock, for example, try reducing it instead. If you always hope to reduce costs by cutting out people, think about keeping your people and setting them the task of expanding volumes instead. If you have attempted to improve communication by setting up cross-functional teams with frequent and unproductive meetings, cut down on the teams, reduce the meetings, put in clear performance measures and allow informal networks to build the communication channels that the changes in the formal organization failed to give you.

How we interact

With the disappearance of traditional hierarchies and the explosion in the number of cross-functional teams and taskforces, the ability to influence others without having authority over them has become a critical skill. Moreover, even when we do theoretically have authority over people it can be quite limited. They are often highly skilled knowledge workers, operating in an area with which we are unfamiliar, and they can easily find other employers if they are dissatisfied with how we treat them. There are many aspects to developing this 'influence without power'. Two key ones are how we understand others and how we communicate (Figure 16.5).

Understanding and empathizing with others

Different people can have quite different ways of viewing and reacting to the world. We all know this, yet many of us could be much better at applying this

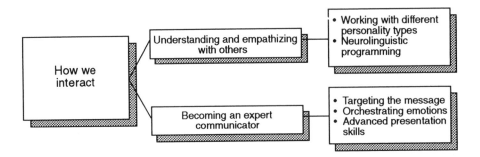

Figure 16.5   How we interact

knowledge. Too often you see managers with different personality profiles failing to communicate, not because they actually disagree, but because each of them does not understand the other's different information needs.

One manager might require a lot of technical detail to be satisfied with a decision's viability, another would be turned off by the detail and would be looking for the overview and market impact, while a third may only approve any proposals if they felt they were in control. A teamworker might be motivated by the idea of group achievement, whereas a specialist is more likely to value the technical content of an assignment.

There are several models of personality and behavior types to choose from:

+ **Myers-Briggs** – extrovert/introvert; sensing/intuitive; thinking/feeling; judging/perceiving
+ **LIFO®** – supporting/giving in; adapting/dealing away; conserving/holding on; controlling/taking over
+ **Belbin's team roles** – coordinator, shaper, plant, resource investigator, teamworker, implementer, monitor/evaluator, finisher, specialist
+ **Enneagram** – perfectionist, giver, performer, romantic, observer, trooper, epicure, boss, mediator.

You can even use astrological types if you feel comfortable with those. But whatever your preferred model, unless you accept that different people will have quite different mental models and consciously try to understand how other people think, you will struggle to build real empathy with them.

Neurolinguistic programming (NLP) has emerged as a powerful tool for helping us understand ourselves and others and change the way we and others think and act. One basic aspect of NLP is the concept that you can classify the way people make sense of the world into three main types – visual, auditory or kinesthetic. By listening carefully to the words and expressions people use, we can start to understand their preferred style and begin to improve our communication with them:

VISUAL	AUDITORY	KINESTHETIC
'I see what you mean'	'I hear that…'	'It feels as if…'
'That looks right'	'That rings a bell'	'I can't quite grasp…'
'Show me that again'	'It sounds as if…'	'We need to get a grip on…'
'It appears that…'	'I've been told…'	'It seems solid enough'
'This will shed some light'	'They say that…'	'I must stress that…'

NLP also proposes some behavioral frames which can help us understand and influence how people think and act. For example:

◆ Some people orientate themselves to **outcomes** (what do I want?), which are forward looking and positive, rather than focusing on **problems** (why am I in this position?) which just look back and are unproductive.

◆ Some ask **how** rather than **why** questions. Asking **how** focuses you on solutions – asking **why** just looks for reasons and justifications without changing anything.

◆ Some think of **possibilities** and not **necessities**. This means trying to find the opportunities in any situation and not just limiting themselves to the constraints.

◆ Some view results as **feedback** to learn from and not **failure** to achieve what they wanted.

◆ Some people are constantly **curious**, trying to find out new information and ideas, while others tend to rest behind **assumptions** and prejudices as if there were no need to discover anything new.

Clearly, we must adopt a different influencing strategy for people who tend to think only in terms of why and necessities than we would use for someone who tends more towards how and possibilities.

Becoming an expert communicator

Any communication can be said to have two main aspects – the content (what we are trying to convey) and the process (how are we transmitting our message). As someone who has had to give and suffer many hundreds of presentations, I still find that too often inadequate thought is given to the process.

Many presenters seem to believe that if they understand what they are trying to say, it will magically be both comprehensible and of interest to their intended audience. Sadly, this is seldom the case.

There are many books about effective communication, but this section will discuss two or three techniques which are not always fully dealt with.

Meeting your audience's expectations

At any presentation or meeting, the audience will generally have a number of questions which they will expect to be answered in the first minute or so (Figure 16.6).

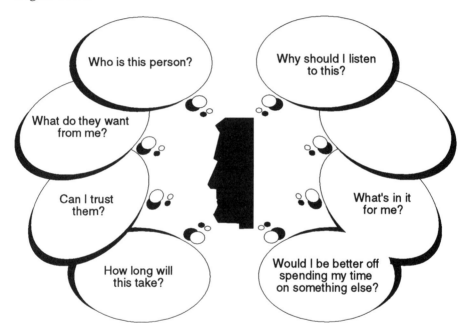

Figure 16.6   We must ensure we answer our audience's expectations

Unless you answer these concerns satisfactorily up front, you'll struggle to retain your audience's interest. Skilled presenters will often start by stating their objectives and then openly asking if their audience has any other expectations. In this way they can check immediately if they are on track and adjust their approach if necessary. This may seem simple and obvious – but it is seldom done. For example, you could start a meeting as follows:

'We have an hour together today. My aim is for us to reach a decision on A. I'd like to spend the first 30 minutes presenting x, y and z. Then we can discuss any points of detail and the way forward. Do you have any other expectations from today?'

Orchestrating emotions

There are few pieces of music that are both monotonous and enjoyable and the same goes for presentations. You'll be lucky if you can find any audience that can remain interested after 10–15 almost identical graphs. Likewise, presenters who try to lighten up their material by showing cartoon after cartoon will soon be taken as seriously as their pictures. Obvious? Yes. Yet time and again presenters fall into the monotony trap.

There are a million and one different ways to structure a presentation. But a key point is to provide sufficient variation to retain people's attention. Figure 16.7 shows a simplified picture of how a presentation might be structured to move an audience through a desired thought process.

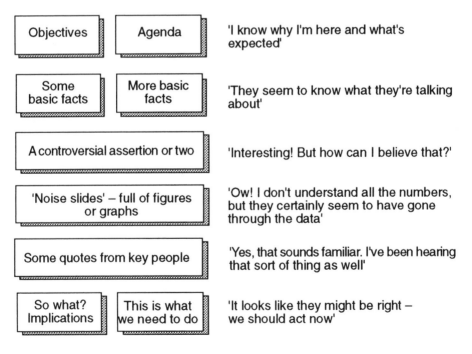

Figure 16.7   Keeping your audience on track

Working with normal information retention

First, three groups of statistics which are probably a reasonable guide to reality – they may not be as accurate as they look, but they are 'directionally correct'.

✦ Of all the information we retain, 83 percent is seen, 11 percent heard and 6 percent touched/smelt/tasted.
✦ When we talk with someone, about 55 percent of the communication comes through body language, 38 percent through voice tonality and as little as 7 percent through the actual words.
✦ At least 40 percent of what we learn is forgotten within 20 minutes and about 60 percent within an hour.

So if you're planning the world's best presentation, with masses of interesting data and plenty of devastating facts, you've got over 100 slides all in glorious technicolor and you're going to need at least an hour to get your important message across – stop! You're probably doing something wrong. People will only retain a few key points and they'll remember them best if they're presented visually. Make those few critical items your subject. You may want to allude to and give examples of all the other useful stuff you've gathered – but you won't be able to put it across effectively in your presentation so don't even try.

Moreover, when you're delivering one of your three or four key points, make sure people know that what you're saying is key to your argument. Not every listener can detect the most important 100 or so words of the more than 10,000 words you'll grace them with per hour of your exposition.

And, of course, move around, use your arms, head and hands, change the tone of your voice, vary the speed of your speech, scan the room looking people in the eyes, show some emotion! After all, the actual words you use are only a small part of what your audience will react to and remember.

Recommended reading

Gillian Butler, Tony Hope & RA Hope (1995) *Managing Your Mind: The Mental Fitness Guide*, Oxford Paperbacks.
John O'Keeffe (1998) *Breaking Out of the Box: Achieve Breakthrough Results by Applying Your Mind*, Nicholas Brealey.
Steven R Covey (1992) *Principle-Centered Leadership*, Simon and Schuster.
Richard Koch (1998) *The 80/20 Principle: The Secret of Achieving More With Less*, Nicholas Brealey.
Denis Waitley (1996) *Empires of the Mind*, Nicholas Brealey.

Part Seven

Changing the Role of the Manager

17

Moving from Manager to Doer

The management task is changing. As organizations become flatter, more flexible, more responsive to customer needs and more dependent on the skills of their staff, managers are having to adapt. While not all organizations are moving at the same speed, even the most bureaucratic institutions are feeling the pressure to move with the times. Government departments are being given service charters and goals; hospitals, schools and local authorities are being ranked on their performance; drug approval agencies in several countries have been told to meet new more ambitious targets; state-owned railways, banks and major companies are being 'cleaned up' for privatization.

The drivers of this change are generally recognized – there are internal factors such as more educated staff and fewer manual workers, greater availability of information through advances in IT, moves towards cross-functional working and teamwork. External influences include a more competitive environment, saturated markets, more demanding consumers and a desire on the part of governments to withdraw from a number of industries and services which they had previously controlled. Figure 17.1 sums up some of the ways in which these trends are affecting the role of managers.

Gradually, but inevitably, the manager's role is turning through ninety degrees – from managing 'vertically' (reporting to a senior and controlling subordinates who are processing information) to managing 'horizontally' (coordinating activities across the organization). Managers are moving from being responsible for directing the actions of subordinates in the same functional area to ensuring that cross-functional business processes work effectively. The old breed of middle managers, part of a long hierarchy of paper pushers, report writers and gatherers of information, has all but disappeared in successive waves of downsizing over the last 10–20 years. Their successors are much more actively involved in the hands-on, day-to-day business of helping their

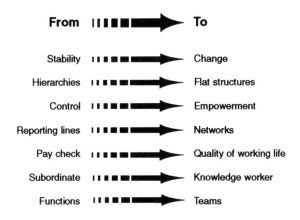

Figure 17.1   The changing role of the manager

organizations function. The following examples show how dramatic the change in a manager's role can be.

In an FMCG company, where the customer base had consolidated from several thousand retail customers making up 80 percent of sales to 10 retail groups now taking more than 80 percent of turnover, the regional sales managers used to work in a clear functional hierarchy, where they were responsible for area sales managers who were in turn managing sales reps. Now, some regional sales managers have become key account managers responsible for working across the organization to ensure that their customers receive the correct deliveries, packaging, promotional and advertising support, credit terms etc. This obviously represents a complete change in role (Figure 17.2).

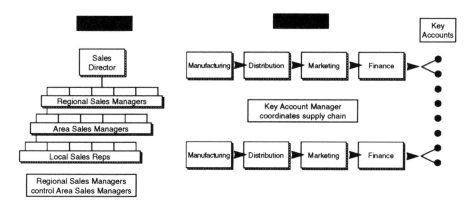

Figure 17.2   Changing roles in an FMCG company

Moving from controller to supporter and doer

Some managers have had problems coping with these changes. Many have resisted, sometimes successfully, and others have gone down fighting, opposing all change until finally the organization reacts and they're moved or fired. Some of the resistance is understandable. Managers are both concerned about keeping their jobs and genuinely worried about how a process will function without their clear managerial control. If you set up a self-managing team in, for example, a packing department and give them responsibility for training, interviewing new members, routine maintenance and detailed scheduling, what is there left for a supervisor or manager to do? And will the team have the self-discipline, experience and maturity to act responsibly without direct management supervision?

One problem might be that those who have resisted these changes have failed to distinguish between the manager as a *position* and the manager as a *set of activities*. If you view the manager as a position, you start to get into all kinds of fruitless discussions around whether certain managerial levels are needed any more or not. Normally this will provoke a fairly aggressive reaction from those who happen to occupy those levels and are naturally quite concerned with protecting their own livelihood. However, if you can see a manager as a set of activities, you can start analysing where and by whom those activities are best carried out. Often the managers themselves will agree that they can usefully pass on certain tasks to others and will also identify other tasks, carried out by superiors or in other areas, which may be more appropriately assigned to them.

It is not necessary for managers to be controllers. This is a phenomenon which developed to suit a certain era, the early part of the twentieth century when the large 'command-and-control' bureaucratic structures evolved which are still in the painful process of being dismantled. When managers understand why and how the context in which they must work is changing, they are usually amenable to discussing how their roles should be altered to match the new circumstances. More often than not, these new circumstances require that managers move away from controlling and reporting on activities carried out by subordinates and towards coordinating teams running cross-functional, customer-facing business processes – from running a sales organization (functional) to managing key accounts (cross-functional), from overseeing an engineering area (functional) to managing a project team (cross-functional). Managers are having to become more involved in the real work of adding value for customers.

Figure 17.3 shows one useful model of how a manager might gradually move out from top-down control to supporting a team.

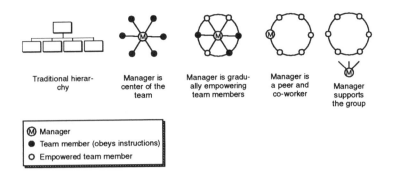

Figure 17.3   Moving from manager as controller to manager as supporter

Managers first replace their hierarchy with a team. Then they gradually give key responsibilities to team members. Next they try to move out from being at the centre of the team to being one of its members by, for example, having other members run meetings, present decisions to affected departments etc. Finally, managers start to withdraw from team meetings and decision making, yet work one-on-one with team members coaching them and are available to help if the team requires.

This may seem slightly idealistic or even mechanical. Moreover, in real life you hardly ever get the chance to go through such a planned, stepwise process. And there are perhaps few occasions where managers might want to go so far in delegating their authority. Nevertheless, the model can be useful as a framework to help managers think through how they are going to move towards a more supportive style of working.

Finally escaping from Taylorism?

Managers are influenced, consciously or not, by the huge volume of management theory which has been developed since the beginning of the twentieth century. In most organizations, many of the main ideas will be represented, to some degree or other, in different areas and individuals. While dealing with the subject of the changing role of the manager, it may therefore be useful to review some of the main schools of thought, and to revisit the work of the much maligned Frederick Winslow Taylor, 'father of scientific management'. Like it or not, his influence is probably more prevalent today than most modern 'enlightened' organizations would like to admit.

Pages 4–11

For convenience, most histories of management theory class the work done into about five main phases. When reviewing the different schools of thought, it must be remembered that they will normally reflect the economic, social and political environment in which they were developed – so what is considered as admirable at one point may be branded 'barbaric' or 'simplistic' by a later generation.

The five main schools of management theory

1. Scientific management

Linked with the work of F.W. Taylor (1856–1917), this can be said to be based on three main principles:

✦ To be efficiently carried out, work must be broken into simple, discrete, measurable tasks.
✦ There is 'one best way' to carry out each task.
✦ Workers will be motivated by money to accept this one best way.

This theory has been linked to the development of large, 'production line' factories and administration systems, where the work is split up into small, boring, repetitive steps requiring little skill. The work study movement which tried to develop times and methods for each task has also been associated with scientific management.

In this kind of environment, the management role was mainly assigning work to an often low-skilled workforce, and closely controlling productivity and output.

2. Trait studies

These studies, which were popular from the 1910s to the 1950s, started to view management as a process of leadership rather than just one of control. Numerous experts conducted studies to try to identify the personality characteristics which successful leaders had in common, with the aim of developing a profile to be used for spotting future leaders. These experts spent a great deal of time and energy disagreeing with each other over what these key characteristics should be.

An implicit assumption of this theory was that leaders were, to a certain extent, born not made. A leading writer (Drucker, 1955) suggested that 'leadership cannot be created or promoted. It cannot be taught or learned.'

It is probably the changing demands put on managers in a changing business environment, rather than anything intrinsically wrong with any of the findings, which has done most to discredit these studies. Much of what made a manager successful in the 1950s is unlikely to be relevant in a high-tech company today. As one commentator noted:

> Fifty years of study have failed to produce one personality trait or set of qualities that can be used to discriminate between leaders and non-leaders. (Jennings, 1961)

3. Human relations or behavioral approach

During the late 1920s some writers began to pay more attention to human and social behavior at work and how this related to productivity. Following the famous Hawthorne experiments (Roethlisberger & Dickson, 1939), it was proposed that increasing production could be achieved less by control and financial incentives, and more by 'humanizing' work through building work groups and giving them more management attention.

These themes were developed between the 1940s and 1960s by the psychologists Maslow (1943) and Herzberg (1959). By developing models of human motivation (see Part Six – Enhancing Personal Performance), they proposed that the management role should be based on motivating  staff through trying to satisfy their needs to belong to a social group, receive attention and credit, and achieve intellectual development.

This theme was picked up in McGregor's (1960) Theory X and Theory Y. To explain this briefly, Theory X managers believe people need to be directed, controlled, rewarded and punished if they are to be productive. Theory Y managers believe people are generally self-motivated and interested in doing a good job. They thus try to encourage people to develop, accept responsibility and enhance their own abilities.

4. Contingency theory

This put forward the perhaps unsurprising thesis that there is no 'one right way' of managing people or organizations (see Fiedler, 1967). Its proponents argued that choice of management approach depended on criteria such as the organization's technology level and environment, the nature of the work task and the manager's personality.

For example, in a stable environment with a simple task (e.g. working on a biscuit packing line), there is probably limited opportunity to empower and develop staff. On the other hand, in a rapidly changing and highly competitive market in a high-technology area, you want people who are able to take the initiative and react quickly.

All this is probably obvious – yet it is extraordinary how often managers in static mass-production plants launch expensive, well-meaning yet ultimately pointless employee empowerment programs, and when employees do come back with proposals these are rejected as 'unrealistic' since managers believe they might interfere with the achievement of daily output targets. And it is far from unusual to see managers put staff in key customer-facing or project-management positions while giving them inadequate budget or decision-making freedom (for example, the project manager responsible for a £50 million program who still has to have trips and travel expenses approved by the departmental director).

5. The learning organization

As the pace of change accelerates, markets become more unstable, technology continues to develop rapidly and economic cycles become more unpredictable, the critical success factor for most organizations will be their ability

to sense and react to the changes in their operating environment. The organization as 'bureaucratic machine' must develop into the organization as 'brain' (see Part Three – Encouraging Creativity). No longer can it mindlessly carry out the 'brilliant' strategies dreamed up by top management – instead it must learn from customers, competitors and even leading companies in quite different industries if it is to adapt and survive (see Garratt, 1988, and Senge, 1990).

This will require the dismantling of hierarchies, empowerment of staff, sup-

portive rather than controlling managers, champions of constructive change rather than defenders of 'the way we do things round here'. It will require an organization that can learn, rather than one that can just execute orders (see Part Nine – Redesigning the Organization).

Theoretically, we've come a long way from the scientific management of F.W. Taylor, the man who:

+ had a 'book' made into which a stopwatch was built, which was specially designed to be operated by one hand, so that he could time the most efficient way of carrying out tasks without workers knowing what he was up to
+ caused strikes in numerous factories and caused the US Senate to ban his time-study methods in defense equipment manufacturing plants due to the industrial unrest they caused

+ said: 'one of the first requirements for a man who is fit to handle pig iron as a regular occupation is that he shall be so stupid and phlegmatic that he more nearly resembles in his mental makeup the ox than any other type. The man who is mentally alert and intelligent is for this very reason entirely unsuited…to work of this character'

+ towards the end of his life became pessimistic about his own work: 'It's a horrid life for any man to live not being able to look any workman in the face without seeing hostility there' and 'I have found that any improvement is not only opposed but aggressively and bitterly opposed by the majority of men' (Dos Passos, 1937).

Although trends such as business process reengineering are reassembling tasks into meaningful and purposeful units of work, there are still too many managers around who would feel quite comfortable sharing a beer and opinions with F.W. Taylor, of whom one commentator said 'the sheer silliness from a modern perspective of many of his ideas, and barbarities they led to when applied in industry, encourage ridicule and denunciation' (Rose, 1978).

Pages 295–304

Empowerment

Perhaps too frequently, empowerment has been portrayed as an option available to enlightened management to create healthy, happy and productive organizations. For many organizations, however, empowerment may be a necessity to be disregarded at their peril, rather than a luxury to be dispensed in moments of generosity.

Empowerment is not the abdication of managerial responsibility. It is a way of working in which the manager's role changes from directly commanding, controlling and processing information to coaching, coordinating and supporting. In the initial stages of empowerment, management intervention is critical to developing staff and creating a safe political environment for them to operate in. You can't just cast employees adrift. You need a 'management steamroller' to remove the capability, skill and organizational barriers.

Later, as employees develop their skills and grow into their new responsibilities, managers can focus on moving into a position that more resembles a sports coach than a traditional authoritarian boss.

It is important to distinguish empowerment from delegation. Delegation has echoes of a manager knowing a situation better than an employee, but passing down extra responsibility to the employee to help them grow and develop. Empowerment seems to refer more to a manager accepting that employees may need some direction, but that they have the skills, knowledge or close contact with the market which may be necessary to find the right solution.

If we look at where effort is focused in most organizations by three main groups (operations staff, middle management and executives), we'll probably get a profile as follows. Operational staff work purely on maintaining efficiency. Middle management spend most of their time focused on current operations with only a small percentage dedicated to improving the way the organization works. And top executives are also buried in general operational management issues, with some time spent on trying to improve these but very little energy applied to what might be called 'leadership' – building the organization's future (identifying new ways of meeting customer needs, developing new products or services, entering new markets, building new alliances with suppliers, customers or competitors and so on).

By building skills such as creativity, teamwork, meeting management and understanding of market needs, we should be trying to move our operational staff towards helping improve the way the organization works, our middle managers towards supporting them, and our executives out of the detail of day-to-day operations management and on to leadership activities.

Summary – choosing a management role

The potential roles of the manager can be shown on a continuum (Figure 17.4) going from autocrat (tightly controlling employee behavior) to coach (dedicated to developing and empowering staff).

Figure 17.4   The continuum of management roles

Most of us would probably like to see ourselves towards the right of the spectrum, as this fits with modern democratic ideas of freedom and individual rights. However, faced with a difficult decision or under other kinds of stress, most of us will tend to gravitate towards the left of the range. This is not necessarily wrong, as many situations require firm leadership and quick decision making. Where managers can go wrong is in constantly inhabiting any one role, regardless of the situation, or in applying the wrong role to a situation. For example:

> The manager of a multinational's UK operation had a reputation for a hardnosed, cost-cutting, 'management by fear' style. When put in charge of the company's European operation, the manager continued to work in the way which had given success in the past. This led to angry and bruising encounters with the various country managers, who spoke of being insulted and humiliated. A particular bone of contention was the once yearly 'inquisition', when country managers spent up to eight hours defending their next year's operating budgets – in spite of holding a very responsible position in their own countries, they felt they were being treated like incompetents.

Finally, of course, there is also a geographic and cultural aspect to choice of management role. Some countries accept, and even expect, authoritarian management, whereas others are culturally biased towards a much more participative approach (see Chapter 19 – The Challenges of Global Management).

Pages 232–45

Recommended reading

Christopher Bartlett & Sumantra Ghoshal (1995) 'Changing the role of top management: beyond systems to people', *Harvard Business Review*, May–June.

Peter Drucker (1955) *The Practice of Management*, HarperBusiness (US)/Heinemann (UK).

F.E. Fiedler (1967) *A Theory of Leadership Effectiveness*, McGraw-Hill.

Bob Garratt (1988) *The Learning Organization*, Fontana.

F. Herzberg, B. Mausner & B.B. Snyderman (1959) *The Motivation to Work*, World Publishing.

E.E. Jennings (1961) 'The anatomy of leadership', *Management of Personnel Quarterly*, Autumn.

A.H. Maslow (1943) 'A theory of human motivation', *Psychological Review*, July.

Douglas McGregor (1960) *The Human Side of Enterprise*, McGraw-Hill.

William Ouchi (1981) *Theory Z*, Addison-Wesley.

F.J. Roethlisberger & W.J. Dickson (1939) *Management and the Worker*, Harvard University Press.

M. Rose (1978) *Industrial Behaviour*, Penguin.

Peter M. Senge (1990) *The Fifth Discipline*, Currency Doubleday.

18

Managing through Effective Negotiation

Most of our interactions with other people are negotiations, whether it's at home discussing which restaurant to go to or who'll change the baby's diapers at three o'clock in the morning, or at work deciding when to launch an advertising campaign or whether to move forward with a project. This ought to mean we're all experienced negotiators. But, with divorce rates of 30–50 percent in most western countries and continual conflicts simmering under the surface of even the most benign-looking organizations, there may still be some room for improvement.

Two significant changes have happened in the field of negotiation:

+ the focus is moving from one-off wins to establishing longer-term relations
+ managers are increasingly having to rely on their ability to negotiate, rather than their hierarchical authority, to carry through their responsibilities.

1. From one-offs to longer-term relations

Five or ten years ago, before the days of supplier partnerships, value chain linking and cross-functional teams, many negotiations could be seen as almost one-off events. The aim was to win the best deal possible, usually on limited criteria:

+ you wanted the best price and delivery terms from suppliers
+ you wanted to keep customers happy without giving away too much
+ you wanted to keep staff loyal, but only for a certain salary level.

It was the outcome of the negotiation which was critical. You were less worried about the relationship – you could always find other suppliers, sell to new customers or hire replacement staff.

But the world has moved on.

+ With the trend towards supplier partnerships, you can't just ditch a supplier if you reach an impasse on price – you may not have anywhere else reliable to go to. Moreover, you've normally built up such an understanding of each other's operation that it would take you years to build similar relations with a new supplier.
+ The concentration of buying power with fewer, larger customers in many markets and the increase in competitive pressure mean that you can ill afford to throw away any customers. Nowadays, losing a major customer can cost you 10–20 percent of your business.
+ With the increase in knowledge workers and the high level of investment that has been put into training many of your employees, you can no longer treat them like easily replaceable cogs in a machine.

In negotiating with these groups you now have to think much more about maintaining a relationship, which goes beyond emerging triumphant from any single negotiation (Figure 18.1).

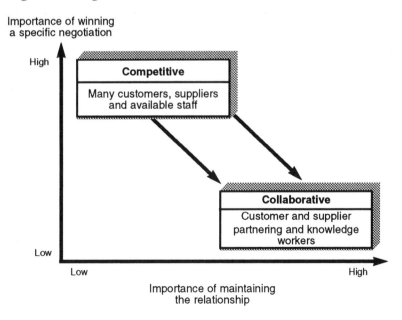

Figure 18.1   Focus on building more long-term relationships in negotiation

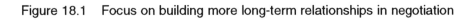

2. From authority to negotiation

As the main part of managers' work has shifted from a vertical, functional focus to a more horizontal, cross-functional one, the good old-fashioned exercise of authority over obedient subordinates has had to be replaced by a greater reliance on collaboration with other functions, who may have quite different goals to you. For example, the regional sales manager, who is put in charge of one or two key accounts, moves from dealing mainly with subordinates such as area sales managers and local sales reps to having to coordinate a whole series of different functions running right across the organization – marketing, finance, distribution and so on (see Chapter 17 – Moving from Manager to Doer).

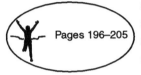
Pages 196–205

And when you will be working with those other functions for years, you can't allow yourself to make enemies by winning one specific negotiation – they can always get their revenge later. Instead, you have to somehow get agreement to proposals which others may not feel are in their interests, without alienating those people.

Many managers have enormous difficulty adapting to this change. In spite of great success in their hierarchical position, they fail as cross-functional negotiators because they lack the very different skills which are needed. This often puts organizations in a difficult situation – they feel they owe the managers some gratitude for their previous loyalty and good performance, but see they are failing in their new positions. Too often, such people are left to struggle ineffectively on, making more and more enemies and becoming increasingly frustrated at their own poor results.

Competitive vs collaborative bargaining

Negotiation theory splits negotiations into two types or extremes. Most negotiations will, of course, tend to fall somewhere between these two poles.

Competitive (also called positional) bargaining is directed at one side winning and the other losing. It assumes that there is a limited cake and that, if one party gets more of it, the other will clearly get less. Price, salary and budget allocation negotiations tend to (but don't have to) fall into this category. This is the traditional win–lose form of negotiation – each side adopts a position and fights tooth and nail to defend that position.

Collaborative (also called cooperative or interest) bargaining tries to take the position that the negotiators are not opponents. It proposes that there is a problem to be solved jointly by both parties for their mutual benefit. It does not see the cake as fixed in size. Here the aim is to work together to enlarge the cake for both sides to share.

COMPETITIVE	COLLABORATIVE
Opponents	Colleagues
Fixed amount to be split	Working together increases benefits
Mistrust, bluff and suspicion	Honesty, fair play, openness
Manoeuvering and outwitting	Building a common strategy
Win this time at all costs	Building long-term relations
Sticking to limited issues	Expanding to cover total relationship
Opposite sides of the table	Same side of the table

Some examples of these two forms of bargaining include:

✦ While some western car manufacturers still squeeze their suppliers remorse-lessly to get price reductions, Japanese manufacturers have worked with suppliers to reduce costs and gain market share from which both can benefit.
✦ While one FMCG manufacturer may be rigid during price negotiations with major customers, a competitor broadens the relationship to include special delivery schedules, joint promotions, customized pack sizes and so on.
✦ While one project manager, frustrated at not getting key resources, stomps angrily out of an obstructive functional manager's office claiming they'll 'take this matter up with top management', another patiently works with the difficult manager, trying to understand why they're obstructing the project and to find some mutually satisfactory compromise.

Competitive negotiation

Although it has become fashionable to talk of turning every competitive win–lose situation into a collaborative win–win one, you may sometimes still be involved in a good old gloves-off, winner-takes-all brawl. If your opponent is determined to slug it out, you've usually little option but to go in fists flying as well. There's nothing wrong with a good get-back-to-basics win–lose nego-tiation – provided, of course, that it's you that wins!

Assuming that it's the last one left standing who wins, here are a few weapons, strategies and tactics you might want to look out for or use yourself.

A basic armory

Information

The more you know, the stronger you can appear. Conversely, one of the easiest ways of weakening an opponent is to highlight an area of ignorance or lack of knowledge of some fact, however marginally relevant this is. Once you've pinned someone down with their own ignorance, you can usually deal some fairly solid body blows before they come back at you.

Time

Understand which of you is under the tightest deadline to get an agreement. If it's the other person, then drag the negotiations out by laboriously working through the detail and watch them crumble on the main issues as the deadline approaches. If it's you, then try to move the agreement forward by setting an earlier deadline to camouflage your real deadline. Try to increase the sense of drama and time slipping away so they feel under pressure too, or else relax and bluff it out as if you don't have any real time problems.

Deus ex machina

A useful device if you're being pushed into a corner is to refer to a higher authority and claim that, although you can quite understand your opponent's point of view, you know that this higher being unfortunately would not accept the offer your opponent is working towards. As this being is not actually present at the negotiation, it's difficult for your opponent to contradict your view.

Stakeholder management

Both of you will be representing stakeholders (a company, department, project group etc.). As they're not actually present at the negotiation and don't hear the other side's position, these stakeholders can often be much less flexible than you have to be. The better you manage your stakeholders' expectations, the less pressure you will be under. The message here is to try to highlight all the difficulties you face to lower your stakeholders' expectations, so you always underpromise and overdeliver.

Personal power

This, of course, depends on you – how persuasive, charismatic, reliable and trustworthy you are, or at least can appear to be. Most people will tend to feel some degree of apprehension and suspicion when entering a negotiation. You may want to make them feel more at ease with you in the hope that they'll be better to work with. Or you could decide to take an uncompromising stance and feed their fear of losing to make them more willing to offer concessions.

Core strategic positions

Three core strategic positions you should always hold to are:

+ **Focus only on this deal**. Don't allow yourself to be distracted by talk of how things happened in the past or might happen in the future – 'Don't you think you're being a little unreasonable? In the past our companies have always seen eye to eye on this.'
+ **Never reveal your final position**, however much the other side appeals to your emotions to do so: 'If we knew where each other stood, we'd make much more progress, don't you think?'
+ **Don't allow yourself to be tricked** into going below what you have already decided will be your sticking point.

Tactics

There are endless tactics which both you and your opponent can use. Some of the more frequent are shown in Figure 18.2.

People will try to use emotion to make you shift your position – 'We've never let you down before', 'Do you think I'd be asking for x if I didn't need it?' or 'You don't think I'd have set a plan I didn't think you could meet, do you?'. Obviously, answering any of these attempts at emotional blackmail directly would be extremely dangerous for your relationship. Whatever you think, you have to defuse these potential bombs by pulling back to objective facts:

+ 'We've never let you down before' – 'I know, but perhaps this situation is different as…'
+ 'Do you think I'd be asking for x if I didn't need it?' – 'No, I'm sure you're right, but given our needs, is there some other way we could…'
+ 'You don't think I'd have set a plan I didn't think you could meet, do you?' – 'Absolutely not. But perhaps some fresh issues have surfaced since then.'

TACTIC	
The surprise low starting position	Roll with, not against, the blow
'I wanted to offer you x, but with things the way they are, unfortunately…'	*'I understand, would you prefer we broke off for now and got back together another time?'*
Real (or feigned) emotional outbursts	Claim to share their irritation
'This is ridiculous, you can't be serious! We've never had this problem before.'	*'Yes, I'm just as frustrated as you, but what can I do? My hands are tied.'*
Delaying agreement to put time pressure on you	Split the issue up to diminish the problem of your deadlines
'If we could just review some of the main assumptions again, that would let us ensure that we've all got…'	*'I think we need to reach agreement on the main points quickly, to give us time for settling all the details afterwards.'*
Using others to gain more concessions	Play the same game if you want
'I'd accept immediately, but my manager…'	*'I know, I think I have the same problem.'*
Using others to wriggle out of having made too many concessions	Play the same game or use feigned emotions to put pressure on them
'Done! Now I just have to check this with… But it shouldn't be too much of a problem.'	*'Oh, I thought we had a deal. I must say I'm really disappointed that you don't have the authority to…'*
Threats or ultimatums	Defuse them, don't counter-threaten
'I'm going straight to see X, we'll see what they think about this!'	*'Normally I'm sure they'd agree with you, but in this case they'd probably…'*
RESPONSE	

Figure 18.2   Negotiating tactics

These tactics may look like weaseling out, but once you get drawn into this kind of emotional web it's extremely difficult to extricate yourself. Generally, once you've defused a couple of these traps, the other side will see that this tactic is not working and drop the approach.

FOs, MSPs, LARs and BATNAs

One way to look at the pattern of negotiation is as a series of positions, which you need to define very clearly for yourself before you go into discussions (Figure 18.3). Failure to clarify these will often allow a smart opponent to use the dynamics and emotion of the meeting to carry you well beyond the point which you had previously thought would be your lowest.

Your Interest		
	FO	**First offer**. This can be above your MSP. But if you pitch it too far above, you risk losing credibility.
	MSP	**Maximum supportable position**. The best position you can support with the facts. Of course, you can always try to use tactics or meeting dynamics to extract an agreement better than your MSP.
	BATNA	**Best alternative to a negotiated agreement** is a point at which you would rather choose some alternative solution than the current negotiation.
	LAR	**Lowest acceptable result** is your bottom line. You should not go below this point, even though a good negotiator may use all kinds of logical and emotional tactics to take you below it.

Their Interest

Figure 18.3   You can view a negotiation as a series of well-defined posi-

Once you have worked out these positions, you're ready to start the ritual dance of negotiation.

✦ **First offer (FO)** – if you're a good negotiator you will probably want to set your first offer above your MSP. If you're less experienced, they should be near each other. Otherwise a skilful opponent will use the gap between your FO and MSP to cast doubts on your credibility and weaken your position. It can be very difficult to recover if you slip up right at the start by pitching your FO too high.

✦ **Maximum supportable position (MSP)** – the more information you have at your fingertips, the higher a position you can support. Obviously the less experienced you are, the more data you should have at your disposal. But it's not unknown for good players to bring in piles of documents (which are never actually used) for dramatic effect or to refer dismissively to all their back-up information without actually ever revealing any of it. Another tactic is to have studied one or two elements in excruciating detail and use your command of these facts to give the impression of detailed knowledge.

✦ **Best alternative to a negotiated agreement (BATNA)** – the stronger your BATNA or the more alternatives you have, the better your position. These alternatives may be real or wishful thinking. If your opponent believes they're real that's enough. But be careful if you're bluffing. You can look pretty foolish if someone calls your bluff – and if they do and you come crawling back, you're going to get a miserable deal.

✦ **Lowest acceptable result (LAR)** – know this and stick to it, unless you're offered something substantial to go below it. If you start going below it, find some way to break off the discussion so you can return better prepared next time.

Moving from competition to cooperation

You may well enjoy hammering an opponent into the ground with facts, figures, dazzling tactical moves and exquisitely timed 'uncontrolled' outbursts of emotion. But, if you're planning a long-term relationship with them, you may unfortunately have to curb your competitive instincts. In this case, you have every interest in trying to turn the situation from a competitive fight over the division of a fixed cake to collaborative working together to increase the size of the cake.

There are four main methods of moving towards this more collaborative approach.

1. Separate the person from the issue

Negotiations can very quickly move from discussions of issues to conflicts between personalities. After all, you're setting two sides up in opposition. And once people's personalities become entangled with the issue under discussion, no amount of logical argument will shift them. If you offend someone's ego, sense of justice or values, their negotiating position will tend to become more intractable.

Once you start blaming people, criticizing, shooting down their ideas, rejecting their proposals (all quite usual in negotiation), they can feel that you're attacking them and they will resent and repulse these attacks. Throughout a negotiation, try to discuss the issues productively while maintaining a very positive relationship with the other person. Until you can depersonalize the discussion and make it a shared problem, human emotions and fears will hamper progress. You need to shift:

FROM PHRASES LIKE:	TO A MORE PROBLEM-SOLVING APPROACH:
'You're five weeks behind schedule.'	'How can we get the project back on schedule?'
'You've overspent your budget.'	'Do you think we made a mistake in setting your budget?'
'Your prices are too high.'	'At that price level we won't be competitive any more.'
'Your results are below plan.'	'What do we have to do to make this year's plan?'

2. Work on interests not positions

Whatever people's stated positions are in a negotiation, these are probably just expressions of how they believe they can satisfy a few basic needs. A buyer may demand a certain price because they are trying to meet profitability targets for their products. An employee may ask for a certain salary, as they feel that to be the appropriate value of their services. A project manager may request specific key resources from a functional manager since they believe they can't be successful at a critical task without them.

Once you start moving behind the direct demands and trying to satisfy the interests underlying those demands, you can often find other ways of satisfying that interest without necessarily giving in:

✦ A supplier may deal with a request for lower prices by suggesting setting up a joint team with the buyer to improve component design and thus reduce costs, or may offer a series of joint promotions to increase sales for both parties.
✦ A manager may not be able to offer a valued employee more money due to budget constraints, company policy or whatever. However, they may be able to offer more responsibility, greater recognition or promotion. These alternatives might satisfy the employee's need to feel valued.
✦ A functional manager might not be able to make available the specific

resources a project manager asks for to work on a critical task. However, they could suggest assigning other people to help with some other part of the project and thus help free up resources to handle the critical task.

3. Generate a range of options

If you can make the issue under discussion a joint problem, you can engage your opponent in a problem-solving process. And part of such a process is applying the three main types of thinking (see Part Three  – Encouraging Creativity). Once you start working with someone on the second phase of the process (generating a range of solutions), you can quickly turn a previously confrontational situation into a collaborative one. Instead of thinking only about how much they can get out of you, your interlocutor is pushed into thinking which of a range of options is best (Figure 18.4).

Phase	Type of thinking		Main aims
1. Defining the problem	Integrative		Make sure both sides have a shared understanding of the nature of the problem and all the main influencing factors
2. Generating solutions	Divergent		Develop a number of options to choose from – don't just move logically forward to what seems like the most likely solution
3. Choosing a solution	Convergent		Working together to narrow down the options to one or two workable solutions

Figure 18.4   Negotiation can be a joint problem-solving process

By engaging both sides in a shared hunt for and evaluation of a range of solutions, you can quickly move from conflicting positions to collaborative working without either side necessarily feeling they have compromised their position.

4. Use measurable criteria

A fourth way to cross the gulf from a competitive to a cooperative approach is to refer to objective standards of comparison:

✦ If someone says they need six months to complete a piece of work, try to find a comparable task and discuss how long that took and why.

✦ If someone demands a certain price, try to work with them to establish what makes up that price or, less threateningly, show them how that price will make your products unsaleable.

✦ If someone demands certain resources, analyse with them what those resources will be doing and for how long and then work with them to see if any of those activities could be done by less key people.

✦ If someone proposes a general concession like 'we'll improve our delivery performance', ask them to help you understand how you'll both measure that they have performed what they promise.

You can also use external benchmarks (how other people have behaved in this situation), examples from similar situations and so on. The key is to keep moving from the general to the concrete. The more specific you are, the more the process of the discussion will appear to be 'fair'.

Breaking out of the ritual dance

The standard negotiation ritual goes as follows:

✦ A comes in with a high/low pitch ⟱⟹	B expresses surprise – a deal is not possible at that level
✦ A modifies their position slightly but gives a pile of reasons why can't go any further ⟱⟹	B still can't accept and starts to give all their excellent reasons why they …

And so on, until time pressure, brilliant tactics, gradual shifts of position or sheer exhaustion cause a settlement to be made or negotiations to be broken off.

But this ritual can damage your relations with the other side. There are a number of techniques you can use to try to break the ritual completely. These should be used with extreme care as they can easily backfire.

1. Offering to overdeliver

Instead of entering the dance, you cut straight to the point and say something like: 'What would I have to offer you for you to leave here with more than you expected?'

Some people might see this as a sign of weakness and use it to try to drive a hard bargain. But most people will be caught slightly off guard, will modify their demands and even come up right away with something that is not far from a position you can agree to. Closing the final small gap can sometimes be reasonably simple.

2. Changing the rules of the game

Here you state openly that you want to move from competitive to collaborative bargaining by saying something like: 'Most people would see our situation as one where one of us has to win at the expense of the other. But I'd rather we approached it as a shared problem we have to work together to solve.'

This gives the other person the choice of joining you immediately in a cooperative style of working.

3. Laying out your objectives

Standard negotiating tactics are that you should never, ever reveal your hand. However, there may be occasions when it pays to break the rules. You might start off the discussion by stating, for example: 'My objectives for today's meeting are to leave with an agreement on price at around x, delivery performance of y and a quality level of z. Does this match your expectations?'

Sometimes this kind of openness and honesty can work for you. It can drive differences out into the open and thus leave you time to work on those differences. But it can also explode in your face if the other person won't play the openness game or else thinks you're just throwing in your highest pitch in the expectation of being bargained down.

4. Revealing your secret weapon

Often people go into negotiations with some new data which they hope will blast the opposition's arguments out of the water. Sometimes this works. But sometimes the fact of dropping such a surprise on opponents causes them to react emotionally. However devastating your secret weapon, they are so annoyed at you that they refuse to listen to reason and the explosion causes almost as much damage to your case as it does to theirs.

A way round this is to be very open up front. Let them know that if you were in their position you'd ask for x, but given the new information you believe that asking for x is no longer viable.

5. Don't meet force with force

The best way of dealing with a powerful aggressor is to avoid a direct clash and instead try to use their force against them. If you meet force with force, you tend just to escalate the situation. But if you continually take their attacks in your stride by asking them to say more, to explain in greater detail what they think and to justify their position, you can wear down and weaken their assault. The more an aggressive opponent can give vent to their feelings, the more likely they are to settle on a compromise in the end. But if you cut them off in mid-flow or fight back, they'll vent their pent up frustration on you, making a compromise that bit more difficult.

Negotiation double-speak

When people say one thing in negotiation, they usually mean another. Some of the most common examples of double-speak are:

THEY SAY:	THEY REALLY MEAN:
'That's my final offer.'	'Come up with a decent proposal.'
'All our customers get those terms.'	'Give me a good reason and I'll agree.'
'There's no point carrying on this discussion.'	'We're getting bogged down, have you any ideas of how to move on?'
'I've heard nothing from you today to make me change my position.'	'You've destroyed all my best arguments, so I'm going to hide behind a refusal to listen.'
'It's been a useful session.'	'I got everything I wanted and more!'

Recommended reading

Roger Fisher and William Ury (1987) *Getting to Yes*, Houghton Mifflin (US)/Arrow (UK).

Tom E. Lambert (1995) *The Power of Influence*, Nicholas Brealey.

Robert Miller, Stephen Heiman & Tad Tuleja (1987) *Conceptual Selling*, Warner Books.

19

The Challenges of Global Management

Whether it's supporting an export order, producing an advertising campaign for a group of countries or being part of a international product design or marketing team, many managers and employees are finding an increasing international component in their work. And when you've just emerged from three days of meetings trying to develop a new marketing campaign which must be as relevant to the southern Portuguese housewife as it is to her counterparts in northern Finland (not to mention Japan, Brazil and Mozambique), you sometimes wonder if 'going global' really is the best way forward.

Some writers have predicted that we're moving to a global marketplace with global products. Certainly, there's plenty of evidence for this claim – global brands like McDonald's, Coca-Cola, Canon, Apple, Toyota and so on. Only certain products have achieved this status, but in general there is evidence that major globalization is being accelerated by a change in the political climate. Twenty or thirty years ago, the entry of a foreign company into a market was seen as a threat to national sovereignty. Now countries are falling over each other, offering grants, tax breaks and interest-free loans to attract multinational companies' investments. Attracting foreign investment is seen as a sign of economic strength, not weakness.

A new set of challenges

Sometimes the pull towards greater internationalization occurs because home markets have reached saturation point and the only opportunity for further growth is through moving to new, usually developing markets. Or else it may be that the arrival of new foreign competitors is forcing firms to find other markets.

Many firms follow a similar development pattern, starting with exporting from a home base, moving to setting up foreign sales subsidiaries or agencies, then on to establishing operating companies in main markets and finally towards managing major products globally. Within this pattern, there appear to be two generations of companies:

+ The pre-1970s generation (Lever, Kodak, Xerox, Electrolux, Ford, Philips, Procter & Gamble) who expanded gradually, often both through local operating companies in the main countries and through acquisitions. These companies tend to reflect their heritage by having quite different market positions in different countries, depending on many factors, including whether the companies they purchased had major or minor market shares.
+ The 1980s–90s generation (Canon, Apple, Microsoft, Toyota, Sony, Hitachi, Honda). These went international much more rapidly, usually without acquisitions and often with much greater consistency across their different markets, quickly achieving global presence.

As each of these companies reaches one phase, there seems to be an irresistible pull towards the next one. Many of the second generation have already achieved so-called global operations. The dominant issue for the larger western first-generation multinationals now is to catch up, by moving from a country-based structure where local country operations had a certain degree of independence to a global focus, to gain synergies from their size and wide geographical coverage. For example:

+ Several major FMCG companies have different brands with different market positions in different European countries. Moreover, where there are common brands, these often have different specifications, pack sizes, product codes etc. This has created a proliferation of product types across Europe and made achieving economies of scale extremely difficult.
+ A household goods manufacturer had been built up mainly by acquisitions. This meant it had a whole stable full of different brands in different countries and very little product harmonization. Again, there were limited economies of scale and this made it vulnerable to an aggressive competitor, which bought up a declining European brand and used this as the platform for a rapid market share expansion based on a single brand with consistent product specifications.
+ A pharmaceutical company had tended to develop products focused on its two main markets. This meant that some important export markets were not started until up to four years after the original launch of the drug, losing mil-

lions in potential sales. With increasing pressure on profit margins from national health authorities and generic drugs competition, the company will be forced to launch drugs more rapidly in all its main markets.

Trying to shift an organization from a largely country-focused situation to one capable of balancing global and local needs has proved to be a more than Herculean task for many companies. And anyone who has been involved at whatever level in the organizational bloodshed that tends to accompany this move towards globalization will know how difficult it is and how frequently it is not accomplished successfully. Managers tend to believe that there is necessarily a win–lose trade-off between local and global interests – they think that the more global a firm is, the less sensitive it will be to local market needs; conversely, the more sensitive it is to local market conditions, the less it will be able to gain the synergies of a global operation. In reality, some local suboptimization may result from a move from local to global focus for companies which are used to having a high level of adaptation to local conditions. But the success of companies such as Canon and Honda has shown that a degree of global standardization does not necessarily have to mean being uncompetitive at a local level.

When deciding to operate internationally or globally, there are three main challenges an organization faces:

✦ **Strategy** – deciding what it is trying to become (multinational, global, key market focused or whatever) and the concrete benefits it expects from this.
✦ **Structure** – working out how it is going to build an organization which can balance local market needs with corporate needs, without either side excessively dominating the relationship.
✦ **People** – finding out how they are going to manage cultural diversity, which if handled well can cause international operations to blossom, but if mismanaged can make them wither away, almost regardless of the qualities of the product or service being offered.

Strategy – how global?

The standard model for assessing the best approach to deciding the form of international operations used a simple two-by-two matrix to assess where the organization stands (see Part Eight – Developing the Right Strategy),

Pages 261–3

comparing the need to achieve global economies of scale against the need to build responsiveness to local markets (Figure 19.1).

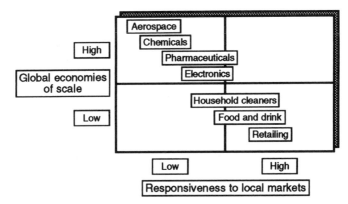

Figure 19.1   A standard approach to balancing global economies and local responsiveness

Then came the idea of the learning organization (see Part Nine – Redesigning the Organization) and a third element had to be added – how important it was to your competitive position to be able to transfer knowledge across borders (Figure 19.2).

Page 305–10

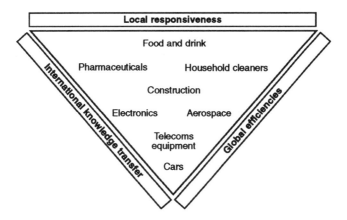

Figure 19.2   Assessing different industries against three criteria

Theoretically, using these models should help you decide how to structure your organization and where the decision-making power should lie:

- ✦ If you had to be very responsive to the local market, obviously you should have strong country organizations (e.g. food and drink).
- ✦ If there were major economies of scale, then production and control should be centralized and the countries become sales and market support (e.g. aerospace) rather than semi-independent operating units.
- ✦ If you needed a high level of knowledge transfer, then you would want a more balanced, collegiate way of working, where neither center nor countries dominated too far (telecommunications equipment or pharmaceuticals).

However, really outstanding companies don't just choose one strategy to compete – they are good at being responsive to local market conditions and at transferring information, yet are still able to gain economies of scale from centralizing some activities.

Moreover, there is an additional complication which limits the value of these 'strategy tools' – any one company or division can offer a number of brands which each have different profiles, some being single-country brands, others regional and others world brands. Several makers of detergents and white goods (refrigerators, ovens and freezers) face this issue. And clearly you cannot create a different organizational structure for each brand, although that is what the above models suggest you should do.

So while strategic models can provide some degree of guidance about how to approach globalization, for most organizations the question is much more complex than a simple 'local vs global' problem – more complicated than deciding if you want semi-independent country operations or a strongly centralized global structure. Firms have to solve the three-part dilemma of simultaneously being locally responsive; gaining global advantages of size; and having the capability to transfer knowledge and learning.

Structure

The return of the matrix

Whichever way you decide to structure a multinational, you're bound to use some kind of matrix organization (see Part Nine – Redesigning the Organization). When you have to balance the interests of countries, corporate HQ, brands, product lines, national and multinational customers, you can't escape from the matrix.

Early matrix organizations often only involved people in the same geographical location. Now, for a multinational to function effectively, organizations often ask their staff to work simultaneously for different bosses in different countries. The most usual matrix now being formed is the country/corporate model, where country brand managers report to a country marketing director *and* to a global brand manager, production managers to a country manager *and* a global supply chain manager, finance director to the country manager *and* corporate finance director, and so on.

As firms rationalize the number of production sites so that one site would serve several countries, or set up international product development teams, reporting structures become much more complex, leading to three- and even four-dimensional matrices – complex on paper and difficult to make function in reality.

If you can imagine being in the position of a production manager serving three or four countries, all with different needs, and at the same time reporting to both your local country manager and a regional supply chain manager, then you've probably got some idea of the mass of conflicting requirements you have to arbitrate between each week and how impossible it is to satisfy all your constituencies. Likewise, brand managers and project managers in international companies tend to get pulled in several different directions as a whole series of stakeholders make demands on their time or resources.

Who gets power?

The big issue in a matrix is 'Who gets power?'. If a country manager wants a certain product type for their market and a global brand manager is trying to harmonize around a different specification, who makes the ultimate decision? If a regional supply chain manager wants to rationalize four factories down to two and the sales managers in the two countries losing their local production sites claim this will damage their ability to compete, which side prevails?

In situations like these, you have three choices, all equally difficult:

✦ If you make your matrix evenly balanced, then large numbers of decisions have to be pushed up to a higher level for arbitration. This can involve truckloads of reports and endless discussions, which slow down decision making and go against the principles of delegation of responsibility.
✦ If you make your matrix unbalanced by giving decision-making power to corporate over countries, you'll create a group of country managers who feel powerless and disillusioned. They will feel that every time they or their people try to make a move, there's always someone from corporate who blocks

their actions 'in the interests of the organization as a whole'.

✦ If countries retain the final say over what happens in their territories, this can lead to country barons who tend to follow local interests, preventing the firm as a whole benefiting from its size and geographic reach.

As the trend has been to move from country baronies to global corporations, there has been a tendency to take most of the country managers' powers and hand them over to regional or corporate functionaries – brand managers, supply chain managers, R&D managers and so on. Most employees in country organizations have probably experienced this 'power grab'. Country managers talk of being responsible for factories, warehouses, sales forces and thousands of people one day and then, a month later, having only a secretary, an accountant and a couple of golf club memberships to manage – from being major figures in the community, they suddenly become expensive figureheads. Yet many organizations have lived to regret too hasty a shift to a shiny new corporately biased matrix.

The issue here, of course, is the difference between theory and practice. In theory, you may want a corporate bias to your matrix because you want to be global. In theory, the country manager's role should almost disappear. But in practice:

✦ Corporate executives can quickly become isolated from specific market needs. Usually they start with good intentions, but the sheer logistics of keeping in touch with 10 or 20 markets become physically unmanageable and they find themselves spending more and more time at HQ, only meeting other people who are also mainly at HQ. Gradually HQ develops a simplified vision of the world which drifts away from operational reality.

✦ People in a country need a local leader to relate to. It's all very well planning that all a country's executives should report to their corporate functional counterparts (finance to finance, marketing to marketing and so on). But this can remove the cohesion of the local operation – without a clear manager as a center of gravity, there is a tendency for local operations to disintegrate.

✦ Most organizations need a final arbiter on the ground in each country to help manage the continuing complexity which comes with international competition. In international organizations, reporting lines can look simple on paper but real life is messy – every day there is a continuous stream of issues, involving several functions, which need fast and locally sensitive resolution. Corporate managers at a HQ thousands of miles away or permanently on planes and in meetings cannot give the necessary speed of response. The country manager can.

The answer is not to try to meet your problems with structural solutions which will just give you a new set of headaches. Keep as close to the structure you have and work on your people's behaviors. Matrices are a way of behaving, not a structural form. If your staff can successfully operate with the duality of balancing local and corporate needs, it won't matter so much which side of the matrix holds ultimate decision-making power. If your people can't operate with the ambiguity of a matrix role or if they rigidly work for their country's or head office's interests rather than those of the whole organization, your structure will fail, however hard you work to get the right balance.

Above all, don't be too hasty in declaring open season on your country managers. In some cases you may be able to remove country managers, but in many other instances they will be needed as the linchpin of your organization – without them, the various sections can quickly begin to fall apart. And if you're a country manager and corporate have just decided to strip away most of your power – don't be too concerned. After a few very difficult months, corporate may move round to realizing that you were indeed necessary, and the pressure to continue effective operations will mean that you'll probably find many or all of your previous responsibilities drifting unofficially back to you.

What do you put where?

As ambitious, freshly appointed corporate executives look out over their new international empires, it often seems as if the opportunities are boundless. When they see 27 brands, 62 pack sizes, 10 factories, 8 warehouses, 5 market research agencies, 14 country-based finance departments and 12 customer service centers, there seems to be so much duplication. They can't help thinking of the financial benefits and the joyous career implications which will arise when they clean all that up with a good dose of rationalization.

Fortunately (or perhaps unfortunately) there are several apparently simple and powerful models to help them decide how to restructure their companies (Figure 19.3). One of the most used classifies activities against what should be centralized and what should remain close to the individual markets.

Of course, you should weed out duplicated functions and unnecessary facilities as you move from a country-based to a global organization. But some words of warning: a rationalization program which appears splendid on a cost–benefit analysis can turn out to be a nightmare in reality:

✦ **Rationalizing facilities** – it's many times more difficult to supply ten countries from five factories than it is from ten factories. Duplication may look

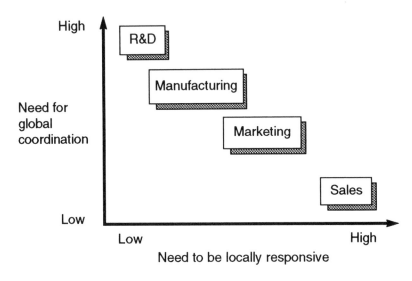

Figure 19.3   A standard way of deciding if functions should be local or
centralized

costly, but the complexity of removing it may turn out to be much more expensive. It's a logistical horror story trying to support different promotions in different countries from one or two sites, even if you have the theoretical manufacturing capacity. You only need to mess up a few deliveries to a major customer and all your so-called savings from closing factories and distribution sites will be out the window.

✦ **Moving authority to corporate HQ** – except in very exceptional cases (such as Asea Brown Boveri), corporate HQs expand. There always seems to be a good reason to add staff and each new addition will tend to generate a huge additional workload for the countries, as corporate staff ask countries to organize information collection, visits, meetings etc. The real cost of each HQ member is probably a minimum of 10–20 times their salary, because of all the extra work they generate in the countries. It may look logical to centralize certain activities, but this can also bring a slowing down in decision making and hidden costs which are in excess of any benefits.

Theory tells us which structural solutions fit which circumstances. Practice warns us to keep organization structure change to the minimum, to avoid adding complexity and to focus on developing staff's behavior so that they work in the way which best supports your global ambitions.

A multinational decided to reduce costs by rationalizing the number of production plants. Unfortunately, the main sites had high-speed, high-volume lines, which were difficult to change over to different specifications and pack sizes. At the same time, most countries had their own product specifications and pack sizes, and marketing were increasingly offering special promotion packs to defend market share against aggressive competitor activity. The result, of course, was that the inflexible centralized sites were unable to cope with the variety they were now asked to produce, the countries who shouted loudest got their deliveries and overall service levels declined resulting in a loss of market share.

Stories like this are the rule rather than the exception as firms try to cost-cut their way to global expansion. There is a more practical view: that you can only grow rapidly if you build some flexibility or slack into your organization. Then, as you put all your efforts into growth, you'll always have the capacity to respond. Successful international operations can be achieved more reliably by trying to create a self-reinforcing virtuous spiral of growth than by short-term structural surgery.

How can culture be handled?

As we move to more global organizations, the question of how best to handle different cultures becomes key. There will almost always be some degree of tension between what is best for the local market and the interests of corporate HQ. Multinationals succeed or fail on being able to manage this conflict constructively.

Building the 'globo-manager'

One way in which organizations have tried to solve the issue of different cultures is to try to ride over them by creating a core of managers who cast off their cultural heritage and replace it with the organization's. They call the process 'socialization', although other less polite words like 'brainwashing' are also used. In a sense, they're almost trying to build a new kind of person.

So you get corporate human resource staff traveling the globe, imposing the latest fashion in teamworking methods, reward and recognition systems in some countries where they are in opposition to the local culture and in others where staff yawn bemusedly as they've always worked that way anyway. And occasionally, senior executives will be yanked out of their jobs for a few days and sent on some kind of team-building course – designed, of course, around the national cultural beliefs of the HQ's country. This approach has led to some companies proudly claiming that you can recognize one of their executives anywhere in the world, because they have the company's rather than any particular nationality's behavior. This may be the correct solution to cultural differences – or it may be a resurgence of a Tayloristic scientific management approach, which tries to bulldoze over individual differences by insisting there is one right way of behaving.

Pages 4–11

Cultural diversity and untidy organizations

The two best known studies of cultural differences between countries were conducted by Geert Hofstede and Fons Trompenaars.

Hofstede (1980) compared managers in around 50 countries against three main criteria:

+ **Power distance** – the degree to which managers expect and accept an unequal distribution of power. France, for example, has reasonably high power distance and Monsieur le Directeur is regarded with respect both at work and outside, whereas in most of the Scandinavian countries a director would be seen as more of an equal by subordinates, particularly in any social (non-work) environment.
+ **Individualism vs collectivism** – how close the ties between people are. Latin countries such as Spain where the family is very important will tend to have a lower score on individualism than somewhere like Britain or North America where family ties are much looser.
+ **Masculinity (how assertive we are) vs femininity (how much we care for others)** – the US has a high masculinity score with its culture of money and achievement, whereas managers in the Netherlands show much more care for other people

Trompenaars (1993, 1994) used five criteria:

+ **Universalism vs particularism** – to what extent we behave according to set rules compared to how much we change our attitudes to situations depending on the particular circumstances.
+ **Collectivism vs individualism** – how far we follow our own interests against how much we identify our interests with those of the groups (families and organizations) to which we belong. Much has been written about the way Japanese managers are loyal to their employers, whereas western managers are probably more loyal to their own career progression and financial well-being.

✦ **Neutral vs emotional** – how openly we display our emotions. Anyone who has driven on a hot day in Rome and a cold day in Stockholm might be able to comment on the difference between the extent to which Italians and Swedes let you know what they're thinking.

✦ **Diffuse vs specific** – to what extent people are the same in all their roles (at work and in social situations) compared to how much they separate their work-related persona from how they behave toward others outside work.

✦ **Achievement vs ascription** – whether society accords people respect mostly according to their individual achievements or more because of their position, age or class.

Without going into the detailed findings (both authors are very readable), it's clear that both studies found very different beliefs and behaviors in managers in different countries. Add to that the communication problems which different languages can bring and you have a fairly significant barrier to effective international operations.

The issue for multinationals is how to manage the double cultural diversity of functional cultures (marketing vs finance vs production etc.) and country cultures (high respect for authority vs egalitarianism, individualism vs belonging to a group etc.).

Organizations have a mania about tidiness – having the same structure in Germany as in Brazil, the same reward system in France as in China, the same management development program in the Netherlands as in the US – even if this urge towards standardization and order goes against what everyone can see to be reasonable. It's obvious that someone from a highly assertive, individualistic culture may be willing to sacrifice their personal life for a rapid rise up the organization hierarchy, but that their opposite number from a family-oriented, quality-of-life-focused country might feel that the benefits from being promoted are not worth the disruption of family life through the constant relocation which promotions can bring. For the former promotion is the key goal; for the latter it is a major disincentive and not viewed as a reward for excellent service. Whereas the former would be a company person through and through, the latter may end up leaving because they feel their job is imposing too much on their personal life.

Building untidy organizations

The problem here is that organizations mix up content and process. The *content* of people's work is what you want them to do, the *process* is how they should do it (Figure 19.4):

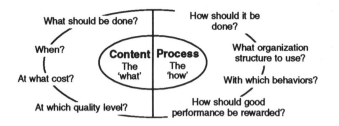

Figure 19.4   The organization may need to manage the content, but should it also dictate the process to different cultures?

✦ You may want a factory manager to run at over 85 percent utilization and to respond to all customer orders within three days (that's the content of the job and these may be quite reasonable demands). But a corporate HQ, thousands of miles away, demanding that the factory manager achieves these goals with a particular standard organizational structure and using a particular form of self-managed work teams (the process of the job) seems more difficult to justify.

✦ It's ludicrous to demand that because your division in the US spends x percent of turnover on advertising and y percent on sales promotions then all other country divisions should do the same. Industry structures and buying behaviors differ by country. In some countries (such as Britain) consumer advertising is the way to shift goods, in others (such as Italy) this is done by establishing long-term relationships with distributors and retailers. Corporate have every right to demand that a country achieves certain sales targets, but again, insisting on the detail of how these should be achieved is counter-productive.

✦ Similarly, just because successful managers in countries like the US and Britain expect to move to a new position every two to three years, this doesn't mean that everyone is equally ambitious. You can design a career path system for them if you want – but why force it into countries and cultures where it's not only not wanted, but even seen as a disincentive?

Different organizational functions can work to quite different time frames. This leads to their having quite different cultures and so they need to be organized and measured differently.

The same is true of national cultures: they must be managed differently. Corporate HQ has every right to specify what each country should deliver, just as management of a single country operation can detail what each function must produce. Corporate may even want to advise on how countries should organize to meet their targets. However, it may look logical from a comfortable office on the 25th floor of HQ that corporate should attempt to dictate organizational structures, team behaviors and local reward and recognition systems, but it defies common sense.

Successful organizations are effective, not tidy. They must allow local subsidiaries the freedom to organize how they see fit, provided that they deliver the results. The organization chart does not need to be a masterpiece of symmetry and balance, it needs to work – the two are often quite different.

Summary – cultural diversity as a strength not a weakness

In a theoretical world, where a theoretical global business could theoretically be built on certain theoretical structural principles, the role of the country manager theoretically disappears and you can theoretically all report in to switched-on corporate executives who completely understand the needs of every market and successfully reconcile these with overall corporate requirements – theoretically!

However, in the real world you allow for human nature, you build untidy organizations with a little excess capacity and you take account of local cultural differences. The country manager is the only person who can protect the cultural integrity of the local operation from the periodic corporate raiding parties on their mission to harmonize an 'unacceptably' untidy world.

And in this real world, you steer clear of technically brilliant but practically overcomplex organizational structures and you build some slack into your systems, because you realize that supplying ten countries from one factory may be theoretically possible, but practically a nightmare.

It's an organizational strength to have local operatives who are close to, understand and fit into, for example, the Italian market. And it can be a disaster to fly in cultureless corporate clones to meet key customers. Customers in Italy want long-term relationships with someone they know and can trust, not brief stopovers from busy young high-flyers, whose only concern is the signed contract and their next geographical and career moves.

So know, understand and build around the different cultures in your organization – they can be your competitive advantage.

Recommended reading

Charles Hampden-Turner & Fons Trompenaars (1994) *The Seven Cultures of Capitalism*, Doubleday (US)/Piatkus (UK).

Geert Hofstede (1980) *Culture's Consequences*, Sage.

V. Pucik, N. Tichy & C. Barnett (eds) (1992) *Globalizing Management*, John Wiley.

Fons Trompenaars (1993) *Riding the Waves of Culture*, Nicholas Brealey.

Part Eight

Developing the Right Strategy

20
Redefining Strategy

Henry Mintzberg voiced the unease which many in the west feel about our traditional notion of strategy when he claimed:

> Strategic planning is to managers what Taylor's approach was to workers. It's analytical and very mechanical, but it lacks creativity. It prevents middle managers, for example, from adding their experience to the decision-making process, despite their close contact with customers and production. (Burton, 1990)

He expanded on his concerns in his 1994 book, *The Rise and Fall of Strategic Planning*:

> Several decades of experience with strategic planning have taught us about the need to loosen up the process of strategy formation.

Other experts have been equally unhappy about how traditional strategy has been applied. In a passionately argued article Richard Pascale, co-author of *The Art of Japanese Management*, wrote:

> Strategy formulation 1) is generally assumed to be driven by senior management whom we expect to set strategic direction; 2) has been extensively influenced by empirical models and concepts; and 3) is often associated with a laborious strategic planning process that, in some companies, has produced more paper than insight. (Pascale, 1984)

And another broadside came in 1989:

> As 'Strategy' has blossomed, the competitiveness of Western companies has withered. This may be a coincidence, but we think not. We believe

that the application of concepts such as 'strategic fit', 'generic strategies' and the 'strategy hierarchy' have often abetted the process of competitive decline. (Hamel & Prahalad, 1989)

Clearly, something was wrong in the previously flourishing world of strategic thinking.

Hierarchical, mechanistic and unambitious

Many of the models and techniques which were developed to assist in strategy formulation – portfolio analysis, SWOTs, learning curves, PIMS, product lifecycles, industry structure analysis, value chain analysis and so on (see Chapter 20 – Key Strategy Tools and Techniques) – are not, in themselves, either wrong or harmful. Most are very useful ways of gaining greater clarity in complex situations and of communicating why certain courses of action have been chosen.

Pages 258–75

However, there are three main aspects of western strategy to which the critics most objected. They saw it as being:

- ✦ too hierarchical, based on the conviction that top management had the best view of the operating environment
- ✦ limited in both range and intellectual reach and too mechanistically applied
- ✦ generally unambitious, more about making small incremental changes, rather than trying to make major improvements in an organization's competitive position.

Hierarchical

In the classical model of strategy formulation (Figure 20.1), the top executives and their strategic/corporate planners analysed the environment and the firm's fit to it, identified opportunities, finalized their strategy in great detail and handed this down to the organization to be implemented.

This allowed information on the strategy to be communicated down the organization, but usually not very much information questioning the applicability of the strategy in real market conditions to pass back up the various hierarchical levels. In an environment with changing customer

Figure 20.1

needs and new opportunities arising all the time, this top-down model was criticized for being heavy, distanced from the market and generally inflexible.

Mechanistic

Many western models produced a limited range of so-called generic strategies, the most famous being the BCG matrix for portfolio analysis (Figure 20.2). These generic strategies were accused of being too limited, unimaginative and mechanistically applied.

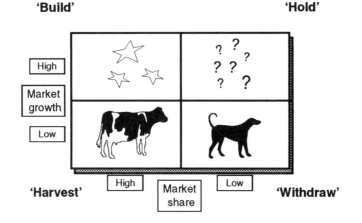

Figure 20.2   How portfolio analysis can lead to four generic strategies

It isn't difficult for managers to build a portfolio of their businesses and apply one of four proposed strategies depending on which box of a two-by-two matrix each business happens to fall into. What would be more challenging would be for them to plan to build and grow all their businesses, regardless of market and competitive situation.

Unambitious

Many strategies seemed to be based on finding a fit between the organization's capabilities and market opportunities, rather than seeing what the opportunities might be and setting stretching targets for the organization to achieve. They were all about standing still ('sticking to the knitting') instead of reaching out to learn new skills.

From strategic planning to strategic intent

In blasting away at the western application of strategic theories, many critics took what they called the Japanese approach to strategy as an alternative model. Gary Hamel and C.K. Prahalad (1989) compared western 'strategic planning' with Japanese 'strategic intent'.

Pages 4–11

Strategic planning was based on executives making a realistic assessment of what an organization could achieve and then planning in great detail how that strategy should be implemented. And the strategy that was most likely to be accepted by top management was the one with the most financial and other detail, as quantity of detail was often taken as an indication of quality of strategic thinking. Moreover, the top-down, hierarchical nature of strategic planning often meant that the final outcomes were of little relevance to most of the organization:

> The strategy hierarchy undermines competitiveness by fostering an elitist view of management that tends to disenfranchise most of the organization. Employees fail to identify with corporate goals or involve themselves more deeply in the work of becoming more competitive.

Strategic intent, on the other hand, requires top management to set a series of goals for the organization and to help develop the networks and skills to achieve those goals. But it is up to the various levels in the organization to work out precisely how those goals will be reached.

Using the examples of the rapid success of Komatsu, Matsushita and Canon in a whole series of market sectors, Hamel and Prahalad point out that, when you don't have a position in a major market, it is difficult to be precise about how you will dominate it in just a few years. But what you can do is to set a target for the organization (for example Komatsu's 'surround Caterpillar' or Canon's 'a copier for $1,000') and through a series of steps – improving quality, gaining economies of scale, product redesign, JIT production etc. – gradually build up the organization's ability to reach that target.

From machine to brain again

This is far from a debate about semantics. It gets to the heart of how we view organizations and their members (see Part Three – Encouraging Creativity):

Pages 73–85

+ as part of a well-organized machine, designed to carry out whatever strategies are programmed into it (however relevant those strategies are to the real world which is constantly changing), or
+ as a thinking organism (a brain) which can use its detailed knowledge of the marketplace and competitor activity to work out how a particular ambition can be realized.

There are still too many organizations in which an isolated central power group decides (with little consultation) which way the organization should go. And there are far too many managers who find themselves forced to implement (or at least give the impression that they're trying to implement) policies and plans which they know are inappropriate:

+ the FMCG country manager, forced by short-term corporate profit requirements to sell off (closer to giving away) a factory which he knew would set up as a competitor two months later making own-label products for supermarket chains
+ the cardiac surgeon who had to allow her patient list to be swallowed up by another hospital, because the hospital strategy no longer included cardiology as a 'core speciality', even though she knew that once the hospital lost cardiology, it would no longer offer a full range of services and would therefore become vulnerable to losing other specialities
+ the pharmaceutical project manager who had to spend millions on a series of clinical trials which she knew would give no results, because the powers-that-be had decided to embark on a poorly thought-through attempt to prove that the drug was more effective than potential rivals
+ the factory manager pushed to making staff redundant to satisfy a corporate plan to reduce employee numbers, even though he knew that a planned increase in production shift work would make him reemploy the same people, but hidden away as temporary, not permanent, headcount.

All these recent cases are typical examples of the top of an organization not only saying in which direction it must go, but also exactly how it must get there. People at middle and lower management levels were not given the discretion to decide how a policy (reduce labor costs, improve profitability, prove a drug's efficacy, maintain a self-financing cardiac department) should best be implemented.

For a strategy to be effective in today's conditions, it must move from being a centrally developed detailed plan, cascading down to each operating level, to becoming a corporate direction or ambition which operational levels must refine and apply as best suits their individual circumstances.

One of the more eloquent descriptions of this way of defining strategy came from Kihachiro Kawashima, who became president of American Honda. Explaining Honda's start-up in the US he said:

> In truth, we had no strategy other than the idea of seeing if we could sell something in the United States. It was a new frontier, a new challenge, and it fit the 'success against all odds' culture that Mr. Honda had cultivated... I reported my impressions to Fujisawa – including the seat-of-the-pants target of trying, over several years, to obtain a ten percent share of U.S. imports. He didn't probe that target quantitatively. We did not discuss profits or deadlines for break-even. Fujisawa told me if anyone could succeed, I could and authorized $1 million for the venture. (Quinn, Mintzberg & James, 1988)

The attack on traditional ways of formulating and implementing strategy has led to a simplistic, but useful, division of strategic approaches into two opposing schools (Figure 20.3). Although these two schools don't actually exist, the purpose of the comparison is to illustrate through opposites where strategic thinking was 20–30 years ago and how it is developing today.

Traditional view	Modern approach
• Keeping up with the competition, following them when they cut costs, improve quality, advertise more etc.	• Find new ways to compete – new alliances/technologies/product offerings
• Carefully planned to the last detail, all eventualities thought through	• Direction is clear, the people will fill in the detail
• Based on 'strategic fit' – what the firm is currently capable of	• Assumes the organization wants to learn and improve
• Primarily aimed at increasing shareholder wealth	• Contains goals which are meaningful to employees
• Built on the assumption that top management are the only group with a holistic view of the business and so the only ones qualified to give worthwhile input	• Knows that top management must set out the ambition, but also that those close to customers, production, development and distribution have valuable input to give as to the means of achieving the ambition
• Assumes the organization will do as instructed	• Understands the difficulties in changing the way an organization behaves
• Sees the organization as a series of business units	• Views the organization as a whole, where one part can help another

Figure 20.3   Two opposing views of strategy development and implementation

Like other aspects of organization (structure, people management, leadership style etc.) the way we view strategy must evolve with the way organizations' environments are evolving. As we move from the organization as a bureaucratic machine to the organization as a brain (the learning organization; see Part Nine – Redesigning the Organization), we must also adapt our concept of strategy.

Page 305–10

The implications – competing on processes

If we accept the general idea of strategic intent or strategic direction, then our concept of how to compete should change. We should move away from a slightly static view of competition – market share, differentiation, low cost, core competences, what an organization achieves – towards focusing on business processes – how an organization operates. We must shift our attention from the expected *results* of our work to the *processes* we use to achieve those results.

For example, using a strategic planning mindset, if we decide to be a low-cost competitor we will organize our people and control systems to reach a low-cost position. When shifts in competitive conditions occur, we will continue to pursue our low-cost strategy because our whole organization has been set up to achieve this.

However, with strategic direction thinking, we would tend to set goals such as being the major company in an industry or being the most innovative competitor. We would then try to layer in the business processes and behaviors necessary to succeed. These would be aimed at developing flexibility through techniques such as sharing of knowledge, building teams and networks, looking for strategic alliances, devolving responsibility and clearly communicating our corporate vision. Here we would not be restricted to a limited series of competitive weapons such as low cost or differentiation or constant product innovation, but would be able to use all of these. We would build up and add to our organization's abilities, rather than narrowly directing our existing skills at a limited goal.

Many traditional telephone companies, for example, have used a strategic planning approach and aggressively cut costs to become low-cost service providers. But they have been outclassed by competitors who have used internal growth and alliances to develop their ability to integrate a range of technologies to compete on a wider base and in a larger number of markets, including business services and cable-supplied entertainment.

Successful organizations are turning away from competing on specific strategies to competing on business processes, away from restricting and directing their people towards concrete goals and toward building capabilities and ways of working so that they can achieve more ambitious results. Thus the focus of managerial effort is moving from defining the strategy ('what we must become'), to building the skills to achieve more than the organization believes it is capable of.

Abandoning core competences

In their desire to maintain clarity and control, many western companies have split themselves into strategic business units (SBUs) or even separate legal entities, aimed at different products or markets. There are obviously many advantages in this. It shows unambiguously where profits  are being generated, allows clear management accountability, assists in allocating capital between businesses and ensures that no area's underperformance is masked by another's market success.

Pages 269–70

However, because business units are seen as almost independent from each other, this control-based split can have a number of harmful side-effects:

✦ it is difficult for knowledge to move between business units, so some units will be unaware of useful developments in other units and will either not benefit from them or duplicate them

✦ the organization will dispose of some units which in isolation appear to be unprofitable but which actually contain some knowledge or experience essential to another part of the business. For example, having disposed of all their color television manufacturing as a mature market unable to compete with Far Eastern (usually Japanese) producers, many western consumer electronics companies found that they had also lost the skills to compete in the video recorder market.

From a control and focus point of view, division into SBUs makes sense. However, this approach sees the organization as a collection of entities whose only common denominator is cash. It takes no account of synergies between business units. For example, part of a business may not be generating cash, yet it may own a technology or skill which other parts need. Standard 'cash-based' portfolio models would tell you to get rid of this business and instead invest your money in a 'star'. However, you shouldn't judge each part of an organization on its own – it also has to be viewed as part of an overall structure. Rather than paring itself down to some limited 'core competence', an organization must identify what skills and technologies it needs to compete, then acquire or retain those skills and technologies and ensure that there are mechanisms to spread them across its business units.

Car manufacturers who have completely subcontracted engine design and manufacture, makers of computers and other electronic devices who no longer have any control over the design and production of microchips, video recorder producers who buy most of their components from competitors or independent suppliers – all are examples of organizations which have made themselves extremely vulnerable by relinquishing control over critical areas of their business. All are now dependent on the goodwill and competence of suppliers, who are often also competitors on end products. And all are probably living on borrowed time, as it is often suppliers and competitors who decide the terms and costs on which they do business.

Summary – a trip down memory lane

Reviewing some of the strategy tools which were once seen as imparting almost divine wisdom can sometimes seem like visiting a museum of seventeenth- and eighteenth-century household appliances – you look at all kinds of strange contraptions and wonder if people ever really used things like that.

As an example of the fragility and potential shortcomings of some of the traditional strategy tools, you could, for example, take the BCG matrix (Figure 20.2) and, quite logically, reverse all the definitions of how you should react to each market situation. This would, of course, lead to you adopting policies diametrically opposed to those traditionally proposed (Figure 20.4).

Under one view you should milk your cash cows and pour cash into your stars. Yet, in the alternative reading, you should bang investment into the areas you know well (cash cows) and avoid stars like the plague, because you can always pick them up cheaply secondhand when someone else has burnt their fingers.

A final, but damning, criticism of this portfolio management approach is that three (divest, hold, harvest) out of the four generic strategies are passive or defeatist – they're all about withdrawing, biding your time or running away. Only one (grow) is aggressive. And none of these generic strategies mentions concepts such as rejuvenating a market through innovation or technology. If three out of four western companies are choosing surrender strategies, it is no wonder much of our industry is limping painfully towards its grave.

Quadrant	Traditional definition	Alternative view
Cash cows	Generate a lot of cash due to strong market position. As their markets are static or only growing slowly, they don't need a lot of investment. Drain off their excess cash and pump it into your stars.	You have a strong position in a static market. You have production facilities, distribution, knowledge of your customers – in fact a good basis on which to build. Try to revitalize the business you know well instead of risking your future on the ever hungry stars.
Stars	Strong position in fast-growing markets. Invest here as they will be the future of your firm, even if they're not profitable in the short term.	These are the fast-growing markets. These always attract a rush of competitors, overcapacity, low market share for everybody and losses for most. Keep a low profile, let others take the start-up pain and move in to buy cheaply when someone else has had enough and wants out.
Question marks	Weak position in growing market. Generate little to no cash due to poor position. Can be turned into stars with sufficient investment.	A weak position in a growing market, which is about to be flooded with eager new entrants. Sell your business quickly to someone dazzled by the market growth. It'll be a while before they realize that all they've got is a very hungry dog in an oversaturated market.
Dogs	Weak position in static market. The only market share that can be gained is from other competitors as the market is not growing. Divest!	A weak position in a static market. Your competitors are probably complacent, they've underinvested for years and they may even want out. Attack aggressively – remember, pianos, ball bearings and zippers were dogs until Japanese companies saw the potential.

Figure 20.4   By looking at each quadrant in a different way, you can reach the opposite strategies to those originally proposed

Recommended reading

John Burton (1990) 'Management mania: how Professor Henry Mintzberg discovered the "bottom up" approach and came out on top', *Scanorama Magazine*, September.

Gary Hamel & C.K. Prahalad (1989) 'Strategic intent', *Harvard Business Review*, May–June.

Gary Hamel & C.K. Prahalad (1990) 'The core competence of the corporation', *Harvard Business Review*, May–June.

Gary Hamel & C.K. Prahalad (1994) *Competing for the Future*, Harvard Business School Press.

Henry Mintzberg (1994) *The Rise and Fall of Strategic Planning*, Prentice-Hall.

Kenichi Ohmae (1983) *The Mind of the Strategist*, McGraw-Hill (US)/Penguin (UK).

J.R. Quinn, H. Mintzberg & R.M. James (1988) *The Strategy Process*, Prentice-Hall.

21

Key Strategy Tools and Techniques

This chapter runs through some of the basic tools used in strategy analysis and formulation. Although the previous chapter questioned the top-down, inflexible approach used for developing strategy in many command-and-control organizations and the limited number of unimaginative strategy options which they often resulted in, the basic analysis techniques can still be valuable and effective, if used in the right way.

The challenge for many organizations in the past has been to assess 'What markets are we in?', 'What is our market position?' and 'How can we best compete?'. For these kinds of questions, rather mechanistic tools like SWOTs, portfolio analysis, two-by-two matrices, lifecycle curves, industry structure analysis and value chain analysis are excellent in helping managers analyse, understand, communicate and react to complex situations.

However, as the issue for organizations moves away from 'How do we compete today?' toward assessing 'What must be changed in order to keep ahead of the changes in our environment?' and 'How do we prioritize, coordinate and manage these changes?', many of the standard analysis techniques are turning out to be unhelpful. New tools are beginning to emerge (such as 'to be' mapping and master change planning), but there is still very little available to help organizations develop appropriate strategies when to survive they are necessarily in a constant state of, sometimes very rapid, change.

Charting strengths/weaknesses/opportunities/ threats (SWOTs)

Although probably the most basic analysis method, SWOT diagrams can still be a powerful way of quickly laying out the main features of a situation. With its simple structure a SWOT diagram can give rapid clarity to relatively complex issues.

Constructing a SWOT consists of drawing a cross, creating four sectors and then entering the strengths, weaknesses, opportunities and threats of a situation in the relevant quadrant (Figure 21.1).

STRENGTHS	WEAKNESSES
• What are you good at? • What new skills does your organization have? • What can you do that others can't? • How can you repeat a recent success? • What makes you unique? • Why do your customers come to you?	• What are you not good at? • What skills does your organization lack? • What can others do better than you? • What recent failures have you had? Why? • What customer groups are you not satisfying fully? • What customers have you lost recently? Why?
OPPORTUNITIES	**THREATS**
• Have there been any changes in your market in your favor? • What skills could you learn? • What new products/services could you offer? • Which new customer groups could you reach? • How could you make yourself unique? • How could your organization look in 5–10 years?	• Have there been any changes in the market which disadvantage you? • What are your competitors up to? • Are your customers' needs changing against your interests? • Are there any economic or political changes which can harm you? • Is there anything which could threaten your organization's existence?

Figure 21.1   The kind of questions you might ask when constructing a SWOT

A particular strength of a SWOT is that it forces you to look, not only at your strengths and opportunities, but also at the reverse – weaknesses and threats. Too many strategies are developed with tunnel vision, based purely on what top managers want to do, without looking at the potential risks and downside:

✦ Would Barings have risked more than the bank's assets on just one series of investments if they had really weighed up the risk they were taking to earn another £20–30 million in profit?

✦ Would private investors have been so eager to put their money into the Channel Tunnel if they had looked at the risks – the poor payback which most large-scale construction projects give and the debilitating cost of compound interest on repayments to banks if there were delays in starting full services?

✦ Would a major cleaning products company have launched a new washing powder, claiming it was 'new' and 'more powerful', if it had fully considered

that the same claim had been made at least once a year for the last 30 years
for their own and various other powders?

When developing a SWOT, ensure you consider both the organization's internal aspects and the external environment:

INTERNAL	EXTERNAL
Structure	Competitive position
Marketing, production etc.	Macroeconomic trends
Cooperation between functions	Changes in customer needs
New product development	Suppliers' situation
Finance	New technologies
Ability to innovate	Social trends
Speed of reaction	Political events
Human resources	Competitor moves
Level of technology	Regulatory changes
Management capability	

SWOTs can be built by individuals, but they are particularly effective when
done by a group. They can help move people from quite different functions,
and with quite contrasting views, much closer to a common understanding of
a situation. You should also stretch your people a little and have them make
SWOT charts for your main competitors and customers. These may open up
a whole new series of opportunities and threats which your internally based
analysis did not reveal. This is particularly true with SWOTs done on your
major customers.

A supplier to supermarket chains had tended to treat its largest five
supermarket chain customers similarly. By doing a SWOT on these main
customers, their different market positions and needs became more
apparent. This helped the supplier develop a different key account strategy and service offering for each of them.

As with any analytical tool, SWOTs can be misused:

✦ By including just one person's or one small group's views, they can be tailored to justify an existing strategy rather than being ambitious in trying to
   think of new and innovative opportunities.
✦ Depending on your point of view, many apparent threats can also be opportunities. Complacent managers tend to see many threats, for example the
   pressure for environmentally friendly products, as out of their control, while

more motivated people would seize them as opportunities and offer products and services built around an ecological selling proposition.

✦ SWOTs can sometimes allow managers to adopt comfortable 'fit' strategies, rather than ambitious stretch targets. It's too easy to look automatically at the strengths and opportunities, choose a few opportunities which match your strengths and hey presto!, you have your plan.

Portfolio analysis and other two-by-two matrices

Chapter 19 discussed the strengths and problems with the BCG portfolio analysis matrix. Another portfolio management matrix was also used in the 1960s – the General Electric (GE) matrix. Jointly developed by the American General Electric Company and consultants McKinsey and Co, this was used to assist in dividing GE's 190 departments into 43 strategic business units (SBUs). There are two main differences from the BCG matrix:

Page 250

✦ the two axes (competitive position and industry attractiveness) are built up from a number of characteristics – for example, competitive position is a combination of market share, profit level, management ability, production capability and technological strength

✦ businesses or products are shown by points or circles, whose size shows their respective sales turnover.

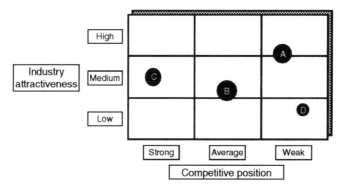

Figure 21.2   The GE matrix

Although supposedly an improvement on the BCG matrix, it is arguable whether by making the two axes combinations of variables (rather than the simpler market growth vs market share on the BCG matrix) this matrix was any more useful. Probably they both shared the same weaknesses – too mechanistic, generating too few strategy options and usually used as a substitute for, instead of an aid to, imaginative thinking. Moreover, this approach to strategy generation could become a wonderfully satisfying self-fulfilling prophecy, in which events always proved you made the right choice. For example:

✦ You're unlikely to put your best managers in charge of a supposed 'dog' and you're not going to plug much investment into it. So given your managerial and financial neglect, it's bound to perform badly, thus proving what you always thought – it really was a dog!
✦ If you milk your cash cows, starving them of investment and management attention, they can hardly grow – once again, your belief that they had no potential will be confirmed.

One useful spin-off from these and other portfolio analysis models was the wonderfully flexible and now omnipresent two-by-two matrix. These matrices are excellent ways of quickly classifying a lot of variables to present a much clearer picture than a verbal description could. Two-by-twos can be used for almost anything. For example, you could use brown papering, process analy-

sis, brainstorming or whatever to generate a number of opportunities for how a key business process could be improved (see Part Three – Encouraging Creativity). To help you plan how to move forward, you could lay out the opportunities on a two-by-two matrix (Figure 21.3), either as points or as circles, where the size represents the size of the improvement opportunity.

Then, depending on your priorities (getting early wins vs fixing the main issues vs focusing effort on the maximum benefit areas), you can start to prioritize the issues on your improvement plan.

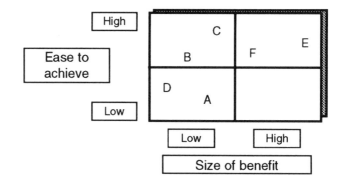

Figure 21.3   Classing improvement opportunities on a two-by-two matrix

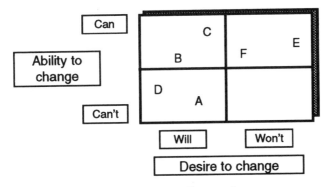

Figure 21.4 Using two-by-twos to classify people

Or you can use two-by-twos for classifying people (Figure 21.4) or other firms. You could plan how to deal with groups of staff – you would take a quite different approach with those who 'want to change but can't' because of skill or personal reasons, than you would with those who 'can change but don't want to', perhaps because they believe they will lose power, prestige or influence.

Likewise, you could use this classification to help you work out how to deal with various competitors – you might seek an alliance with, or try to buy, one who is small, 'has the technology skills but not the finance'. Or, you might try to sell your skills to one who 'has finance but low technology skills'. You would keep your eye on the one who 'has both the financial and skill capability' to benefit from the technology change, as they theoretically represent the greatest threat.

Industry structure analysis

First proposed by Michael Porter at Harvard Business School (1985), this analysis is aimed at understanding the basic drivers of the level of profitability in an industry. Five forces were identified as driving industry structure and thus profitability (Figure 21.5) – level of competitive rivalry, the power of buyers and suppliers, the barriers to entry into the industry and the availability of substitute products to those offered by the industry in question.

Depending on the relative strengths of the five forces, different industries will have different levels of profitability. For example:

✦ **Competitive rivalry** – if there are a large number of competitors, profitability will tend to be low; if competitors have built up large manufacturing facilities they need to fill, this will tend to drive down prices and profitability.

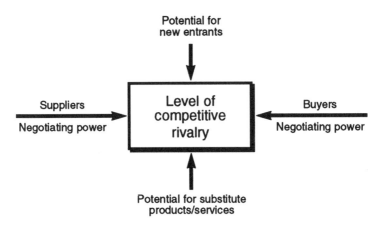

Figure 21.5   The five main forces driving industry profitability

Political reasons may keep a competitor in an industry (Airbus) and this can push prices down; or products may be so similar (gasoline) that price cutting is one of the few ways of competing.

+ **Supplier power** – if suppliers have control over a critical resource (gold, diamonds), if it would cost a lot to switch from an existing supplier to a new one or if the industry is not an important customer for those suppliers, then suppliers will tend to extract significant profits from the industry.

+ **Buyer power** – buyers can take profits from an industry if they take large volumes from that industry, if they can easily switch suppliers or if they can threaten backward integration (buying a source of supply).

+ **Substitutes** – either there can be direct substitutes for an industry's products (rented accommodation is available if builders raise new home prices), or else there can be substitutes for the same expenditure (food, entertainment and travel all compete for our spending). If, for example, music companies raise their prices too much, people switch their spending to another area. Obviously, the greater the availability of substitutes, the lower the profits in an industry will tend to be.

+ **New entrants** – even if an industry has little internal competition, low buyer and supplier power and few real substitutes, it may not be able to achieve high profitability if it is easy for new entrants to come into the industry. Many industries manage to maintain high profitability by keeping out new entrants through building 'barriers to entry' – high cost of setting up manufacturing plant (chemicals), access to potential consumers blocked by incumbents filling up supermarket shelves (FMCG and food), government restrictions keeping out potential competitors (airlines) or high brand power (Sony).

If, as with pharmaceuticals, there are no real substitutes to what the industry can offer, there are extremely high cost and regulatory barriers to entry, there has been limited competition within each therapeutic area and if (as has been the case until recently) buyers and suppliers have had little bargaining power, then profitability for all players in the industry can be very high. Even so, buyers are starting to gain power and regulatory authorities are under pressure to bring down the cost of medical care, so profitability is starting to decline.

The breakthrough which this model provided was in clearly and simply linking a firm's strategy to the features of its market. This helped take strategy development away from an excessive internal focus on a firm's various functional departments.

Standard strategy formulation proposes that once a firm has an understanding of these five forces driving profitability, it can start to build a strategy to give it above average profitability for its industry, by:

✦ trying to influence one of the forces – for example, setting up alliances with powerful suppliers, customers or competitors, or trying to influence the availability of substitute products

✦ choosing a low-cost supplier position – being able to supply an equivalent product to other firms, but at a lower cost through better design, production, distribution or marketing

✦ differentiating its product sufficiently from the competition (extra features, performance, service, reputation or strong branding) so that buyers will be prepared to pay a premium price for its products.

Of course, an aggressive firm will build a strategy including all three of the above options. It will look for advantageous alliances, while at the same time differentiating its product and seeking internal efficiencies to bring the cost down. This would allow it to fight on cost or on differentiation or both.

Japanese cars made rapid inroads into many markets through offering high quality at a low price. When volume restrictions were imposed on them, they had sufficiently differentiated their products (through quality and extra features) that they could raise the price and extract maximum profits from the number of cars they were allowed to sell. They also used close relationships with suppliers, quality and feature differentiation *and* cost advantages to enable them to compete on several levels simultaneously.

Product/industry vs needs lifecycles

There are two main lifecycle methods – a traditional, rather mechanistic view of the way markets develop (product/industry lifecycles) and a more challenging way of looking at how needs are satisfied by different products and technologies over time (needs lifecycles).

Product/industry lifecycles

This is the more well-known, standard approach. These lifecycles can be useful in helping an organization formulate an appropriate strategy depending on whether an industry is in growth, maturity or decline or whatever (Figure 21.6).

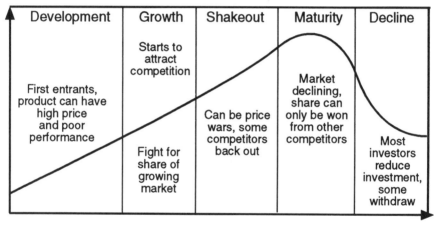

Figure 21.6   A standard industry lifecycle diagram

The assumption here is that the competitive conditions will be different at each stage of the lifecycle. For example:

✦ **Development** – the product/service will be bought by 'early adopters'. They tend not to be price sensitive and so profits can be high. On the other hand, investment in developing better performing and more mass-market priced versions can be high and will generally soak up profits.

✦ **Growth** – the market starts to expand, new competitors are attracted in and firms jostle for position. Pioneers will try to maintain their leading position, but new entrants may have advantages because they are not burdened by pioneers' high start-up costs and they can learn from these organizations' mistakes. Although the market is growing, price wars may break out as firms try to establish themselves as leaders. Typically, many newer and lower-price product/service versions will follow each other rapidly, each one adding to the market size.

✦ **Shakeout and maturity** – market growth starts to slow and plateau. There are fewer new variants on the product/service and most changes are now cosmetic. Some competitors will treat their investments as cash cows, others will aggressively invest in marketing to gain some share points, others will cost-cut to ensure that expensive manufacturing plant is kept busy.

✦ **Decline** – sales fall off, competitors withdraw or allow their participation to wither away (as dogs) or sell out to other companies. And when everyone else has given up the sector as a lost cause, some imaginative firm exploits a new technology or shift in consumer taste to launch a whole new lifecycle.

It is possible to mechanize further what may already seem like a fairly mechanistic process for analysing your strategic position. The grid in Figure 21.7 helps you compare your competitive position to the stage of market lifecycle and then, depending on which sector you fall into, a number of alternative strategies are available. A summary of this approach can be found in Johnson & Scholes (1988).

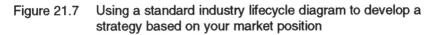

Position	Development	Growth	Shakeout	Maturity	Decline
Strong		Dominate by cost, new versions and marketing		Defend through low cost and distribution power	
Average				Treat as cash cow or find profitable niche	
Weak		Catch up through innovation		Milk then sell	

Figure 21.7   Using a standard industry lifecycle diagram to develop a strategy based on your market position

At first sight, this may seem like producing strategy by a simple spreadsheet program rather than using one's brain. Moreover, by assuming that events must inevitably follow a certain lifecycle pattern, this approach can be accused of being defeatist and leading to predictable, rather than creative and regenerative, strategies.

Needs lifecycles

A more productive way of using the lifecycle concept is to develop needs life-cycles. Here the assumption is that consumers (individuals, private or public organizations) have certain needs which they want to satisfy (entertainment, education, transport, social interaction, generating information etc.). Different products will satisfy these needs at different times.

The key is to avoid focusing on your particular product and believing that it will continue to satisfy a particular need for ever. Technologies will develop, demographic profiles of the population will evolve over time, the political environment will tend to swing between different power groups and tastes will change. Instead of fighting to protect your particular product, fight to ensure that you continue to satisfy the need which you currently know how to meet. Because, even though the way a need is satisfied may change, the skills and knowledge required to meet the need are often similar, putting existing competitors at a great advantage if they are broad-minded enough to understand this.

> Many television manufacturers saw themselves as being in the mature market of TVs and not in the growing market for home entertainment. So they abandoned the market, only to see it explode into growth with video recorders, home computers and in future HDTV (high definition television). The skills of producing televisions – electronics, screen technology, consumer marketing etc. – were relevant to these new ways of satisfying the home entertainment need. Now some firms who left the television and VCR markets are trying to get back into HDTV, but they have largely lost the skills, technical knowledge and component manufacturing infrastructure which they need.

Looking at markets as satisfying a core number of basic needs, rather than centered around specific products, has major implications. You can no longer blame your fate on a supposedly 'mature' or 'declining' market – if you are in trouble, it's because you failed to anticipate the next way of meeting a particular need.

Segments, not just new customers

There is another variant of the lifecycle model which is also critical for developing strategy. Standard lifecycle analysis proposes that markets develop, grow, plateau and decline. What really happens is much more subtle and offers much more opportunity for the firm that understands the process. Markets don't just add and lose customers – they add and start to lose customer segments.

Using a 'segment' approach, you view the market lifecycle as consisting of a process of new customer segments (rather than just new customers) joining and leaving a market (Figure 21.8).

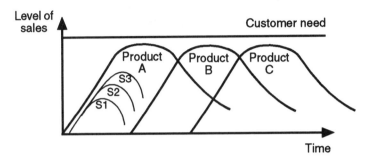

Figure 21.8   Markets change in size as different segments join and leave

Each segment will have different reasons for joining and leaving a market. To be successful, you must tailor your offering to match the needs of each new segment. Organizations which think in terms of new segments and not new customers will most successfully meet each new segment's needs.

Consider electronic calculators. There is a basic need for mathematical calculation. At one time this was satisfied by slide rules, logarithm tables and mechanical calculators. When electronic calculators were introduced, they were first bought by scientists, then engineers and accountants, followed by students and general businesspeople, consumers and finally schoolchildren. What is obvious from this example is that firms which continued to produce better and better calculators for scientists, engineers and accountants (and there were some firms which did that) had no hope of ever tapping into the additional segments which joined the market. These later segments were not just an expansion of the customer base (as a traditional lifecycle model would suggest) but groups which had quite different product and price expectations to the earlier segments.

Those companies which did stick to the specialist early segments were usually forced out of business. Firms which adapted to all the joining segments built up such economies of scale and experience that they were able to dominate the mass market and then fight the specialist manufacturers from a lower-cost position, driving them out of the market and gaining the high profitability which the specialist segments could offer.

Value chain analysis

Value chain analysis has become much more frequently used as organizations go from viewing themselves as a grouping of functions to conceiving of themselves as a series of customer-facing processes. Constructing a value chain consists of identifying the sequence of 'direct' activities – those that directly add value to the customer – and 'indirect' or 'support' activities – those that enable the 'direct' activities to take place (Figure 21.9).

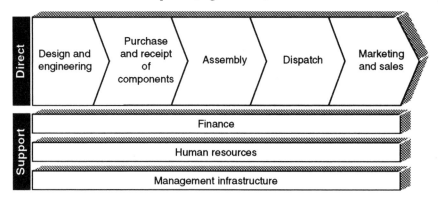

Figure 21.9   Value chain for a car manufacturer

Value chain analysis can be used in a number of ways: to improve effectiveness, manage costs and value, control support costs and provide differentiation.

Improving effectiveness

As discussed in Chapter 23 – Don't Restructure – Reengineer, many of the most valuable improvement opportunities in an organization come not from improving individual functions, but from better linkages between the activities running across the business to serve the customer: better coordination between purchasing, production and sales, for example, or greater understanding between design, production and marketing. By focusing attention on the activities which deliver value to the customer, value chain analysis provides the basis for ensuring that the key linkages are functioning effectively.

Managing costs and value

Once you start to record the costs of each activity and the value it provides to the customer, you can see if there are any imbalances – for, example, an activity which costs a lot but delivers little customer value. Questions need to be asked: Can the costs of that activity be justified? Can it be done some other way? Or more effectively by someone else?

You may also find that some activities cost relatively too little. The whole process of design and assembly of cars sometimes only accounts for 30–40 percent of the production cost. This means that some manufacturers are contracting out 60–70 percent of their added value. Yet most of their managerial attention is concentrated on the internal 30–40 percent and there can be insufficient focus on the subcontracted 60–70 percent.

Other organizations carry out all the activities on a value chain for historical reasons – they've always done them, so why change? In many cases, it can make sense to subcontract some of these activities to another organization – to reduce cost, to improve quality, to create extra capacity for peak periods or to allow management to focus on higher value-added areas.

Controlling support costs

Anyone familiar with the Peter Principle (in a bureaucracy, people will always rise to their level of incompetence) and Parkinson's Law (work will expand to fill the time available) will suspect that administrative costs will continue to rise without necessarily giving any improvement in output. Putting costs on the value chain can help you identify the cost of non-value-adding support activities. And it is more than likely that these are already too high and somehow are still growing. You can then set some targets for support cost and service levels and start to manage these towards a more appropriate balance.

Providing differentiation

In any industry, you can only achieve profitability above the industry average if you provide the product/service for a lower cost or if you manage to differentiate your offering so that customers will pay more for it. Too often, firms focus on the final product as the only source of differentiation. But in many cases, breakthroughs occur when a firm chooses another part of the value chain as a source of differentiation. For example:

✦ One of IBM's innovations and strengths during the era of mainframe computers was its ability to offer more varied financing arrangements than competitors.
✦ Marks & Spencer has always managed to maintain a reputation for higher quality products because of the unusual strength of its buying departments.

Linking value chains

Performance improvement and/or differentiation do not need to come only from within the organization. Often you can achieve considerable change by linking value chains in a new or better way:

✦ **Links to suppliers** – a car manufacturer wanted to reduce component costs, as it was under competitive pressure and components made up 70 percent of the car's production cost. By building more involvement of suppliers' engineers into major component design, component cost reductions of 10–20 percent became possible.
✦ **Linkages to buyers** – a flooring manufacturer was under considerable price pressure from its customers, the wholesalers. They in their turn were finding that the costs of large stockholdings were eating away their margins – yet if they tried to reduce stock or variety, they risked losing customers and sales. By working with its customers, the manufacturer set up a 'hub and spoke' system of stockholding, whereby slower moving items would be held by wholesalers at only a few central depots or by the manufacturer who promised replenishment within a 24-hour period. Faster moving items, which needed next-day delivery to customers, would be held at all depots. This eased both the stockholding costs for the wholesalers and the price pressure on the manufacturer.

Process time analysis

Few organizations realize the disruptive effect which too much time taken up by their business processes can have on their ability to serve their customers. Of course, some effects are obvious – excessively lengthy product-development cycles prevent you from competing effectively and overlong delivery leadtimes build up stock and block your ability to react rapidly. But too much time in a process can have a negative multiplier effect on almost all aspects of an organization.

In most business processes (manufacturing, delivering a service, developing a new product etc.) the percentage of process time during which value is added for the customer is seldom more than 1–2 percent. The rest of the time is spent waiting, being scheduled, being moved and so on. But each of these delays adds more than time to the process, it adds uncertainty and cost. For example, the longer ahead a forecast is made, the more inaccurate it is likely to be, so the more stock has to be carried to offset forecast inaccuracy. This in its turn requires more purchasing, more materials handling and storage, giving greater potential for error – in fact, it creates a whole series of costly trans-actions, which would be reduced if forecast horizons could be shortened.

Many organizations try to deal with the issue of forecast inaccuracy by acquiring ever more sophisticated forecasting tools, which may help. But the real solution is to work on reducing the time between forecast and delivery – for example, by linking your production-planning systems into those of major customers, instead of trying to second guess what they will be producing or selling in six months' time.

A similar concept could be used for new product development. Developing new products faster is not just to do with launching new models faster, it also significantly reduces the cost of development and increases the chances of success. For example, the longer it takes to develop a new product, the more likely it is that the work done in the earlier stages of development will be wasted, as it takes place long before the eventual launch. By reducing the development time, this work is reduced. The shorter the time between design and launch, the lower the risk of mismatch to customer needs.

To take another example, the longer ahead hospital operations have to be scheduled, the more chance there is of a patient's condition deteriorating, of cancellations and changes, of extra administration and medicine.

Excess time leads to a vicious spiral of unnecessary transactions (work, parts purchasing, stockholding, meetings, reports, administration, studies etc.). Most organizations underestimate how much unnecessary time there is in their processes and what this is costing in cash, decreased competitiveness, reduced customer focus and lowered productivity. By applying tools such as process analysis (see Part Three – Encouraging Creativity), they can identify where value is really being added in a process and, of course, where it is not. Time when value is not being added is not just 'neu-

Pages 95–7

tral' time. As the above examples show, dead time adds uncertainty and cost – it thus destroys value.

'To be' mapping and master change plans

This technique starts to address the issue of how you build up a strategy for an organization which is already in a state of continual change. It is a dynamic, rather than static, view of the organization's opportunities.

A 'to be' map lays out the key aspects of an organization's operations and requires managers to visualize how each must develop over the coming few years (Figure 21.10).

Activity	Next 2 years	2–4 years	4–6 years
Customer service	New customer service function operating	Customer queries down to 0.05% of deliveries	Service staff on customer site at 5 top accounts
Technology	30% of added value coming from electronics	Alliance formed with microchip manufacturer	Product development time down to 18 months
Human resources	Project management training for 30%+ of staff	People's bonuses 50% for project and 50% for functional work	Restructure around customer segments
Sales and marketing	Key account management in place	50% of budget in direct sales support	Sales and marketing functions combined
Production	Consolidated to 7 sites	Consolidated to 5 sites	Consolidated to 3 sites

Figure 21.10   Part of a 'to be' map

Once you have produced a clear picture of how each of these main areas must develop, you can do a comparison with their existing state, identify the size of the gap between actual and wished-for state, estimate the degree of change required and the likely benefits, and build up a master change plan for the organization (Figure 21.11).

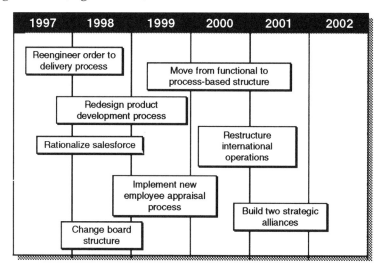

Figure 20.11   A simplified master change plan

The power of 'to be' maps and master change plans is that they help you visualize chronologically all the change programs you will have to manage. Also they can assist as a communication tool to help all an organization's members understand how a series of improvement initiatives fit together.

Summary

This chapter has presented only a few of the basic strategy tools. As methods for understanding and communicating complex situations, these tools can be extremely powerful. However, they must be used to focus and stimulate people's thinking and not as a replacement for imagination and effort. If there is one weakness in most of these tools, it is that they tend to see situations as static – most organizations are already in a constant state of change and there are usually several existing improvement programs.

So the challenge for many organizations is less one of analysis of current markets or organizational competences and more one of knowing how to combine, coordinate and prioritize all the initiatives into a coherent and ambitious program aimed at maintaining corporate health and employees' jobs. It is in this area that sufficiently powerful strategy tools are still not available.

Recommended reading

Gerry Johnson & Kevan Scholes (1988) *Exploring Corporate Strategy*, Prentice-Hall.

L.J. Peter & R. Hull (1969) *The Peter Principle*, William Morrow.

C.N. Parkinson (1986) *Parkinson's Law*, Penguin.

Michael E. Porter (1985) *Competitive Advantage*, Free Press.

G. Stalk (1988) 'Time: the next source of competitive advantage', *Harvard Business Review*, July–August.

Part Nine

Redesigning the Organization

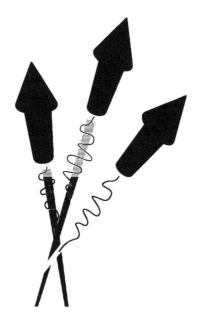

22

Going Beyond Structural Surgery

It's difficult to start a chapter on organizational structure without repeating the well-known but timeless quote from the Roman satirist Gaius Petronius. In AD 66, almost two thousand years before our current obsession with how our organizations are structured, he wrote:

> We trained hard – but each time we began to work effectively as a group, we were reorganized. I learnt later in life that we have a tendency to meet each new situation with reorganization and also what a wonderful method this is of giving the illusion of progress when it only results in chaos, ineffectiveness and demoralization.

Most people in organizations have suffered from managers who are afflicted by an almost manic urge to reorganize. Some organizations swing from centralization to decentralization and back again. Others toy with devolving responsibility and two- or three-dimensional matrices and then either boldly head off towards project teams or, having burnt their fingers, retreat back into a good old-fashioned hierarchy. Yet others are more direct and go for the throat, launching waves of delayering, restructuring, downsizing and rightsizing (when 'right' always means smaller). Eastman Kodak downsized three times in six years, Honeywell twice in four years (Burrough & Helyer, 1990) and in many other organizations (Ford, General Motors, the British coal industry) cutting staff can sometimes seem like a yearly or biannual ritual. The recently privatized British utilities (telephones, gas, water and electricity) are celebrating their new-found freedom by a veritable massacre – 40,000 people out of one, 20–30,000 from another and tens of thousands from the others.

Faced with a problem or a change in the marketplace, it's too easy for managers to reach for the weapon of reorganization. After all, if you really believe that any problem can be solved by shifting around the boxes on the organizational chart and reducing the number of staff, then why not?

We all want an organization that is adaptive, entrepreneurial, innovative, empowered and open to change. When we're constantly told that the way to achieve this is to strip out headquarters like ABB, run project teams like 3M, have team-based factories like Procter & Gamble and build cross-functional networks like Honda, the temptation to grab at the restructuring panacea becomes almost irresistible. We're told it worked in other companies, so why shouldn't it also work for us?

Confusing structure and behavior

Since the 1960s an immutable truth within strategy and organization design has been that 'strategy drives structure' (Figure 22.1).

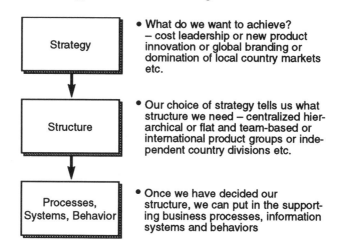

Figure 22.1   The classical view of how strategy defined structure

It was believed that if you wanted to be the lowest-cost producer, then you needed top management pressure, a clear hierarchy and tight control systems to drive down cost. If you had ambitions of establishing a global brand, then executives would split that product off into its own SBU and measure its financial performance. If you wanted to be close to local markets, then you built your structure around local country barons.

When organizations were driven by central control and were less reliant on how their people were motivated, this model may have worked. But now managers are looking for new attributes – flexibility, risk taking, empowerment, innovation – which are based on people's behaviors. And these cannot be structured in. You can structure your organization so that certain brands are managed globally to ensure consistency across markets – but you cannot, for example, put in a central control system to ensure that managers are delegating.

Of course, there are times when you have to reorganize. Heavy hierarchical structures, with their ponderous reporting and control systems, can stifle initiative and ambition. But axing the structure is not guaranteed to encourage the new behaviors. What is so frequently overlooked is the extraordinary effort that organizations such as ABB, Matsushita, Apple and 3M have put into changing their people's behavior and attracting staff with the right personal as well as technical qualities.

Extremely competent, motivated and open-minded employees can usually work their way around an inappropriate structure, although this is inefficient and wasteful. However, sycophantic corporate careerists, whiling away the time until unearned, well-rewarded retirement, are not going to turn into competitive tigers just because you shake the organizational structure around a bit.

Managers' thinking has to shift in focus from the classical 'structure follows strategy' to a new model, where business processes and people's behaviors help define the way they should be organized (Figure 22.2).

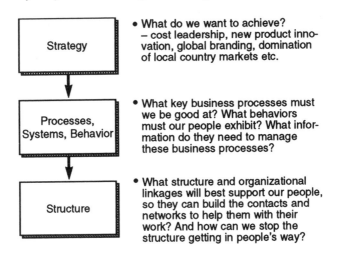

Figure 22.2   Building structure around processes and behavior

In a sense, our whole concept of the role of structure must be changed. Over the last 60–70 years, structure has been a way of organizing and controlling unreliable human beings to reduce the number of errors they made and to increase their productivity. Limits, controls, boundaries and efficiencies were its aim.

Now that people are starting to be viewed as of added value, as being able to contribute with their flexibility and ideas, the structure should be targeted more to enabling and less to controlling; although of course some element of control has to remain. The issue is to get the structure of the organization out of people's way and, where possible, to use it to support staff.

Where we've come from

Before looking at what structure to choose and how to implement it successfully, it may be worth quickly reviewing the five most common building blocks of organization design.

Primary organization

Small, owner-run companies are theoretically close to the market, responsive and able to change quickly. However, they are totally dependent on the personality of the owner – if he or she refuses to or is unable to adapt to a changing market, then the organization will probably disappear. The fact that about 70 percent of small companies fail within two years shows the vulnerability of these structures.

Functional organization

Division into functions is usually the first step after a primary organization has started to grow. People are grouped by functional skill – finance, R&D, manufacturing, marketing etc. – to gain economies of scale and good communication between functional specialists.

The functional structure starts to break down as an organization moves into new products/services and new market areas. The specialized functional groups are usually seen as too unresponsive to deal with the different demands of differing markets. The main problem is likely to be that once any function grows beyond a certain size, its focus turns inward on itself and it starts to treat requests from the areas it is meant to serve as irritating distractions from its own routines. In one aircraft factory the administration is said to have kept on not only functioning but actually growing, two years after the last plane was produced.

Product organization

When functional structures start to become unwieldy, many organizations split

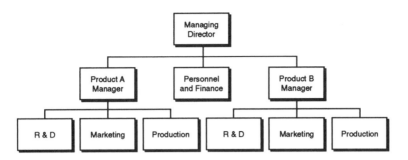

Figure 22.3 A simplified product organization

up according to products/services or market sectors (Figure 22.3). This can imply a duplication of functions (for example, each product may have its own finance department, though they could also share some functions). However, it also gives a greater focus on the organization's outputs and, by bringing together people into groups with a shared interest, should improve information flow and decision making.

Divisional structure

Divisional structures were popular in the 1970s, when the move was away from large corporate control centers and towards creating semi-autonomous strategic business units (SBUs) (Figure 22.4).

Pages 255–6

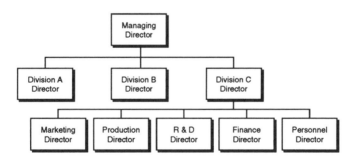

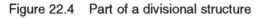

Figure 22.4 Part of a divisional structure

By splitting an organization up into divisions, cost and profit responsibilities are passed down to the divisions which act almost as independent companies. The role of the center becomes one of setting strategy (deciding which divisions to keep, acquire or divest) and acting as an internal capital market (allocating investment between divisions).

The move to divisional structures has recently been attacked by some experts as a failure. They have accused managers of being unable to support increasingly complex organizations and of seeking simplicity by carving them up into 'manageable' and more easily measurable units. Moreover, the SBU structure tends to create a short-term mentality, as each unit tries to maximize its individual profitability and ability to attract corporate investment – synergies between units (particularly development and use of new technologies) usually suffer.

Matrix organizations

All organizations function to a greater or lesser extent as matrices. People in any function or product group will inevitably have contacts with departments or teams outside their group. What formal matrix organizations did was to bring the duality of people's roles to the surface and try and find a structural solution. If you were in the product design department and worked simultaneously on three projects, the matrix tried to lay out your reporting relationships. Figure 22.5 shows a simple matrix where country managers are the ultimate decision makers, but their functional managers are each supported by a series of centralized corporate functional areas.

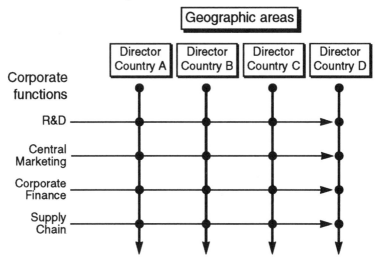

Figure 22.5   A matrix structure where the country managers have more power than the corporate functions

As a theoretical model, the matrix seemed a good solution. Some experts claimed that if people could relate to two parents, then they should also be able to work for two managers. In reality, many people find it extremely stressful trying to balance the often conflicting demands of, for example, a local hierarchical and a corporate functional manager.

Another problem was that the matrix could become stupendously complex. For example:

✦ You're in a British advertising agency's creative department. You're assigned to two local country accounts, another one for a pan-European client and one worldwide account run from New York.
✦ You work in the global product design area, but live in and are paid from France. You are part of the electronics group whose manager is in Switzerland. And you're working on one local French project, a worldwide new product and also as part of a team trying to upgrade your organization's electronics skills.

In cases such as these, deciding who owns your time and who evaluates your performance can start to look like a Kafkaesque nightmare.

Matrix organizations were once heralded as the 'great breakthrough' in organizational design. However, too often the structure was imposed with little effort given to encouraging appropriate behaviors. When they are successful, matrix structures can be exciting, dynamic and innovative places to work. When they fail, people feel that they spend their time in endless, decisionless meetings and that there is constant conflict between the two sides of the matrix.

In fact, as with teams and networks, there is a question about whether matrices are really a form of organizational structure. Most probably, all three are ways in which people behave, within what may be another structural form.

Do you really want to tear it down and start again?

There are two approaches to reorganization.

The 'iconoclasts' tend to write about reorganization rather than doing it and are all for flattening hierarchical structures, ripping out bureaucracy, throwing everybody into fast-moving entrepreneurial teams and networking. 'If you're not reorganizing today, you're dead tomorrow' seems to be their motto. Theirs is a kind of kneejerk reaction – they seem to be saying that everything you did before must be wrong and it all needs to be thrown away.

In their proselytizing, they're quick to seize on what's different about successful organizations, often proclaiming that they've found the new organizational Holy Grail, and they are prone to glossing over what has actually remained stable in those organizations. And they tell you which structure you should adopt, although few stick around to share with you the painful process of implementation and the often even more painful process of coping with the after-effects of a theoretically ideal, but in practice unworkable, structural model.

The 'realists' understand that organizational development is a cumulative process. As organizations grew, small groups started to coalesce into hierarchies and then gain efficiencies of knowledge, different areas specialized in specific activities (finance, manufacturing, sales etc.) and formed what came to be called 'bureaucracies'. At no point in moving to a bureaucracy were small groups and hierarchies abandoned. They were simply built into the next structure.

Save the hierarchy and the bureaucracy?

Hierarchies are not in themselves bad. Nor are bureaucracies (which are simply the splitting of people into specialized functions). What is important is how people *behave* within these structures. A small team of overambitious empowered entrepreneurial managers who hijack a large organization (for example many highly leveraged management buyouts) can be just as dangerous as a smothering, control-obsessed bureaucracy.

A cross-national study of management (Hampden-Turner & Trompenaars, 1994) suggested that managers in the three 'economic miracles' (Japan, Singapore and Hong Kong) believed that their organizations were very hierarchical, while those in two less successful economies (the US and the UK) thought that their organizations were quite flat. This may seem to defy conventional wisdom – after all, aren't we constantly told a thousand times that we need flat organizations if we are to transfer complex information and be flexible to market changes? And haven't many western companies spent the last ten years ripping out supposedly excess layers of management?

In fact, hierarchies seem to be used in different ways in the west compared to the east. In the west, the hierarchy is too often about control. Managers believe they know best. Strategies and commands are thrown down from above. The hierarchy splits functions one from another and makes cross-functional working difficult as each function pursues its suboptimal local goals. And there are few channels allowing information, which may challenge orthodox thinking, to rise up through the structure. In the east, the hierarchy is aimed more at integrating information so that the right decisions will be made. Each level accepts that the level below may have valuable insights and experiences to offer. Managers see their job as bringing together a wide range of information from different functions and helping their people to interpret it correctly. Western hierarchies tend to control, eastern hierarchies are targeted more at coordination (Hampden-Turner & Trompenaars, 1994).

Many Japanese companies are quite clearly split into the traditional functions we know so well. They get round the problem of narrow functional specialization not by doing away with functions and replacing them with cross-functional teams, but by continually moving managers between different functions so that they gain a broader viewpoint and also develop their own cross-functional networks. But this, of course, only makes sense if managers are planning to stay for some years. When, as in the west, some managers see each company as a brief stepping stone in their careers, it's obviously not worth the investment to give them this wider range of experience and so many never graduate beyond a narrow functional range.

So what should change?

However flat, innovative and market responsive you want your organization to become, you're still going to want some degree of hierarchy and you're always going to require some level of functional excellence in your core skill areas. But, at the same time, you have to build back in to the larger organization the sensitivity to the market, entrepreneurial spirit and willingness to take risks which are more likely to be present in small groups. Some degree of reorganization can remove many of the barriers to achieving the required behavior change:

✦ **Small groups** need to be reemphasized to foster the productive, motivating and innovative power of teams and networks (see Part Five – Building Effective Teams). This means focusing on developing cross-functional teams based on business processes and encouraging information- and experience-sharing networks.

✦ **Hierarchies** should be reduced. Information technology has decreased the need to have multiple levels, all reprocessing data for the levels directly above and below. Deprived of their *raison d'être*, excess levels will try to create new work and controls to justify their existence. New reports and coordination activities suddenly start appearing. These need to be stopped and the excess levels removed.

✦ **Functions** should be opened up as the organization's focus turns from vertical command and control toward horizontal customer-focused business processes. Functions are the guardians of your core skills (manufacturing, medical knowledge, technology, marketing ability etc.). While you may want to break down the restrictive power of the functions by moving their people into cross-functional teams, you're unlikely to abandon functions completely, as doing so would probably lead to a rapid erosion of your core skills.

An aerospace company puts as many staff as possible on to project teams. But it still gives staff a 'functional home' (avionics, airframe design etc.), otherwise it will lose these critical competences.

Likewise, an FMCG manufacturer may start building key account teams, but it will still maintain functions such as marketing, distribution and production as there are economies of scale from these skills being applied across all customers.

Structures which are clear and can function effectively don't abandon hierarchies and specialized functions. Instead, they reduce the power of functions and supplement them with teams to give them powerful cross-functional, project- or customer-focused goals (Figure 22.6). And they reinforce information-sharing networks, both within and outside the organization, to enable adaptability and learning.

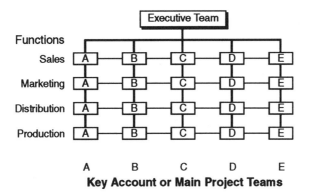

Figure 22.6   Most customer- or project-based organizations will still need to retain functions to grow core skills

When do reorganizations succeed?

1. When you ensure a fit between structure and all the other elements of your organization

Obviously there's no 'one right structure'. Different environments, industries and tasks require different structures:

✦ A franchised fast food operation, which must give exactly the same product/service offering as 50,000 others in the same chain, will clearly not be looking for a loose teamwork structure in which everyone can use their initiative. Here control has to be tight, everything the staff say to customers (even down to how and when they smile) is carefully scripted and the product must be completely standard.

✦ A leading-edge research department, on the other hand, will clearly need a looser, more collegiate than hierarchical environment to encourage experimentation and exchange of ideas.

So one aspect of fit is finding the right structure for the task at hand. Most models of fit try to match structure to the complexity of the task and to the rate of change in the environment (Figure 22.7).

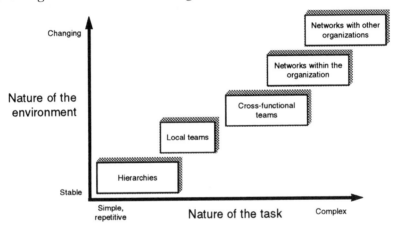

Figure 22.7   One model for fitting structure to task

The second aspect of ensuring structural fit is having consistency between structure and the other elements of the organization – reward systems, behaviors, goals, management reporting. When a structure is misaligned with any of these elements, confusion and ineffectiveness usually result:

✦ A well-known branded products company wanted to 'globalize' its brands. Rather than create a whole new management level of global brand managers, it decided to give its current country managers a dual role. In addition to being in charge of the operations in their country, now each would also be responsible for a global brand. However, in making this change the company left the bonus system unaltered. Naturally, country managers focused primarily on what they were measured and rewarded on – their country's performance – and the global brand manager role took second place and was seen as unsuccessful.

✦ A food manufacturer put self-managing teams into its packing areas. Unfortunately, almost all its problems originated in areas before and after packing. Being unable to affect these areas, the teams quickly became disillusioned. No benefit was gained from the new structure until the manufacturer opened up the rest of the organization and implemented the improvements which problems in the packing area showed were necessary.

Clearly, there is no point in developing self-managed teams if they have no power to cause change or if you're constantly pressuring them to increase productivity. Similarly, it's fruitless to start up project teams if people don't have the information they need (schedule adherence, costs, milestone achievement) to manage the projects effectively. And you can't expect employees to give their hearts and souls to your total quality program if their bonus system only rewards them for output and lumps together grade one, two and three products as having equal value in a situation where it's easier to churn out tons of grade three product than it is to produce grade one.

2. When you manage to deal with the organization's internal diversity

Most managers have experienced organizations which are confused by their internal differences. Some of the most classic are:

✦ Sales believe marketing don't understand the customers and marketing can't understand why sales are so unappreciative of their latest campaign.
✦ Production believe sales will promise customers anything to make their monthly targets, however much this disrupts schedules, yet sales cannot see why production always has such problems with delivering on time.
✦ It's obvious to production that a new product design is impossible to turn out, but engineering are exasperated by production's apparent inability to make some simple changes in manufacturing processes.

In an attempt to overcome these barriers, some managers have tried to impose a single structure and reporting system on all areas – usually with little success. Another approach has been the clumsily named but useful concept of 'differentiation' and 'integration'. The basic concept is rather obvious in theory, but frequently overlooked in the rough and tumble of organizational life:

✦ **Differentiation** – different functions will have different skills, goals, time horizons, behaviors and so on. You would hope, for example, that an accounting department in an advertising agency would not have the same attitude to its work as the so-called creative group. To cater for these differences you must allow for different structures, measurement systems, cultures, etc. – you must differentiate between areas, encouraging rather than trying to suppress their differences.

+ **Integration** – given that you have to manage all these differences, you need integrating mechanisms to enable such diversity to work effectively together. These mechanisms can be things like management action, coordinators, shared planning and information systems, project or customer teams, weekly or monthly meetings and setting common organizational goals.

The kinds of timescales which different departments work to, for example, can show the radically different attitudes they have to their work and give an indication as to why they often have so much trouble understanding each other. While research departments operate in terms of years and product design in months, both the operating horizon and speed of reaction required from production planning and machine operators can be as short as days and minutes respectively.

Why do reorganizations fail?

The main reason for reorganizations not delivering the expected results is that they were never a realistic solution in the first place. If you really need behavior change, then change behavior – don't waste time playing Chinese checkers with the organization chart. But, while you're changing behavior, ensure that your organization structure enables, rather than hinders, the behaviors you want.

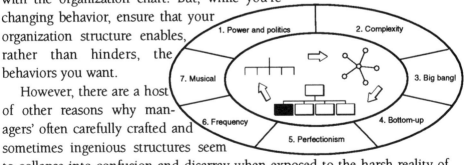

However, there are a host of other reasons why managers' often carefully crafted and sometimes ingenious structures seem to collapse into confusion and disarray when exposed to the harsh reality of operational life. These can be called the 'seven deadly sins of reorganization'.

1. Power and politics

Reorganizations will inevitably involve a redistribution of power and influence.

Those who believe they might lose out will fight to retain whatever power they think they have, while those who should be about to gain power may have less influence currently and thus less influence over the course of the reorganization.

You need a very powerful negotiating process to prevent a reorganization from being hijacked by those who are currently most powerful or most vociferous. Otherwise you end up with a botched solution – a new structure but with power still, inappropriately, in the hands of those who had it in the first place. It's not unusual to see an organization that has moved to project teams, but these team leaders have no access to top management. During the reorganization, executives caved in to functional manager pressure and let the latter keep their cherished positions on the management group, thus excluding the project managers.

2. Complexity

Many situations are so multifaceted that if you did try to build an organization to cope with them, the structure you would end up with would be almost baroque in its intricate complexity. It would also be unworkable. There are many organizations where the organizational chart is so involved that even mid-level managers can't explain clearly how it all hangs together. There comes a point when you have to stop looking for structural solutions to complexity in the operational environment.

3. Big bang!

Often executives are so pressured or so keen to have their new structure in place that they go for the 'big bang' implementation approach. This means making the structural changes quickly and simultaneously throughout the organization. This can be successful, but more often than not it isn't. The big bang approach means little time to prepare people, no time for piloting, testing or refining, and it tends to lead to top management forcing a structure on employees without allowing front-line workers to adapt it to their particular circumstances.

Moreover, big bang implementations tend to be based on the view that once the new structure is in place, everything else will work – hence the urgency to get the structure in. If you believe that structure must be a result of required processes and behaviors, then the big bang approach, with its focus on a structural solution, must be wrong.

4. Bottom-up

However much you may want to empower employees, you cannot leave the whole design to front-line staff. They probably lack a holistic vision of the organization's direction and they are unlikely to propose designs which put them personally in a worse position, even if this is in the interests of customers and the organization as a whole. Any design requires a combination of clear top-down direction and contributions from those at the coal face, who will have to make the structure work.

5. Perfectionism

Another frequent lapse is management's desire to have all the detail covered – reporting lines, job descriptions, reward and recognition systems, information systems support etc. Assembling all this can take 2–3 years and by the time you're ready, you're either drowning in detail or else the environment has changed and your fabulous structure is no longer appropriate anyway.

6. Frequency

If you've just put in a new structure 2–3 years ago and another one 2–3 years before that, the likelihood is that neither has had the chance to settle down and work properly. Some business gurus claim you should reorganize every year or so to remain competitive – but most Japanese companies have remarkably stable structures and many of them are quite a bit more competitive than western companies. Moreover, few organizations can focus effectively on serving their customers if they're continuously buffeted by restructuring, however well meaning. Disorganization inevitably reduces the value which employees can add.

7. Musical chairs

Finally, many so-called reorganizations are just like a game of executive musical chairs, only they never reduce the number of chairs available to support the players. In fact, they sometimes add new ones by creating fine-sounding but meaningless new posts. A few top executives and their hangers-on shuffle around taking new positions and titles, but little really changes. This is all about 'jobs for the boys'. Long-servers who aren't up to it any more are put out to pasture by being given supposedly 'non-critical' positions.

Although executives often announce these as great steps forward, usually nobody in the organization is fooled and these 'reorganizations' just lead to cynicism and apathy. But much worse, these games of musical chairs can jeopardize an organization's future. For example, when the good old boys are put out to pasture, they're given the jobs that, in the past, have not been critical. But times change. Positions which were not key to the organization can suddenly become its heart and soul. Distribution in FMCG, licensing in pharmaceuticals, subcontractor management in aerospace, purchasing in car manufacturing – all these have recently moved on to center stage as market requirements have changed. And in all of them, you can often find people quite unable to cope, who were shunted aside to those positions when the posts were not considered important. These people, through their inaction, limited abilities and lack of motivation, are often unwittingly destroying whole organizations.

Back to behaviors

The main structural issue facing most organizations is how to maintain a clear, workable structure, while moving more to a style of working which is customer focused and operates via cross-functional teams. Some firms are trying to solve this with purely structural solutions. Others are experimenting with a mix of structural and behavioral change. Many fail because, while restructuring to focus more on customers, they destroy people's involvement by grabbing quick savings through staff reductions.

Given the complexity of some structural solutions it is likely that success will go to those organizations which put the emphasis more on changing behaviors. Rather than relying on structural rearrangement, these organizations are building in matrices, teams and networks in different areas.

✦ Matrices – being able to deal with ambiguity and balance the demands of two or three activity areas.
✦ Teams – knowing how to work effectively in a multiskilled and, to some extent, self-managed group.
✦ Networks – having the skill and motivation to communicate openly with and seek ideas from many individuals both within and outside the organization.

Matrices, teams and networks are not replacements for structure – they are the small group behaviors which must be put in place within the structure to achieve the innovation, empowerment, entrepreneurship and responsiveness which most organizations want. You don't replace your divisional structure with teams – you strengthen it by improving teamwork within it and by building networks with other divisions to share knowledge and experience.

Toward the virtual organization

The concept of the organization itself is becoming looser. Only a few years ago you could clearly see the boundaries of most organizations, but now those boundaries are becoming less obvious. Many organizations are linking their value chains – Procter & Gamble with K Mart and Marks & Spencer with its suppliers being two well-known examples. Other organizations are forming strategic alliances with former competitors – Lucas and Bosch, British Aerospace and Matra, Apple and IBM, and for a time Volvo and Renault. Others are linking themselves to firms in complementary sectors, such as Disney and McDonald's. And some private sector companies are aligning themselves with public sector organizations – for example, drug companies are offering disease-management services to the British National Health Service.

Quite simply, organizations are realizing that they can no longer survive alone, and that it is more effective and economic to form alliances than always to try to acquire the technologies or market openings which they need.

A similar situation is developing in the area of competences. A few years ago, most organizations would have met a skills shortfall by hiring the appropriate resource. But today many have understood the increased flexibility and economic benefits of subcontracting in specific skills merely for the time they are needed. This has led to rapid growth in the numbers of freelance staff and a corresponding decline in full-time employment. There has also been an explosion in services such as IT facilities management as organizations seek to contract out activities not seen as core. Up to 70 percent of the value of most cars, for example, is now made by suppliers, with the end product manufacturer only being responsible for overall design, final assembly and marketing. Likewise, pharmaceutical companies are starting to contract out services such as clinical trials to small, specialized companies so that they themselves can concentrate their resources on the discovery and development of new drugs.

Summary – where we're going

Many organizations seem to have tried every structure under the sun – not always with the greatest of success. But their managers are not yet giving up the search for the perfect structure. Now there's much talk of new organizational forms – clusters, clover leaf structures, the donut organization, adhocracies, heterocracies, the information organization, the virtual organization and more. Managers should think very carefully indeed before trying to load one of these ingenious, but often theoretical, models on to their long-suffering staff.

Some trends in design are fairly clear and quite positive:

+ a continued shift from static functions to project teams assembled only for the life of the project and disbanded at its end
+ a move to align structures more to customer-facing business processes and less towards functional specialisms
+ a rebirth of matrices (although probably under another name) as organizations try to balance the many different elements of their operations, such as the benefits of local responsiveness with the synergies of large size, with the advantages of being ahead in leading technologies and with the economies of scale of centralizing some less customer-related activities
+ a further increase in alliances, either joining several organizations' value chains together or else sharing technology between companies to gain mutual advantages.

Some of these moves, for example building alliances, becoming more team based and aligning to customer-facing processes, are very valid ways to improve an organization's competitive or regulatory position. But there are others, such as a hollowing out of organizations as they try to look for ways to contract out activities not seen as core, which may in some cases be more management copouts than real structural improvements. So when managers talk of 'removing functional structures' or 'outsourcing all but core activities', you need to ask yourself: Have they found a real solution to a real problem? Or are they just hoping for yet another structural 'miracle cure' to all their ailments?

Reorganization has too often been a substitute for effective leadership. So look carefully at the latest reorganization plans to see if they're just repeating the easy errors of the past – if they've caught the 'restructuring disease' yet again.

Recommended reading

B. Burrough & J. Helyar (1990) *Barbarians at the Gate*, HarperCollins (US)/Jonathan Cape (UK).

Charles Hampden-Turner & Fons Trompenaars (1994) *The Seven Cultures of Capitalism*, Doubleday (US)/Piatkus (UK).

Charles Handy (1976) *Understanding Organisations*, Oxford University Press (US)/Penguin (UK).

23

Don't Restructure – Reengineer

When faced with the challenge of how best to restructure your organization, one answer is, of course, to keep whatever structure you already have. This is probably no better or worse than any alternative, and at least it's familiar. So, instead of looking to a new structure as the answer to most of life's problems, consider improving the *flow* of products, services and information through your existing structure. Instead of reorganizing your organization chart, reengineer your business processes.

Business process reengineering (BPR) will probably emerge as one of the most influential management theories of the 1990s. It has been described by critics as 'Big Personnel Reductions', 'the fad of the moment' (*The Economist*, 2 July 1994) and as a 'rebottling of well-known industrial engineering methods, which had been around for 30 to 50 years' (Harvey, 1994) – while supporters describe it as a way for managers to 'reinvent their companies' and as 'the fundamental rethinking and radical redesign of business processes to achieve dramatic improvements' (Hammer & Champy, 1993).

It is generally agreed that the concept emerged during a study conducted by the Massachusetts Institute of Technology (MIT) from 1984–9 into best management practice. But MIT professor and consultant, Michael Hammer, is normally credited for bringing the idea to a wider market in a 1990 *Harvard Business Review* article and then in the co-authored best-selling book *Reengineering the Corporation*.

If we believe that markets are more turbulent and that the rate of change is accelerating, then we must accept that effective processes will be critical for organizations. In a time of change, it is not market position or financial muscle which gives competitive advantage, but rather the ability to move quickly into markets, develop products and services faster and seize opportunities before the competition. Strategic success has moved from being based on static power to

Pages 248–57

depending on sensitivity to the market, adaptability and speed of reaction – and these come from effective and flexible customer-focused business processes (see Part Eight – Developing the Right Strategy).

What makes business process reengineering different?

First, BPR can be seen as a more radical change than some previous methods of business performance improvement (Figure 23.1). Whereas some previous improvement programs would be content with a 10–20 percent measurable change, BPR frequently looks for figures comfortably in excess of 40 percent.

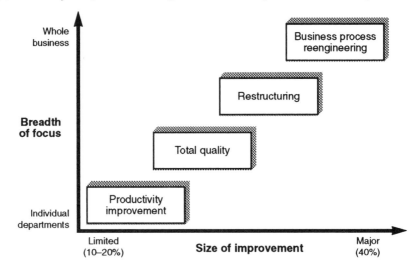

Figure 23.1   BPR is seen as a more radical level of change

Second, it has been seen as a reversal of the basic principles of Taylorism or scientific management. Under Taylorism, work is believed to be most efficiently carried out if it is broken down to small, often repetitive tasks, performed by different individuals and frequently in different departments. This approach suited the US in the early part of the twentieth century, with a large number of, often illiterate, immigrant workers (the environment in which Taylor developed and tested his ideas). The original Ford manufacturing plants were seen as the ultimate application of these principles. But more recently, they have clearly become dysfunctional:

+ a mortgage or insurance policy might pass through five or six departments before being issued, taking weeks to complete the process
+ a car component may go through five or even ten workstations and inspection areas before being sent to an assembly plant, so a few minutes' machining may take weeks to complete.

BPR reassembles tasks into meaningful units of work, frequently using information technology:

+ with a good information database, an insurance policy or mortgage can be fully processed by one person in minutes (not weeks) – the way telephone banking and insurance shook up two previously conservative industries shows the power of IT-based reengineering
+ with modern computer-controlled equipment, multiple machining operations on a complex car component can be carried out by a single operator, eliminating waiting time, reducing stock levels and reducing cycle time.

But perhaps the most important and innovative aspect of BPR is that it requires organizations to look at improving processes rather than functional activities. Many of the inefficiencies in modern organizations exist less in individual departments and more in the handovers between departments. Different departments in an organization will have different aims, methods, time frames and cultures. The more a product or piece of information must pass between functions, the more likely it is that there will be delays, miscommunication and the destruction (rather than addition) of value. BPR is seen as a way of moving an organization from being what Xerox chief executive Paul Allaire has called a 'large functional machine' (Harvey, 1994) toward being more flexible and knowledge based, structured around serving customer (not internal organizational) needs.

Typically, reengineering might take an insurance company from a classical, functional structure (Figure 23.2), where a policy must pass through up to six different areas and can take weeks to be issued, to a series of multiskilled teams with expert support, who can issue policies almost immediately (Figure 23.3).

How to reengineer a business successfully

The activity of running a BPR project is not theoretically complex and can be shown as a logical series of steps, which are little different to how any other improvement program might be run (Figure 23.4). The complexity comes from two main areas – working with processes and managing cross-functional change.

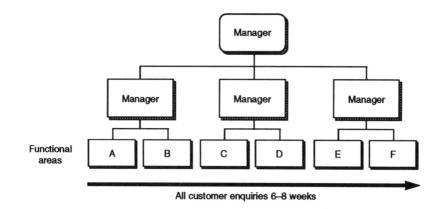

Figure 23.2   An example of long process times in a traditional functional
               structure

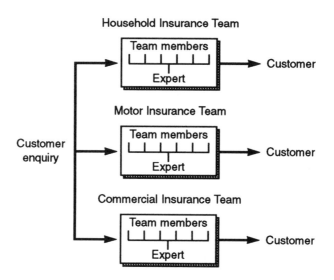

Figure 23.3   An example of a market-focused team structure in an insurance
               company

1. Working with processes

Organizations are used to thinking about themselves as functions – sales, marketing, production, research, finance etc. – not as processes. When you ask
people to identify processes, they will probably give examples such as order
entry, new product design, preparing annual budgets. These are, of course,
processes. But they are what might be called 'local' or 'sub' processes as they

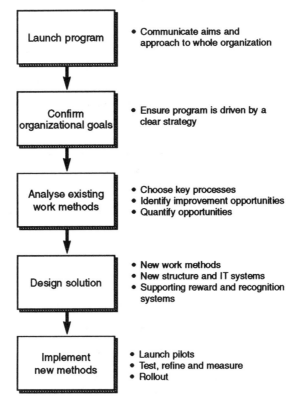

Figure 23.4   The main steps in a BPR program

tend to take place in only one or two functional areas and they are not linked to providing a clearly identified customer benefit.

In fact, preparing annual budgets is just part of internal organizational control and adds no value for the customer. Many BPR programs make the mistake of choosing 'easy' targets and attack these internal or local subprocesses. They are not that difficult to reengineer but, on the other hand, improving them tends to provide very little benefit. Examples of processes which give added customer value and reach across functions are:

✦ Pharmaceutical company – development of a new cancer drug
✦ Advertising agency – design of a new campaign
✦ FMCG manufacturer – serving large supermarket groups

Reengineering these processes that cut across functional and professional boundaries requires a much more sophisticated, dedicated and imaginative effort from management than does rebuilding a few purely 'local' processes.

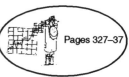

Pages 327–37

2. Managing cross-functional change

A significant change in behavior is necessary for people to move their attention and loyalties away from their functions to a cross-functional business process. Putting through such changes in an organization with several thousand employees and worldwide presence is extraordinarily difficult. Executives  who have carried out reengineering are often quoted as saying things like 'we needed leg-breaking', 'people have to be clouted', 'it was more difficult than we ever imagined' and 'it ain't cheap and it ain't easy'.

Why BPR has been criticized by many experts

First, the results from BPR are far from impressive – one survey claimed that '85% of reengineering projects fail' (CSC Index, 1994); although this low level of achievement may not be that unusual, since similar claims were being made only a few years earlier about the disappointing results from quality programs (Fuchsberg, 1992). While probably reasonably accurate, such statistics must be handled with care – they are often produced by specialists and consultants keen to create a need for their services.

Second, BPR has been accused of being another euphemism for firing staff, just like downsizing, rightsizing, delayering, strategic realignment, restructuring, productivity improvement, transitioning employees out, refocusing the organization and other such terms. And it is true that many of the major BPR programs have led to significant job losses – Bell Atlantic claimed to have been able to take out 20,000 employees in the years 1988–93 and British Telecom is aiming at an even higher number. It's no wonder that one executive called BPR 'trying to get the turkeys to vote for Xmas' (*Management Today*, August 1993). If you remove inefficiencies in a process equivalent to 40 percent or more of work effort, then you end up with a lot of people with much less to do. Only a very few organizations are lucky enough to experience such high levels of growth that they can find something useful to occupy these people.

This leads to the main criticism of BPR – that it is primarily aimed at managing costs downwards and does not sufficiently contribute to real business growth. BPR has been called 'surgery' (cutting out any sick parts) rather than 'therapy' (helping the organization become better). BPR supporters will say that BPR may have been used for cost reduction, but that by focusing on the customer it will really lead to growth. However, one commentator echoed the views of many of the critics by writing: 'after the wave of interest in reengineering passes, organizations will shift from managing costs to managing real business growth' (Lipnack & Stamps, 1994); and two of the most influential strategy experts suggested that, while BPR was a legitimate management task, it has 'more to do with shoring up today's businesses than creating tomorrow's industries' (Hamel & Prahalad, 1994).

The ten commandments of BPR

BPR can be necessary, but it is complex and difficult. It involves rethinking how the organization works and how it faces its customers. Moreover, it almost inevitably requires a major shift in power from functional barons to process managers – and it is extremely rare to find a functional manager willing to give up power without a determined fight. To implement a BPR program successfully, you must at least do all of the following and you probably need to do a lot more:

1. **It must be a top-down/bottom-up program.** Unless it is strongly driven from the highest level of the organization, it will founder on functional resistance. However, only the people close to the actual work are able to develop effective new ways of working.

2. **It must be customer focused.** It's too easy for organizations to decide to reengineer in order to reduce costs or shorten development times and these may give useful financial benefits. But unless the aim of the BPR exercise is to improve the way an organization works with its customers, it will not ultimately lead to any competitive advantage.

3. **Processes must be designed from the outside in.** It's not enough to conclude that all customers want lower prices or better service. Some customers will want faster deliveries, others a wider product line, others the lowest price, others 100 percent delivery reliability, others better payment terms. Unless you design your processes to give the appropriate benefits to each of your main customer groups, you will end up alienating all those whose needs you are not meeting.

4. **Top management must drive the process for the whole project.** Too often, executives launch the project with a great fanfare and then, when they lose interest, delegate it to a middle manager (often giving them the grand title of BPR manager) who doesn't have the power to overcome the inevitable resistance.

5. BPR is no cure for poor products or strategy. If your product/service is losing out in the market, BPR may slow your decline, but it can't reverse it. If your company direction is wrong, then BPR will only help you get to the wrong place faster.

6. You must be prepared to break down functional barriers and dismantle departmental empires. After all, BPR is about working effectively across, as well as within, functions.

7. You must change promotion, reward and recognition systems to support the program. You can't expect someone to dedicate themselves to a new cross-functional team, if their performance evaluation, bonus or promotion is still 100 percent dependent on how their departmental manager views their work.

8. You must make it worthwhile for people to participate and be honest about what action you intend to take with people made superfluous as a result of the process improvements made. If you don't say anything, people will assume the worst and find all kinds of ways of slowing down the program. Moreover, if you just aim at reducing your staffing levels, clearly people will block the program. But if you make your target building a better future for the organization, you're more likely to get the necessary employee support.

9. You must base your program on multidisciplinary teams. If you use functionally based teams or even leave out some functions, you will get functional solutions which are not accepted as relevant by the rest of the organization. For example, one major company asked part of a technical area which temporarily had a lull in its activity to redesign a major business process – they did a good job, but not knowing all areas in detail and not fully involving people in all areas, they could not come up with a comprehensive, universally acceptable solution.

10. Above all, always aim at finding the ideal solution, then work back to what is possible (Figure 23.5). This stretches people's imagination and helps them break free of their normal ways of thinking. If you just try to analyse existing processes and find solutions to any operating problems, you will tend to come up with solutions which resemble current methods and produce only small improvements.

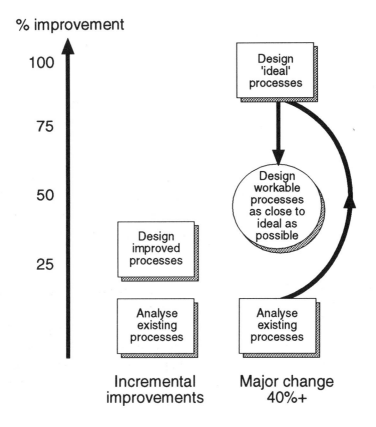

Figure 23.5   BPR will achieve more if it works back from the ideal process

Summary

Like all popular management ideas, BPR perhaps suffers from its proponents' desire to 'brand' their product as new and different. It does contain new elements, particularly the insistence that we view a business as a collection of customer-focused processes rather than internally focused functions, and that we remove any activity not aimed at benefiting some customer or end-user. But much of the methodology for analysing, redesigning and implementing new work methods is not significantly different from that used in other types of performance improvement programs.

BPR is a valid and useful contribution to management practice. And it is extremely difficult to implement successfully. However, with its tendency to focus more on what can be taken out today, rather than on how the future can be built, it is not quite the total solution its partisans would claim it to be.

As a recent article in the *Economist* commented: 'It is clear that it [BPR] was hopelessly oversold, and that it is much more use to some types of firm, or business people doing some types of thing, than it is to others. In other words, it is a useful tool, not a complete answer.'

Recommended reading

CSC Index (1994) *State of Re-engineering Report*.

The Economist (1994) 'Re-engineering reviewed', 2 July.

Gilbert Fuchsberg (1992) 'Quality programs show shoddy results', *Wall Street Journal*, 14 May.

Gary Hamel & C.K. Prahalad (1994) *Competing for the Future*, Harvard Business School Press.

Michael Hammer (1990) 'Re-engineering work – don't automate, obliterate', *Harvard Business Review*, July–August.

Michael Hammer & James Champy (1993) *Reengineering the Corporation: A Manifesto for Business Revolution*, HarperCollins (US)/Nicholas Brealey (UK).

David Harvey (1994) 'Reengineering: the critical success factors: special report', *Management Today*.

Jessica Lipnack & Jeffrey Stamps (1994) *The Age of the Network: Organizing Principles for the 21st Century*, Oliver Wight (US)/Omneo (UK).

Management Today (1993) 'Shocking to the core', August.

24

Building a Learning Organization

Few of us could honestly claim that the organizations we work for use all our talents and creativity. Most people have experienced the frustration of seeing a course of action which they know to be right being rejected by an organization which they feel is too distant from operational reality to make an informed decision. And many of us are precisely the people who are guilty of rejecting proposals from employees who are much closer to the market than we'd ever want to be.

However, many people will view the concept of a learning organization with some degree of suspicion. Having been through waves of total quality, rightsizing, decentralization, teamworking and so on, they might feel it's just the latest fad that management theorists and HR departments have come up with to justify their existence. Yet there is some evidence that some organizations are able to build on the skills of their employees in a way that bewildered competitors fail to grasp.

Two factories, part of the same company making similar products for the car and truck industry, both had the same production line machinery installed. There were a lot of problems with the equipment.

The engineers at the British factory bemoaned the situation as yet another example of corporate incompetence and added staff and rework stations to put right all the quality problems the equipment caused.

At the French factory, they set to work redesigning parts of the equipment and even added a whole series of new, electronically controlled features. Quality performance was superb. Seeing the difference in results between the factories, management sent teams of British engineers over to France to see what the French had done differently. With depressing regularity, the teams reported back that the French had made some modifications, but these were really not relevant to the situation in Britain.

Two cleaning product producers were bitter rivals.

Producer A's model for business success was to focus constantly on achieving short-term profitability. Costs were continuously being cut and, it was rumored, they also tried to boost profitability further by reducing the level of 'goodies' (the active agents in the product), thus lowering the quality of the product.

Producer B improved the quality of the product year after year and gradually increased market share. Increasing market share generated more profits, which could be invested in product improvements and marketing, increasing market share even more.

Producer A, however, had a trick up their sleeve – a brand new way of making a better product than their rival could ever produce. With a huge publicity campaign, the new product was launched. Unfortunately, there were some performance problems and the launch flopped. Press estimates of the losses were in excess of £100 million.

The compelling need to learn

Experts have expressed the need that organizations have to learn in many different ways. One of the most powerful (Garratt, 1987) is the idea that, for an organization to prosper, its rate of learning must be greater than (or at least equal to) the rate of change in its external environment: $L \geq C$.

Another approach is the idea that knowledge is doubling every seven years (Davis & Botkin, 1994). This means that by the time a university student graduates, much of what they learned in their first year will be out of date. It also means that it is ludicrous to expect a single business model or product design to last more than a few years. Changes in technology and taste can destroy a supposedly stable market in a matter of months.

A third way of expressing the imperative to learn (Sveiby & Lloyd, 1987) is  the idea of there having been a shift from 'financial' to 'knowledge' capital (see Part Three – Encouraging Creativity). There are scores of examples – GM vs Honda, IBM vs Apple, Caterpillar vs Komatsu, Xerox vs Canon – of

Pages 86–8

huge, apparently invincible organizations with vast financial resources being rapidly overtaken by once tiny competitors. At one time, manufacturing and marketing muscle was sufficient to ensure continued success. Now, the organization that can learn faster than its competitors is the one that will be successful. But all of an organization's assets depreciate over time. Knowledge capital depreciates as customer needs and technology changes. Organizations must move from thinking about investing only in physical assets to a mindset where they also constantly try to renew their knowledge capital.

Pages 317–18

What should an organization learn?

It's all very well to talk about building a learning organization, but this is hardly specific enough to suggest what each organization should be trying to learn.

There are two main areas in which an organization must learn – managing its internal functioning (processes, structure, systems etc.) and adapting to changes in its external environment. Obviously the two are connected – a sudden shift in technology, for example 60 percent of the added value of a product moving from mechanical to electronic features, will clearly have a major impact on internal ways of operating.

There are many tools for analysing an organization's situation:

◆ External market – portfolio analysis, lifecycle analysis, industry structure analysis (see Part Eight – Developing the Right Strategy).

Pages 258–75

Pages 327–36

◆ Internal operations – activity-based management, service level analysis, benchmarking (see Part Ten – Increasing Profitability).

◆ Match between external environment and internal capabilities – SWOTs, process mapping, S-curve modeling, value chain analysis.

Using these tools, managers can identify many of the weak areas to be rectified, potential threats to be managed and potential opportunities to be seized – although these slightly mechanistic models should be used with care and be an aid to, not a replacement for, imaginative thinking.

What does a learning organization look like?

Four main features are critical to developing a learning organization:

1. Moving from single- to double-loop learning

A learning organization can be very different from a highly trained organization. Training is all about how to do specific activities well and is usually based on single-loop thinking (see Part Three – Encouraging Creativity). Learning is aimed at being able to assess constantly whether what you are doing is right. Training gives you greater efficiency (doing things better) – learning builds effectiveness (doing the right things).

A learning organization continually tries to improve its processes, but at the same time is able to question whether those are the right processes by using double-loop learning (Figure 24.1).

A single-loop learning organization would deal with a quality problem by putting in more inspectors, tightening up control systems and training employees.

Figure 24.1

With double-loop learning, there would be an attempt to understand the cause of the problem, redesign parts or equipment and even work with suppliers to reach a better way of making the product or constructing the service.

A single-loop learning organization would react to a drop in market share by increasing promotions to end-users or discounts to retailers and by bumping up advertising expenditure. With double-loop learning, the company would compare product performance and advertising effectiveness, review consumer taste and see if there are ways of better linking their value chain with that of their retailers and consumers.

A single-loop learning organization would set a strategy and monitor how well various sectors are implementing it – a double-loop organization would set a strategic direction and let individual units work out how best to adapt it to their particular operating environment.

2. Seeing change as continuity not upheaval

Even organizations that are not learning organizations are capable of change. However, while a learning organization would generally change in line with the changes in its environment, non-learning organizations tend to slip behind the rate of external change, go through massive and painful upheaval to catch up again, start slipping again and once more have upheaval.

Upheaval means lost jobs, closed factories and intimidated but obedient staff. Learning brings growth, opportunity and personal development. In the west we've become experts at upheaval, but are considerably less capable of encouraging learning.

3. Having a non-linear systems mindset

Chapter 4 (Chaos and Management) discussed the differences between linear cause-and-effect thinking and a more complex non-linear systems mentality. Managers who see their organizations as simple closed systems Pages 34–5 believe that by applying a series of levers – reducing costs, increasing advertising, adding extra production shifts etc. – they can produce a series of known outcomes.

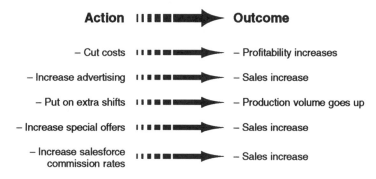

Managers who view organizations as more complex open systems constantly reacting with the environment, partly in predictable and partly in unpredictable ways, understand that apparently simple actions can have unexpected results. One of the most common mistakes cause-and-effect sales managers make, for example, is to believe in a direct link between offering increased commissions and discounts and the level of sales.

Frequently, sales managers who are falling behind target try to increase sales by offering special bonuses to sales staff and/or extra discounts to customers.

Sales staff are galvanized into action and persuade customers to take advantage of the special offers. Customers stock up on the product and sales targets are reached. However, the discounts have made the sales less profitable than required, the rush of orders causes extra costs in production and customers now have so much of the product that their orders are extremely low at the start of the next period.

To ensure that the next period's targets are met, sales managers must again offer discounts and increased commissions and the whole unprofitable process starts all over again. This is the start of a potentially vicious spiral fuelled by three forces – erratic sales patterns, lower profitability and increased production costs.

4. Encouragement of diversity

Learning and creativity come from the clash between opposites. You may enjoy spending an evening with a group of people who went to the same school or the same university as you and who share the same opinions. And it appears much easier to work with like-minded people than with a group whose members are always at odds with each other. But uniformity leads to monotony and shared experience usually results in groupthink and unimaginative strategies.

One challenge in managing a learning organization is to encourage a diversity of opinions, however threatening this may seem to the existing power structure.

Getting there – build on specific improvements

Moving an organization from closed-minded, top-down, authoritarian behaviors to open-mindedly handling two-way information flow as part of building organizational learning is a major task – you're often trying to change deep-rooted cultures and behaviors which are supported by structures, power distribution, information systems and ways of interacting. In fact, you're changing everything. If, for example, you leave a heavy hierarchical structure in place while trying to encourage learning, the structure will continually work against the behaviors you're trying to promote. Or if you leave power with functional managers while you're trying to set up market-sensitive cross-functional teams, the power structure will always be blocking the changes you're hoping to make.

You can't build a learning organization directly. You could, of course, try teaching people all about learning, meeting techniques, creative thinking, openness, networking and so on. They are likely to enjoy the time off work in the workshops and classroom sessions, but little to nothing of what was com-

municated would be put to use in day-to-day operations. A learning organization results from radically changing the way people behave at work. So getting
there has to come from changing behaviors on concrete, task-related issues,
rather than attempting to instil something as nebulous as a 'learning climate'.

You have to go back to a basic model of learning to understand where to
start. There are two main ways of changing behavior:

+ external methods – threats, rewards, incentives
+ internal – changing the way someone sees the world and thus the reasons
  they act in a specific way.

When you want to increase productivity, boost sales or speed up a project, you
can use external methods. The threat of being fired or the offer of large
bonuses can do wonders in helping people cope with what they had claimed
were insurmountable problems. But you can't threaten or bribe your way to a
learning culture. That leaves method two – changing people's beliefs. This happens most easily when people experience practical proof that there may be
another, better way of viewing and doing things (Figure 24.2).

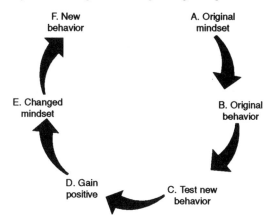

Figure 24.2   To change behavior you must change the mindset which
drives that behavior

It takes time to move through all the steps from A (original mindset) to F
(new behavior). Some organizations hope that a good dose of training and
workshops will take them directly from A to E or even from A to F, although
it seldom works that way. You may get some early results and think you've
achieved your goals, but unless the new behaviors and mindset are well
embedded through constant on-the-job use, people normally slip back to their
old ways of thinking and working.

So achieving a learning organization is unlikely to be a question of a huge, organization-wide training program. It most probably means starting with one very specific targeted improvement program – revamping a customer-facing process, running a development project in 30 percent less time than it normally takes, setting up an international brand management team, reducing the throughput time of a supply chain by 20–40 percent or whatever. Around this improved process you build new structures, reporting relationships, reward systems and power distribution, and you  protect it continuously from being dragged down by the rest of the organization's non-learning culture (see Part Four – Managing Change).

Once you have created this island of best practice, you can move on to the next key process or area and run another improvement project. And so on until you have created such critical mass that the rest of the organization begins to fall into line (Figure 24.3).

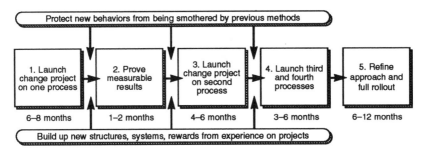

Figure 24.3   Build a move to a learning organization around a series of measurable key process improvement projects

Why organizations don't learn

Learning is, or at least should be, a natural human activity. As our young children stumble around our homes scattering all our possessions, tugging at plants, electric wires, the dog's tail or whatever, they're fulfilling their curiosity and trying to learn – although sometimes it may look like the aim is pure destruction rather than building experience.

But at school, great efforts are put into controlling our natural curiosity and convincing us that learning is concerned with committal to memory of volumes of facts, rather than adding to our experiences. Then as we start to work in an organization, we quickly understand that things are done in a certain way – except in the most enlightened organizations, deviation from that norm, however valid the reasons, will usually bring disapproval, sanctions and in extreme cases expulsion. We either leave or quickly learn the behaviors which ensure survival and success.

The forces for moving towards a learning organization may seem strong in theory, but the practical obstacles can sometimes appear almost insuperable:

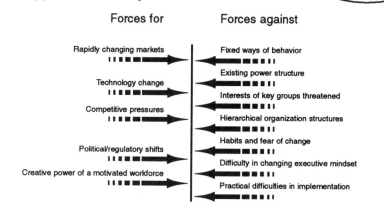

Pages 120–9

Forces for   Forces against

Rapidly changing markets   Fixed ways of behavior

Existing power structure

Technology change   Interests of key groups threatened

Competitive pressures   Hierarchical organization structures

Habits and fear of change

Political/regulatory shifts   Difficulty in changing executive mindset

Creative power of a motivated workforce   Practical difficulties in implementation

Figure 24.4   The forces against building a learning organization are formidable

Knowledge management

Within any organization there are usually just a few key skills that are critical to high performance. These may be linked to how new products are developed, how suppliers are managed or how customers are dealt with. And while there may be areas of best practice, too often these depend on a few individuals or groups and are not captured so they can be disseminated throughout the organization. Sometimes personal or departmental rivalries even prevent best practice being spread.

Any learning organization needs to have knowledge-management processes for codifying existing best practices, developing new ones and ensuring that they are transferred to the people who should be using them. Best practices must also be continually upgraded in the light of new learning, to avoid them becoming restrictive and out of date.

Knowledge management requires new roles, responsibilities and systems. It usually also requires a cultural change to overcome a 'not invented here' mentality. Staff have to move from scarcity thinking, where knowledge is jealously hoarded, to abundance thinking, where knowledge is openly shared.

Summary

The performance of those learning organizations that do exist is often way beyond the limited imagination of their more hide-bound, arthritic competitors. But learning is not something that can be taught to a whole organization. It should be built gradually on a base of concrete, well-targeted, operational improvement initiatives. Choose a key process, redesign the way people work with that process, protect them from inertia or even interference from the rest of the organization, prove the benefits of the new way, then move on to the next process. This may take time, but there is probably no other realistic way.

Recommended reading

S. Davis & J. Botkin (1994) 'The coming of knowledge-based business', *Harvard Business Review*, Sept–Oct.

Bob Garratt (1987) *The Learning Organisation*, Fontana.

Peter Senge (1994) *The Fifth Discipline Fieldbook: Tools, Techniques and Reflections for Building a Learning Organization*, Doubleday (US)/Nicholas Brealey (UK).

K. E. Sveiby & T. Lloyd (1987) *Managing Knowhow*, Bloomsbury.

Part Ten

Increasing Profitability

25

Accountant or Manager?

The large industrial organizations which have dominated commercial activity for much of the twentieth century developed certain ways of functioning which suited the period in which most of them were formed:

+ heavy, hierarchical structures splitting employees into functional specialities
+ a 'command-and-control' mentality, where those at the top did the thinking and those lower down carried out instructions
+ fractionalization of activities into small tasks that could be easily taught, measured and controlled.

They also developed financial reporting and control systems to suit these ways of functioning.

The environment in which these organizations operate has changed dramatically – foreign and domestic competition has increased, technology has made products rapidly obsolete, saturated markets and an overabundance of products have made consumers more demanding and new methods (just in time, total quality, business process reengineering) have revolutionized the way we think about work.

Organizations have tried to adapt:

+ heavy hierarchical, functional structures are being replaced by fast-moving, cross-functional, business-process-focused teams
+ command and control are giving way to attempts to empower employees on the front line
+ fractionalized, repetitive tasks are being reassembled into meaningful and customer-focused units of work based on cross-functional business processes.

But one aspect which does not seem to have adapted is the way organizations measure and report financial performance. In fact if anything, with the move to common accounting standards, an outdated and inappropriate financial reporting system has been reinforced, instead of being adapted to changing needs.

Businesses in the west have become dominated by those who control and set rules rather than those who know how to produce value for customers. In Britain two in every thousand people are accountants, in the US it's one in every thousand and in Japan it's one in every twenty thousand people – quite a difference!

Huge energy is expended in organizations at the end of each month, quarter and year to close the accounts. It's true that annual accounts do give investors and the stock exchange a more or less reliable standard against which to judge a company's performance. However, there are five major reasons that most accounting systems are not only unhelpful to managers, but may actually cause them to take decisions which can seriously harm the organizations they're paid to lead (Figure 25.1).

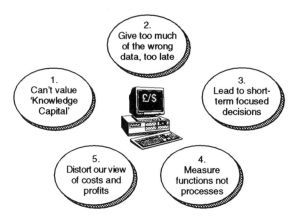

Figure 25.1   The five main weaknesses of financial accounting systems

1. Inability to value knowledge capital

Twenty years or so ago, General Motors had vast financial assets (factories, machinery, stocks, cash) and Honda had very little in comparison, Xerox was a giant whereas Canon was tiny, IBM was a colossus while Microsoft had not yet been formed. According to the assets valuation on the balance sheets GM, Xerox and IBM were monsters with the power to crush any upstart competition. But then the balance sheets only measured physical capital – not the ideas, talent and flexibility of the workforce. Most investors nowadays would rather put their hard-earned savings into Canon, Microsoft and Honda than the bruised and battered former heavyweights.

What has happened is that competitiveness has moved from being a result of vast financial resources to depending on an organization's ability to acquire and deploy knowledge (see Part Pages 86–8 Three – Encouraging Creativity). While accounting systems measure financial capital, successful competitive performance in the real world often stems more from a company's knowledge capital (Figure 25.2).

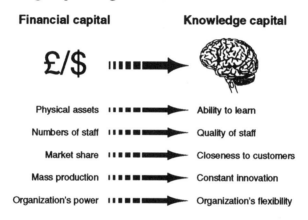

Financial capital		Knowledge capital

Physical assets	➡	Ability to learn
Numbers of staff	➡	Quality of staff
Market share	➡	Closeness to customers
Mass production	➡	Constant innovation
Organization's power	➡	Organization's flexibility

Figure 25.2   Competitive success is going to organizations with knowledge rather than financial capital

Working out how to measure knowledge capital may not be that easy. But managers must at least understand the potential for standard asset valuation to overestimate major companies' strengths and to underestimate the power of smaller, smarter competitors. Then those managers who feel sheltered within the fortress-like walls of some multinational commercial giant may feel less complacent about their future and may be more inclined to be active in developing their operations – while those in struggling minnows may be less daunted by the apparent strength of a massive market incumbent.

2. Too much, too limited, too late

Each month or quarter there is a feverish level of activity in the finance department. They're closing the books. And then, half-way through the next month or quarter, truckloads of figures come spouting out of the corporate computer.

But what is this mysterious 'closing the books' on which so much time and effort are expended? Has it anything to do with the daily management of the business? Not usually. Does it matter if the books don't completely balance? Not really. Closing the books, balancing debits and credits, is all about matching income to expenses. It doesn't help you develop more products, be more innovative or grab greater market share. It's accounting convention, not operational management.

Running a business can be compared to flying a plane or driving a car. In each of these activities there are certain things you want to know:

✦ Flying a plane – altitude, weather pattern, geographical location, ground speed etc.
✦ Driving a car – speed, distance from the side of the road and other cars, direction etc.
✦ Running a business – sales, new product performance, project schedule adherence, delivery performance to key customers, new product development times, advertising effectiveness etc.

Most of the indicators you need to run a business are not included in the monthly, quarterly or annual accounts. But more importantly, if you're flying a plane there's no point being informed by your navigator two weeks after the event that his reconciliation of the ground and the plane's position shows you're ten meters below ground level. Likewise, you can't drive a car only looking in the rear mirror to reconcile your position with that of the road and traffic coming from the other direction.

In business, you need a constant stream of meaningful operational indicators which tell you how you're doing and which you can use to take action to adjust your position. You don't get that from monthly, quarterly or annual accounts. There's lots of detail in the accounts and the figures may be more or less accurate and they cost you a lot to produce – but too often they can't be used for anything very productive. Financial accounting systems give us too much of the wrong information, too late to be useful.

Management is not an exact science – accounting pretends to be. Management requires real-time operational data – accounting provides after-the-event financial figures based on a number of convenient assumptions or accounting conventions. Management is about using information to lead – accounting is obsessed with getting data to balance.

3. Short-term focus

There is a serious mismatch between, on the one hand, the time frames of our traditional accounting systems and the managers who use them and, on the other, the time required to make a significant impact on an organization's performance by, for example, developing and launching a new product, implementing an operational improvement program or gaining market share.

When accounting systems were developed, most expenditure was probably relevant to the financial reporting period in which it fell. Product lifecycles were long and managers spent years in the same position. Now as product lifecycles have shortened, more and more money is having to be channeled into R&D to develop the next product model. And as managers only expect to spend two to three years in any position before their next promotion, they are under intense pressure to get financial results to justify their next move upstairs or to a better position in another organization. The result of these two trends is depressingly predictable.

Put into a new position and measured on monthly or quarterly financial results, managers will look around for where they can easily have an effect to show their value to the organization. Most current expenditure is probably committed (factories, materials, staff etc.) so there's not much that can be done there. Increasingly, organizational expenditure is being focused on the future – new IT systems, R&D, marketing, organizational change programs, setting up joint ventures with suppliers, customers or even competitors. Yet monthly or quarterly financial reporting measure only the immediate. So the more we spend for the future, the worse our immediate results look. Conversely, of course, the less we invest now for the future, the better our immediate results appear. Given that situation, it's fairly obvious that ambitious managers will be only too willing to ransack our investment for the future if they can gain some short-term career advantage from doing so.

Moreover, accounting conventions can actually discourage investment in improving a firm's performance. By allowing the cost of acquisitions to be excluded from the income statement, profits and earnings per share are inflated. So investments in internal growth, which have to be written off against revenues, are seen as much less attractive than takeovers to some financially driven companies. This situation has led to a spate of acquisition-driven companies which saw rapid apparent growth and usually even more rapid decline, because much of the growth was funded by unsustainable levels of debt rather than real earnings improvement. Polly Peck, for example, showed a profit of £155 million in 1988 by writing off £170 million against reserves. In reality it was later discovered that it made a loss of £15 million for the year. And when investors understood the fragility of the rapid growth and apparent profitability of Saatchi and Saatchi, the share price fell from £7.0 to £0.2.

4. Measuring functions not processes

With few exceptions, accounting systems are set up to measure the costs and revenues of the various functional departments. But they tend to be mismatched to the new view of key customer-facing processes. Accounting systems can tell us how much we spend on manufacturing in a month, but they normally can't tell us how well we served our main customers or even which customers were the most profitable.

If we are to run our organizations as a series of customer-facing processes, we will have to develop a whole new group of horizontal operational performance indicators, which most current financial reporting systems are unable to provide.

Pages 22–33

5. Distorting our view of costs

But perhaps the most serious shortcoming of traditional accounting systems is that they often lead organizations to believe that loss-making or marginal products are making a healthy profit and that other products are not producing revenue when they are in reality extremely profitable.

In most industries, product or service variety is continually increasing to match the needs of more demanding customers and more fragmented markets – for example, the number of varieties of coffee, shampoo and sauces increased by over 40 percent between 1989 and 1993.

If you're now making ten different versions of a product, instead of the previous two, it's obviously important to know the respective costs of the different versions so you know what to charge your customers. Because of the way traditional accounting systems allocate costs to different product types, most organizations don't have a clear view of the costs of each product version and frequently sell products at a loss when they believe they're making a profit.

Typically a company will have an impression that each of its products adds to its profits (Figure 25.3). The real picture may be much more dramatic, with some products immensely profitable and others making hidden losses. The way this apparently perverse situation has developed is as follows:

1. The proportion of indirect or overhead costs in most organizations has risen steadily over the last 10–20 years.
2. Traditional accounting systems usually allocate these indirect costs to products or services on a very simple basis such as labor and materials content or just percent of sales – so a product that accounts for 60 percent of sales gets allo-

cated 60 percent of overhead costs and one that is 5 percent of sales gets 5 percent of overhead allocated.

3. This is all very logical in theory and was quite an acceptable approximation, when overheads were only 10–20 percent of costs. But now that overheads can be 40–60 percent of costs, such approximations can be misleading and even dangerous.

4. What you normally find is that the products/services which make up the larger part of your sales are the high-volume ones, which require very little support activities, while the smaller-volume products/services are short runs requiring a lot of planning, equipment set-up and so on, or else are 'specials' needing more design, attention, handling etc.

5. The standard method of overhead cost allocation does not usually take account of the fact that these smaller-volume products/services often are the driver of more complexity and more overhead cost.

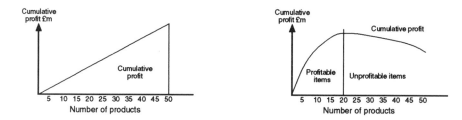

Figure 25.3 Traditional accounting systems often give the impression that most products add to overall profits. In reality, many apparently 'profitable' products may be losing money.

This can have dramatic effects on a business. For example, it often means that you are selling the (more commodity) part of your range, which is easier to make (and where you probably need to be most competitive on price), at too high a price. The part which is difficult or expensive to make, where you add the most value for your customers and where there is less competition, is probably being sold at too low a price. Normally, you could even charge more for these lower-volume items. However, you don't charge more because you think you're making a reasonable profit on them, even though you may be making a loss.

As an example, take two construction projects, one large (Figure 25.4) and one small (Figure 25.5). Overheads are assigned to both projects at the rate of 5 percent of direct costs. This makes the large project look like it made a profit of $1 million and the small project a profit of $100,000. However, assume that as a percentage the indirect costs of the smaller project are a little over 8 per-cent ($500,000) while the larger project had real indirect costs of only about

3 percent ($2 million). This completely changes the picture, making the real profitability of the larger project double that shown by the accounting system and highlighting that the smaller project actually made a loss not revealed by the accounting system.

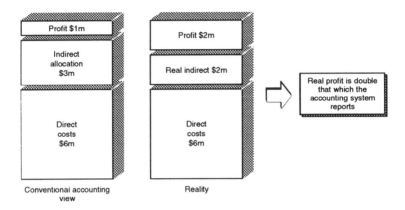

Figure 25.4   On larger projects (or higher-volume products) accounting systems often underestimate profitability

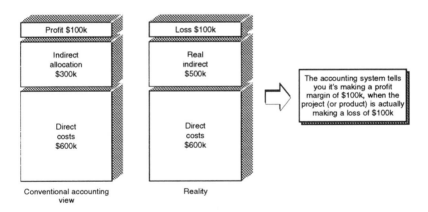

Figure 25.5   On smaller projects (or lower-volume products) requiring proportionately more overhead, accounting systems often overestimate profitability

This misleading impression of profitability which standard accounting systems give is not just a problem for the accountants to sort out. It can sometimes lead to a vicious spiral in which:

1. Managers believe that smaller projects or lower-volume, more complex 'specials' are profitable (when in reality they make a loss).
2. Managers are thus encouraged to sell more of these.
3. Because these smaller projects or specials tend to be more complex and require more overhead (planning, designing, handling, control etc.) overhead costs increase.
4. As overheads increase, the high-volume items attract more than their fair share of these new overheads in the accounting system and so seem even less profitable. Managers are thus encouraged to sell even more specials. Overheads increase more, and so on.

Short production runs, small projects, customers who order in limited quantities and complex products all often have hidden costs, which are not usually reflected in the conventional accounting view of a business:

HIDDEN COST PRODUCTS	HIDDEN COST CUSTOMERS
Require extra planning	Order in small quantities
Made in short runs	Pay slowly
Need long setups or changeovers	Need a lot of technical support
Need more management attention	Create extra administration
Complex packaging	Disrupt production plans
More waste	Occupy management time

Once managers are aware of the severely distorting effects of outdated methods of accounting and cost allocation, they can start to look beyond the picture presented by traditional accounting systems, as these do not usually take proper account of the growth in indirect costs or of the different levels of indirect costs which different activities entail. Some firms are trying to do this by introducing the concept of activity-based management (ABM). This tries to understand the real drivers of cost so that costs can be allocated to the products or services which cause them rather than according to a convenient accounting convention.

Thus ABM helps managers take decisions based on a better understanding of the drivers of cost and profit. This could lead to increasing the price for the short-run 'specials' to make up for the extra cost and complexity they cause, or eliminating some of them from the range altogether. Also, it can allow high-volume, 'commodity' products to be sold at a more competitive price and still be profitable. And, of course, once the real drivers of cost are clearly identified, managers can control them more effectively.

Economic value added

One idea developed to overcome the weaknesses of traditional accounting measures of performance such as profit is economic value added (EVA). The concept is to deduct from net operating profit a charge for the amount of capital (both debt and equity) that the firm employs. A positive EVA means that value is being created, a negative result indicates that value is being destroyed. Many firms are starting to link directors' bonuses to EVA rather than profit or share price, as they believe that it is a better measure of the real creation of value.

There have been a number of criticisms of EVA. Three of the most important are:

+ It can discourage executives from making significant capital investments as these will tend to lower EVA. There is a risk of managers boosting EVA in the short term by starving their firms of capital spending.
+ Efficient use of capital is only one measure of a firm's success. It says nothing about the organization's ability to innovate, develop its people or out-strategize the competition.
+ In the new knowledge-based economy, where human capital is more critical than financial capital, EVA can be meaningless. In particular, it is less relevant for younger, growing companies where efficient use of capital is a minor concern.

However, EVA can be a useful tool in some circumstances and for some companies. It helps focus managers on the real costs of doing business.

Open-book management

Some organizations practice what has been called 'open-book management' (OBM) to attempt to bridge the gap between financial results and the daily reality of employees' lives. With OBM you use a regular forum – monthly meetings, cascade briefings, newsletters – to make staff aware of the current financial results. Ideally, this should be accompanied by training in interpreting the numbers correctly.

The aim of OBM is that understanding how each person can affect the organization's financial results should help build a sense of responsibility and focus people's efforts on the areas of greatest financial leverage.

> A metal casting unit was always measured on tonnes produced and man-hours used. Staff didn't really know key information about their work – which products were most profitable, how much an hour of machine downtime cost, what the total cost of quality was and so on. After managers introduced and communicated a simple monthly profit and loss report, people could immediately see the effect of their actions on the financial results and concentrate on the most rewarding areas. Moreover, a new sense of motivation was created by managers guaranteeing that a certain percentage of monthly profits would be reinvested in new equipment.

Summary – accountant or manager?

Of course, accounting systems have a role to play – we need to know an organization's financial results. However, we also need to take financial managers' claims that you can 'run a business by the numbers' with a pinch of salt. Even if such a sweeping statement were true, you would have to have the right numbers and they would have to give a reasonably accurate depiction of reality. Most accounting systems no longer meet these two criteria.

 Pages 22–33

Managers need to understand the shortcomings of our standard accounting systems and put them into context. A mechanistic belief in the plethora of numbers which accounting systems produce can lead to disaster – an intelligent application of the parts that can be useful can aid good decision making.

Recommended reading

John Case (1998) *The Open-Book Management Experience: Lessons From Over 100 Companies that Have Transformed Themselves*, Nicholas Brealey.

Tony Hope & Jeremy Hope (1995) *Transforming the Bottom Line: Managing Performance with the Real Numbers*, Nicholas Brealey.

H.T. Johnson & R.S. Kaplan (1987) *Relevance Lost: The Rise and Fall of Management Accounting*, Harvard Business School Press.

26

Adding Value for the Customer

It has become fashionable to extend the concept of 'the customer' from outside to within the organization itself. Different parts of the organization are often referred to as 'suppliers to' and 'customers of' each other. Our mental picture of the organization has thus moved from a traditional functional model to a series of processes along each of which there are a number of customers and suppliers (Figure 26.1).

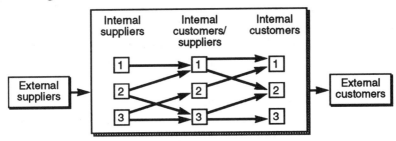

Figure 26.1   Many organizations have moved to a supplier/customer view of their operations

The aim of this shift is to get departments thinking of each other as customers or suppliers linked in a mutually beneficial process of serving external customers, rather than seeing each other as sworn enemies. The growth of cross-functional business-process-based teams and project teams should have gone some way to reducing the age-old internecine warfare, but in some instances they have just added a new level of conflict as organizational complexity increases.

Most of the problem lies in organizations not having learned how to direct their members' efforts towards a unifying common goal (see Part Six – Enhancing Personal Performance). But part of this organizational conflict may

Pages 179–82

also stem from the fact that, although we talk about internal suppliers and customers, we've seldom had the willpower or courage to apply the concept rigorously. If we did it would mean that:

✦ Customers can decide what services they need, what quality they require and should be able to negotiate a fair market-related price for those services.
✦ Suppliers should not provide services for which there is no customer demand.
✦ All activities or services should be, as far as possible, aimed at adding value for the external customer. Some internally focused functions are necessary, but these should be kept to a minimum.

Frequently, support departments provide services that other areas have no use for or could obtain much more cheaply from another source. And many of an organization's activities are aimed purely at satisfying internal requirements and add no value to end (or even intermediate internal) customers.

Two tools which can help overcome these problems and refocus an organization on adding value for intermediate and end customers are service-level analysis (SLA) and value-added analysis (VAA).

Service-level analysis

One of the main trends in almost all organizations over the last 10–20 years has been a switch in the ratio of direct productive workers (manufacturing, sales, distribution) to support staff (finance, planning, IT etc.). It would have been normal 20 years ago for there to be five to ten direct staff for every one person in support activities. Today there are often as many support staff as direct workers and in some organizations indirect staff are in the majority. With advances in IT and automation and a greater tendency to outsource, there are now many fewer people working in what can be called 'direct/productive' jobs – making things or dealing with customers – and ever more people and cost moving into support areas – accounts, product development, planning, IT etc.

It has always been relatively easy to measure the value of direct workers (amount produced or sold, number of customers dealt with and so on) and to increase or decrease their cost depending on the level of business. But it is much more difficult to know how well support functions are performing or even whether much of what they do is necessary at all.

Moreover, often it is the support activities, which usually include general management, who decide what level of support will be given to direct areas.

This gives direct departments little say over what services the organization provides them with and how much these services will cost. However, administrative support areas have a tendency to grow almost independently of the real evolution of an organization's activities. Studies have shown that support departments often grow at a rate of 3–5 percent a year whether the organization's activity level is itself growing, static or even declining.

Service-level analysis is one way of helping the customer, rather than the supplier, make the judgment of what is necessary. It treats the direct areas as 'customers' for internal services and thus sees the internal workings of an organization as a series of transactions between suppliers (the support areas) and customers (the direct departments). So, just as outside an organization the customers decide what they want to buy, the internal customers get the opportunity to help define what they want the internal suppliers (the support functions) to supply.

Conducting a service-level analysis

There are three main parts to a service-level analysis (Figure 26.2).

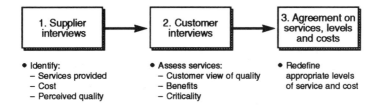

Figure 26.2   A basic SLA can be done in three phases

1. Supplier interviews

The first step is to analyse the services being provided. The best way is to interview key figures in each support function to find out:

✦ what are the main services they supply and to whom
✦ how they measure the volume and quality of those services
✦ the approximate cost of providing each service
✦ how highly they rate the quality of each service
✦ what ways they see of improving the quality or reducing the cost of the services they provide.

Supplier Forms

5–10 Key Services	Customers	Associated KPIs	% cost on each	Performance Rating (self assessment)	Improvement Potential
Name service	Direct depts which use the service	List how service is currently measured		(1 to 10)	(1 to 10) and explanation of potential

Figure 26.3   A form that could be used for supplier interviews

Obviously, these first interviews must be handled carefully. Service providers will normally be very sensitive about what their section offers to the rest of the organization. They will tend to overcomplicate the nature of their work to justify their existence and may even try to use these interviews as an opportunity to prove they need more – more money, more space, more resources or more whatever.

2. Customer interviews

Here you go and see the main customers of the services to establish their view of:

◆ what services they believe they receive
◆ the quality of the services they receive
◆ the cost of those services and their value to the customer
◆ the importance of each service to the customer's operation
◆ other ways in which they could receive that service
◆ how they rate the performance of the service
◆ opportunities to improve services.

Customer Forms

Service provided	Cost of the service	The supplier	Need for the service	Alternatives	KPIs	Performance rating	Improvement potential
			Scale of 1 to 5	More Reduce Consolidate Outsource Eliminate etc.			

Figure 26.4   A form that could be used for customer interviews

3. Achieving agreement on desired service level and cost

Once you have conducted a few supplier and customer interviews you start to find two main things:

+ **Suppliers give more services than customers either want or need.** Many of those services may exist for historical reasons and nobody has ever reviewed their rationale. Or suppliers may have provided some services which were useful to the customer, but when the customer finds out the high cost they can think of new ways of working which dispense with the need for those services.
+ **Customers are dissatisfied with the quality of many key services and yet receive others which are far in excess of their needs.** They may only need a critical few to be of a very high quality.

Suppliers will naturally be willing to spend the organization's resources ensuring that a wide range of services are all of equally high quality. But often this quality level is essential for only a few services and others can be done in simpler ways. For example:

+ Accounts may produce extremely time-consuming and detailed analyses of costs and income. But much of the detail may not be of any use to line managers for decision making.
+ IT may be developing an expensive system giving 'real-time' information on sales and stocks. For a twentieth of the price, they could have put in an off-the-shelf batch system giving daily closing figures by 10 am the next day. The cheaper solution might be quite satisfactory for users.
+ Market research may be spending half their budget on very detailed weekly market-share data. This may have been useful when a company had many thousands of small retail outlets as customers and constantly had to monitor how its products were performing in the market. But now that the level of business is largely decided by annual contracts with a few large customers, the information can't be used for effective decision making. Monthly or even quarterly figures might now be quite sufficient.

There are a number of ways to proceed from this point:

+ Work individually with customers and suppliers to try to bring them closer together using the data you have gathered as the starting point for your discussions.

✦ Organize a meeting or workshop with both customers and suppliers, to analyse jointly each service and agree on the appropriate service level, quality and cost.

Critical to your success in achieving agreement will be a clear and powerful presentation of the data received from the interviews. You are dealing with extremely sensitive issues and potentially threatening some departments' self-image, power base and even existence. If you just present a series of opinions from users, you will only end up in unproductive arguments about people's perceptions, with suppliers claiming that users don't have sufficient grasp of the operation to be able to define what is necessary. This particularly happens when conducting an SLA on a corporate headquarters. When unnecessary activities and costs have been clearly identified, the people carrying out those activities eventually fall back on arguments attacking the competence of operating units and suggesting that only those in the center can have a valid view of business needs.

It is thus important that your presentation of the results is objective and well argued. A possible structure for feeding back the results of the SLA might be as shown in Figure 26.5.

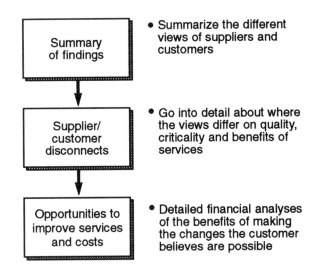

Figure 26.5   The presentation of the SLA results must be clear and logical

Value-added analysis

One of the weaknesses of a service-level analysis is that it takes the existing level of services as a starting point for the discussion. When you do this, it can be difficult to encourage people to think creatively about whether existing services are needed at all. People tend to assume that if an activity exists, there must be a need for it in some form or other. So SLAs can often end up giving only incremental rather than major levels of improvement.

One way to try to break out of this thought process is to base the study on identifying which activities add value to external customers (distributors, retailers, users) and which do not. So in a way you're almost rebuilding the business from the ground up – starting from zero.

A value-added analysis (VAA) has four main steps (Figure 26.6).

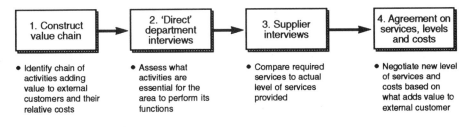

Figure 26.6   A basic VAA can be done in four main phases

1. Constructing a value chain

The first phase consists of mapping out the basic business process as a value chain, showing direct and support activities and the costs of each. Figure 26.7 shows how this might look for a car manufacturer.

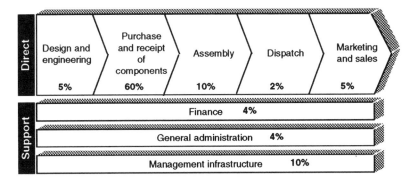

Figure 26.7   Simplified value chain for a car manufacturer

2. Direct department interviews

Working with each direct activity, you then construct a process flow detailing the main activities and information flows. Brown papers (see Part Three – Encouraging Creativity) are a useful tool for making the process flow realistic and meaningful to the area you are working with.

Pages 95–7

Basing your discussions on the activities and information mapped out on the brown paper, you can now start going through each of them, questioning what value they provide external customers or internal departments. This should give you a list of activities, both within each direct area and coming from support areas, which can be reduced, simplified or suppressed altogether.

Typically you will find:

+ there are too many steps in each flow and some can be taken out or combined, making the operation simpler
+ information is provided too late, in an inappropriate form or even reproduced manually in many areas as people don't have confidence in the information coming from outside their area
+ the interfaces between different areas are not clear and there is constant duplication of contacts as different levels try to find out what is happening
+ there is a considerable amount of waiting or idle time between different steps of the process (particularly between different departments) which makes throughput times at least two to three times longer than necessary.

3. Supplier interviews

For all the questionable services coming from support areas, interview those areas to establish:

+ the cost of those activities
+ the rationale for providing them at that cost and that level
+ ideas which the support departments have for improving service provision or reducing service cost.

4. Negotiating agreement

As with service-level analysis, you now need to enter a process of negotiation with both service providers and recipients to agree a level which is aimed at adding value to external customers with a minimum of internal support cost.

Internal contracting

Many organizations are taking the idea of internal customer service relationships to its logical conclusion and are setting up formal contracts between different parts of the organization. In railways, for example, there are often business contracts between maintenance and operations. These define the prices that operations will pay for a variety of maintenance activities and the service levels which maintenance has to live up to.

These contracts can be a powerful way of improving results, as each department pushes other areas to higher levels of performance – railway operations, for example, will pressure maintenance to reduce costs and service times, while maintenance will press for greater scheduling reliability. However, there can be a reverse effect which must be avoided. If individual departments start trying to optimize their local operations at the expense of the organization as a whole, the benefits of these contracts can quickly dissipate. For example, under pressure to reduce costs, maintenance might try to smooth its workload by producing an inflexible six-month plan. This may permit maintenance to reach its cost goals, but may restrict the ability of the organization as a whole to react to fluctuating levels of customer demand. To guard against this, it is important to reinforce cooperation between the two parties to the service contract by setting up some form of joint team between supplier and customer staff. By fostering two-way communication and an understanding of each other's operating situation, this team can act as a counterbalance to excessive focus on local departmental interests.

The role of HQ

Closely linked to the question of how support departments add value is the issue of the role which should be played by the headquarters of an organization. It is rare to see an organization question the role and even the existence of a head office at all. As competitive conditions harden and organizations need to develop faster reactions, it is time for many of them to analyse objectively whether their head office is adding or destroying value.

The wave of demergers in the 1990s has shown that many organizations have realized that parts of their business would function much more successfully if they weren't controlled by the corporate HQ. Oil companies such as Shell, Exxon, Standard Oil and BP sold their mineral businesses after achieving an average pre-tax return on sales of -17 percent in the mid-1980s compared to metal companies' average of +10 percent. ICI increased its market value from £7.6 billion in July 1992 to £13.2 billion by December 1994 following its demerger into two separate businesses, chemicals and pharmaceuticals.

Organizations should ask a series of questions:

+ Is HQ adding or destroying value?
+ How can HQ best add value?
+ What processes and structure are appropriate for HQ to add this value?
+ What activities should HQ stop doing as these are destroying value?

Clearly, if part of a business already has good control systems, there is no point in duplicating these at head office. Likewise, if an area has very specific technological skills, then involvement from head office may only slow down decision making rather than improve it. However, if a business is operating in several countries, the HQ may play a valuable role in coordinating design and product specifications and spreading new technologies and ideas.

Once you have worked out how a head office can add value to its businesses – whether through strategic leadership, being a source of innovation, a migrator of best practices, a financial controller, a provider of funds or expertise, a coordinator of activities, a builder of networks or whatever – you can start to build the business processes required to fulfil this role and the most appropriate structure. The mistake which many organizations make is to assume that head office must naturally fulfil *all* the above roles. Depending on the sector in which the organization operates, some roles may be most appropriately performed by head office; but in others, head office will only obstruct and even misdirect decision making, and destroy rather than create value.

Summary

With the growth in indirect costs in most organizations and the corresponding fall in direct costs, it is becoming more difficult to assess whether the organization is getting value for the money it spends – the efficiency and necessity of many support functions are notoriously hard to measure objectively. Because of this, many organizations have seen a poorly controlled mushrooming in support activities, some of which may not be fully aimed at providing useful services either for external or internal customers.

In discussions about overhead cost levels, direct departments often come off worse as the indirect areas are usually most closely linked to corporate management and thus are closer to the sources of power and decision making.

If we are not to drown ourselves in ever-expanding support costs, we need tools and methods which allow us objectively to assess support activities from the point of view of the external and internal customers.

Organizations should exist to serve their customers. But most of us will have experienced organizations where a huge amount of energy and resource goes into satisfying internal organizational needs – adding no apparent value for external customers. Unless activities can be justified as being useful to internal direct departments or to external customers or partners, those activities should be removed. Service-level analysis and value-added analysis are two tools which can help you tighten your area's or organization's focus on customer value and eliminate unnecessary administrative activity.

27

Building a Smart Supply Chain

Mention the words 'supply chain' to most managers and you're unlikely to excite much interest. For most of us, it sounds too much like lorries and warehouses – fairly boring, the job of the logistics or distribution manager and certainly not anything that is central to our organization's survival.

However, this is not the case for a few leading companies. For them the supply chain is anything but a tedious chore bolted on to their business. What they have done is to make the supply chain the key driver of their whole organization rather than an afterthought. They use it to channel energy into providing innovative and differentiated products and services (Figure 27.1).

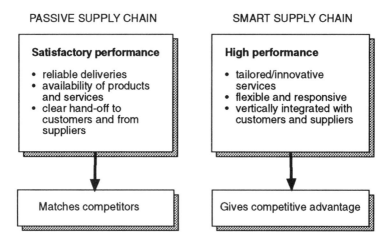

Figure 27.1   Passive vs smart supply chains

The passive supply chain may well provide competitive products and services with reasonable efficiency. But the smart supply chain continually develops new ways of adding value.

Organizations with passive supply chains often find themselves reducing price and dreaming up numerous special offers and promotions to generate business. The smart supply chain achieves such an increase in value for the customer that price decreases in importance as a competitive weapon. In a wide range of industries and services, the ability of a few organizations to develop smart supply chains has given them a breakthrough in performance that less able competitors have struggled to match.

How the smart supply chain is different

To demonstrate some key aspects of the smart supply chain, we can take a simple value chain that could belong to almost any organization (Figure 27.2) and look at it from two angles:

✦ what we normally find
✦ how the smart supply chain does things differently.

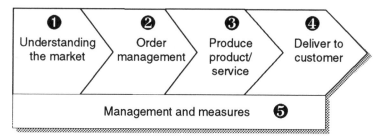

Figure 27.2   A basic value chain

What we normally find

1. Understanding the market

There are two basic facts that apply to most markets or populations. First, there is a predictable concentration – the 80/20 rule can be applied to the majority of markets or groups that use a service:

Pages 199–200

✦ 20 percent of customers usually account for 80 percent of turnover
✦ 20 percent of the users of a service take up 80 percent of resources
✦ 80 percent of profits tend to be generated by 20 percent of customers.

Second, different sectors have different needs. Most markets or service users can easily be segmented into a few clearly differentiated groups, each with a specific set of needs:

+ Older people make up about 20 percent of the population, consume about 80 percent of healthcare spend and have quite different needs from younger patients.
+ For advertising agencies, lawyers, accountants, consultants and so on, large accounts make up about 20 percent of customers by number but represent about 80 percent of turnover. They will have quite different service needs from smaller customers.

Of course, most organizations know who their large customers are or who uses most of their services. But time and again you find that there is only a small difference between how organizations handle the critical 20 percent and the less important 80 percent.

2. Order management

The way most organizations take orders and convey them to production or the service provider is, with very few exceptions, passive and administrative. However orders come in – from the salesforce or by e-mail, fax or letter – they all tend to go through the same bureaucratic process – registration, entry into a system, a wait to see when they can be scheduled and then a confirmation issued or appointment made. This process usually applies to large and small answers, repeat orders and totally new ones. It is unintelligent, just a matter of pushing paper around and keying in data.

3. Produce product/provide service

In general, the manufacture of most products or provision of many services tends as far as possible towards being standardized and repetitive. The aim, of course, is to operate at lowest cost. But the distinction between key customers and less critical ones is lost and the specific needs of different clients are insufficiently addressed.

4. Deliver to customer

Warehousing, transport and delivery are normally an afterthought. They are handled by the logistics or distribution manager and many people in the organization would be hard pressed to tell you much about how the process works.

5. Management and measures

There is seldom an executive responsible for the supply chain. It falls through the cracks between other functions such as sales and marketing, R&D, production, finance and human resources, which do have their own managers.

The ever-increasing power of information technology has allowed us to measure almost anything we want at whatever frequency we desire. But most performance measures are either financial or focused on the operations of each main function. It is rare to find an organization that satisfactorily measures the functioning of its total supply chain.

With no executive clearly responsible for the supply chain and no adequate measures of its performance, we can hardly expect it to be managed effectively and proactively as a key competitive weapon.

How the smart supply chain does things differently

Obviously, organizations in different sectors will have quite different supply chains, so there is no one correct way of running a supply chain. However, there are certain principles of the smart supply chain that can, in one form or another, be applied to supply chains in many industries and services.

1. Understanding the market

Organizations with a smart supply chain clearly understand the principles of concentration of demand (80/20) and segmented needs. They actively split their customers into at least three main groups (Figure 27.3):

◆ the critical few customers who can account for up to 80 percent of volumes and profits
◆ the group of mid-range customers who make up 10–15 percent of profits
◆ the largest group by number who contribute little volume and profit.

With the smart supply chain there is a different strategy for each group:

◆ **Critical few** – really invest in delighting these customers. Provide excellent service: faster leadtimes, higher quality, better support etc. Try integrating your supply chain with the supply chains of these customers, so you create

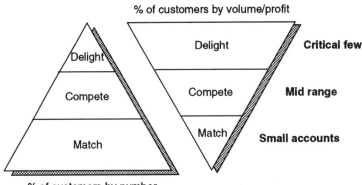

Figure 27.3   Different strategies for different customer groups

dependency and increase the costs and risks for them of switching to another supplier.

✦ **Mid range** – ensure that you compete effectively. Place yourself in the top quartile of performers for your sector.

✦ **Small accounts** – match the industry. It's probably too costly to try to out-perform competitors with these customers. Because of their size you will probably never receive an adequate return if you invest too heavily.

2. Order management

When you take an order or make an appointment with a customer, this provides an excellent opportunity to gather information and market the better service you can provide. Whereas typical order management is normally just a bureaucratic process, in the smart supply chain it can be a competitive weapon.

For example, given the right up-to-date information (Figure 27.4), order-management staff could compare the incoming order with the customer's past history to identify any changes in ordering pattern (positive or negative) and ask why this is happening. They could inform the customer of the status of all outstanding orders and confirm that any special requirements were still necessary. They could see if there were any credit problems. They would have access to the production plan and availability of resources so they could immediately quote a delivery date. They could offer the customer profitable services that have not been used in the past. Unfortunately, this is not how things happen in many organizations.

Similar principles can be applied in service organizations (banks, hospitals, engineering design, management consultancy etc.). Given good information on customer histories, resources availability and services offered, receptionists,

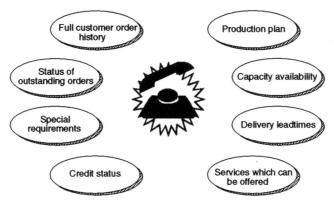

Figure 27.4   With the right information, order entry can be a proactive service weapon

customer service representatives and telephone service staff could provide a more proactive and radically better operation than most now do.

3. Produce product/service

In the smart supply chain, those producing the product or service always know for which customer or group of customers they are working. They know something about that customer – how they work, their particular requirements, what their own customers need and so on. Ideally, in manufacturing industries, some key opinion leaders from production will have been to visit your key customers and will understand precisely how your products are used or sold and under what sorts of constraints your customers work. Knowing what makes the difference for your key customers will help your staff make intelligent decisions that are in the best interests of all concerned.

Similarly in services, those providing the service should have participated in customer/client research to deepen their understanding of how users perceive the service, which aspects they value and which are less critical. Again, their enhanced knowledge of their customers' worlds should help them adapt and improve the service they provide.

4. Deliver to customer

If we understand how our key customers use our product we can arrange different delivery frequencies for different products, offer to hold a central just-in-time stock of slower-moving items, help customers reduce inventories, deliver direct to customers' production lines, manage replenishment stocks on their premises, plan deliveries better to minimize transport costs and so on.

In services you can improve delivery performance by involving the customer in the process. You may receive the best medical attention in the world, but if you don't receive a satisfactory explanation about why you're being treated in a certain way you won't appreciate the full value of the service you're getting. Many service organizations fall short of their full potential because they assume that providing the service is sufficient. This is particularly the case when an organization believes it is the best in its field – medical experts, IT specialists and advertising creative groups with numerous awards under their belts often suffer from this blind spot. Organizations with smart delivery mechanisms understand the value of maximizing customer involvement.

5. Management and measures

Managing the smart supply chain is probably the most complex aspect of implementing the concept. You face the same dilemma as any organization that has a functional structure (sales, R&D, production etc.) and is trying to improve the way cross-functional processes are run. It's always clear who is responsible for each function, but usually unclear who owns the main cross-functional processes. Yet as soon as you appoint someone to be accountable for a cross-functional process there will be confusion over responsibility for results – is it the functional managers or the process managers?

With the smart supply chain, you may decide to have three main supply chains based around the main customer groups (Figure 27.5).

The decision on whether to appoint someone to be responsible for one or all of these supply chains will probably depend more on the personalities,

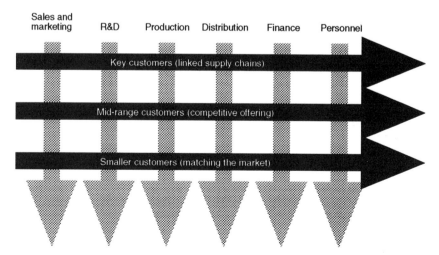

Figure 27.5   Deciding the best management structure is a complex issue

cooperativeness and skills of your management team than on any best practice model. With an emotionally mature management group who work well together, you could make one executive accountable for supply-chain performance. If your managers already tend to turn each issue into a political or personality battle, appointing a supply-chain manager might make the infighting even worse. In the latter situation, the chief executive could decide to take personal responsibility for supply-chain performance and use this as a way of elevating the attention of the management team above their local, functional interests and aligning them around clear, cross-functional goals.

Or you may decide to maintain your functional structure, but to implement a set of performance indicators that measure the overall effectiveness of your supply chain(s). Then your management group has joint accountability for driving these performance indicators in the right direction.

Typically you would design a hierarchy of measures for supply-chain performance so that each organizational level and area can see overall performance, but is only being measured against what they can actively influence. At top management level you might be monitoring service-level performance by customer group and the overall cost of the supply chain. At department manager level you would measure each department's contribution to these two indicators:

♦ In order management, you could measure numbers of orders processed per week, average time to enter and confirm an order, percentage of orders confirmed in 1 day/2 days, cost per order, margin per order etc.
♦ In warehousing and distribution, you could focus on amount of stock, average age of stock, percentage of orders received/despatched on planned day, cost per completed order and so on.

Summary

Different organizations will choose different ways to outperform competitors or provide better value to users of their services. Your organization's main strength may be new product development, marketing, technology, information systems, employing the best experts, creativity or whatever. But no matter what you choose as the differentiator, you can radically improve your market position or service quality by managing your organization as a total supply chain and ensuring that each aspect of that chain is not passive but smart.

Index